21世纪高等学校专业英语系列规划教材

市场营销

专业英语教程

（修订本）

李 娜 主编

清华大学出版社
北京交通大学出版社
·北京·

内 容 简 介

本书共分五大部分：第一部分为市场营销概论，主要介绍市场营销的基本概念、国际市场营销概况、市场营销环境和市场营销信息系统等；第二部分为消费者分析，从不同的视角对消费者展开分析，包括顾客价值理论、消费者需求及其购买行为分析；第三部分为市场分析，包括市场概述、市场调查、市场细分、市场定位及市场拓展；第四部分为策略分析，分别对市场竞争策略、目标市场营销策略、产品策略、价格策略、促销策略、渠道策略及合作策略进行分析；第五部分介绍了市场营销管理方面的内容，预测了市场营销的未来发展趋势。

本书可供高等院校英语专业、商务英语专业及市场营销专业学生使用，同时也可供市场营销工作者或其他英语爱好者使用。

本书封面贴有清华大学出版社防伪标签，无标签者不得销售。
版权所有，侵权必究。侵权举报电话：010-62782989　13501256678　13801310933

图书在版编目（CIP）数据

市场营销专业英语教程/李娜主编．—北京：北京交通大学出版社：清华大学出版社，2016.2（2020.1修订）
21世纪高等学校专业英语系列规划教材
ISBN 978-7-5121-2662-6

Ⅰ.①市⋯　Ⅱ.①李⋯　Ⅲ.①市场营销-英语-高等学校-教材　Ⅳ.①H31

中国版本图书馆CIP数据核字（2016）第029539号

市场营销专业英语教程
SHICHANG YINGXIAO ZHUANYE YINGYU JIAOCHENG

责任编辑：孙晓萌

出版发行：	清 华 大 学 出 版 社	邮编：100084	电话：010-62776969	http://www.tup.com.cn
	北京交通大学出版社	邮编：100044	电话：010-51686414	http://www.bjtup.com.cn

印　刷　者：北京鑫海金澳胶印有限公司
经　　　销：全国新华书店
开　　　本：185 mm×243 mm　　印张：20.25　　字数：514千字
版　　　次：2016年2月第1版　2020年1月第3次印刷
书　　　号：ISBN 978-7-5121-2662-6/H·444
定　　　价：49.00元

本书如有质量问题，请向北京交通大学出版社质监组反映。对您的意见和批评，我们表示欢迎和感谢。
投诉电话：010-51686043，51686008；传真：010-62225406；E-mail：press@bjtu.edu.cn。

前言

飞速发展的中国经济日新月异，需要与世界经济接轨；日益繁荣的文化产业也需要与世界文化交流；越来越多的中国人需要了解外国市场管理和市场营销策略，以取长补短。目前，市场上有很多市场营销方面的教材，要么过于侧重于理论，实践性不强；要么教材的内容过于陈旧，无法适应市场的需求。

本书在汲取以往教材优点的基础上，结合当今市场营销活动中的热点话题，将基本的营销理论与营销实践融为一体，以期达到理论性与实用性并举的目的。

为顺应新世纪经济和社会发展对高校教学的要求，进一步提高我国高等教育水平，在北京交通大学出版社的精心组织下，我们编写了这本适合高等院校使用的《市场营销专业英语教程》。本书有以下几个特点。

（1）实用性。本书适用于高等院校英语专业、商务英语专业、市场营销专业学生，旨在让学生在掌握基本市场营销理论的基础上，了解一些常见的营销活动，既学习语言知识，又开阔眼界，为其将来走进社会、走上工作岗位奠定坚实的基础。

（2）针对性。本书编者多年从事专业英语教学，深知学生的特点，所以本书的内容遵循由浅入深、循序渐进的原则，层层深入，逐步培养和提高学生对市场营销理论与实践的驾驭能力，以及语言的表达能力。

（3）广泛性。本书多方位、多层次、多视角地为学生呈现了各种不同的市场营销活动，使学生有机会领略市场营销的庐山真面目。

本书由李娜（北京联合大学师范学院）担任主编并完成全书内容的编写。

由于编者水平有限，书中难免有疏漏、错误之处，望同行专家和广大读者不吝赐教。

编　者

2016 年 1 月

目 录

PART I Introduction to Marketing

Unit 1 Marketing ……………………………………………………………… (2)
Unit 2 International Marketing ……………………………………………… (15)
Unit 3 Marketing Environment ……………………………………………… (32)
Unit 4 Marketing Information System ……………………………………… (44)

PART II Consumer Analysis

Unit 5 Customer Value ……………………………………………………… (60)
Unit 6 Customer Demand …………………………………………………… (79)
Unit 7 Analysis of Consumer Buying Behavior …………………………… (97)

PART III Market Analysis

Unit 8 Market ………………………………………………………………… (112)
Unit 9 Market Research ……………………………………………………… (128)
Unit 10 Market Segmentation ……………………………………………… (141)
Unit 11 Market Positioning ………………………………………………… (153)

I

Unit 12 Market Expansion ··· (165)

PART IV Strategy Analysis

Unit 13 Marketing Competition Strategy ·· (184)
Unit 14 Target Marketing Strategy ··· (202)
Unit 15 Product Strategy ·· (216)
Unit 16 Pricing Strategy ··· (230)
Unit 17 Promotion Strategy ··· (245)
Unit 18 Marketing Channel Strategy ·· (260)
Unit 19 Collaborative Strategy ··· (274)

PART V Marketing Management & The Future of Marketing

Unit 20 Marketing Management ·· (292)
Unit 21 The Future of Marketing ·· (305)

参考文献 ··· (317)

PART I

Introduction to Marketing

Unit 1
Marketing

In the planned economy era, enterprises didn't have to worry about selling things, and they merely set up a supply department responsible for the procurement of raw materials. There is simply no such a concept of marketing. Later on, with the arrival of market economy, gone are days when enterprises depend heavily on the higher authorities in charge of sales of the products.[1] They have to rely on their own to find markets to sell their own products. In order to maximize the profits, many companies began to set up marketing departments. As market competition intensifies, there seems to be a growing awareness that they should attach more importance to not only sales but also a variety of sales-related work.[2] Thus the concept of marketing is gaining increasing popularity among people. It has changed and evolved over a period of time and there are many different definitions.

- The Chartered Institute of Marketing defines marketing as "the management process responsible for identifying, anticipating and satisfying customer requirements profitably". This definition looks at not only identifying customer needs, but also satisfying them (short-term) and anticipating them in the future (long-term).
- Marketing is the process used to determine what products or services may be of interest to customers, and the strategy to use in sales, communications and business development.[3] It is an integrated process through which companies build strong customer relationships and create value for their customers and for themselves.[4]
- Marketing is the process of developing, pricing, distributing and promoting the goods or services that satisfy the needs of the potential customers.
- Marketing is the all-embracing function that links the business with customer needs and wants in order to get the right product to the right place at the right time.
- Marketing is not about providing products or services; instead, it is essentially about providing changing benefits to the changing needs and demands of the customer.
- Marketing is essentially about marshalling the resources of an organization so that they

meet the changing needs of the customer on whom the organization depends.

The above-mentioned definitions are all right. The better definitions are focused upon customer orientation and satisfaction of customer needs, thus making the customer, and the satisfaction of his or her needs, the focal point of all business activities. Marketing is founded in the belief that profitable sales and satisfactory returns on investment can only be achieved by identifying, anticipating and satisfying customer needs and desires.[5] The adoption of marketing strategies requires businesses to shift their focus from production to the perceived needs and wants of their customers as the means of staying profitable.

Now that you have been introduced to some definitions of marketing and the marketing concept, remember the important elements contained as follows.

- Marketing is about meeting the needs and wants of customers. In other words, it focuses on the satisfaction of customer needs, wants and requirements.

- Marketing is a management responsibility and should not be solely left to junior members of staff. Only with the joint efforts can an organization identify the needs and wants of the customer and deliver benefits, while at the same time ensuring that the satisfaction of these needs results in a healthy turnover for the organization.

- Marketing involves an ongoing process. The environment is "dynamic". This means that the market tends to change—what customers want today is not necessarily what they want tomorrow. Therefore, the company is supposed to create long-term demand, perhaps by modifying particular features of the product to satisfy changes in consumer needs or market conditions.

- Successful marketing requires a deep knowledge of customers, competitors, and collaborators and great skills in serving customers profitably. Marketing therefore combines market research, new product development, distribution, advertising, promotion, product improvement, and so on. In other words, marketing begins and ends with the customer. Truly successful marketing understands the customer so well that the product or service satisfies the needs so perfectly that the customers are desperate to buy it.

Marketing activities are numerous and varied because they basically include everything needed to get a product off the drawing board and into the hands of the customer. The broad field of marketing includes activities such as: designing the product so it will be desirable to customers by using tools such as marketing research and pricing; promoting the product so people will know about it by using tools such as public relations, advertising, and marketing communications; setting a price and letting potential customers know about your product and making it available to them.

People have to spend 80% of their time marketing their new business. The reason lies in the fact that marketing encompasses many different parts of the business. Generally speaking, there are seven functions associated with marketing and these functions are the basis of all marketing activities.

● Pricing: setting and communicating the value of products and services. Setting the price at the right level.

● Selling: communicating directly with potential customers to determine and satisfy their needs.

● Distribution: determining the best ways for customers to locate, obtain, and use the products and services of an organization. It involves moving the products from the producer to the consumer.

● Product/Service management: designing, developing, maintaining, improving, and acquiring products and services that meet consumer needs.

● Financing: budgeting for marketing activities, obtaining the necessary funds needed for operations, and providing financial assistance to customers so they can purchase the business products and service.

● Market information management: obtaining, managing, and using information about what customers want to improve business decision making, performance of marketing activities.

● Promotion: communicating with customers about the product to achieve the desired result—customer demand for and purchase of the product. It includes advertising, personal selling, publicity, and public relations.

Each function can have a positive or negative effect on business. The point is to be aware of each of them and include them in our marketing decisions.

Vocabulary

enterprise	n. 企业	focal	a. 焦点的，中心的
procurement	n. 获得	return	n. 利润，盈利
maximize	v. 最大化	adoption	n. 采纳，采用
intensify	v. 变得更剧烈	perceived	a. 感知到的
trend	n. 趋势	turnover	n. 营业额
evolve	v. 发展，演变	dynamic	a. 动态的
identify	v. 识别	modify	v. 修改
strategy	n. 策略	collaborator	n. 合作者
anticipate	v. 预测	desperate	a. 迫切的
profitably	ad. 营利地	varied	a. 各种各样的
potential	a. 潜在的	desirable	a. 想要的
all-embracing	a. 包括一切的	pricing	n. 定价
marshal	v. 整理	available	a. 可利用的，可使用的
above-mentioned	a. 上述的	encompass	v. 包括，包含
orientation	n. 方向，导向	distribution	n. 分销

Unit 1 Marketing

maintain v. 维护，维修
locate v. 定位
involve v. 涉及，牵扯
acquire v. 习得，获得
budget v. 预算

operation n. 运转，操作，实施，运营
assistance n. 帮助，援助
performance n. 业绩，表现
publicity n. 宣传

Phrases and Expressions

in the planned economy era 在计划经济时代
raw material 原材料
market economy 市场经济
set up 成立，设立
marketing department 营销部
attach importance to … 重视
meet the need of … 满足……的需求
gain increasing popularity 越来越受欢迎
be of interest to sb. 激发某人的兴趣
now that 既然
be supposed to do sth. 应该做某事

joint effort 共同努力
market research 市场调查
product improvement 产品改进
drawing board 筹备阶段
marketing communication 营销信息交流
lie in 在于
financial assistance 财政资助
business decision making 商业决策
desired result 预期的结果
personal selling 人员销售
public relation 公共关系

1. Later on, with the arrival of market economy, gone are days when enterprises depend heavily on the higher authorities in charge of sales of the products. 后来，到了市场经济时代，企业完全依靠高一级领导来销售产品的时代一去不复返了。
本句中使用了 when 引导的定语从句，为了保持句子平衡，避免头重脚轻，本句采用了倒装结构，正常的语序应该是 "days when enterprises depend heavily on the higher authorities in charge of sales of the products are gone"。类似这样的结构还有：Round the corner walked a policeman. (A policeman walked round the corner.)。

2. As market competition intensifies, there seems to be a growing awareness that they should attach

more importance to not only sales but also a variety of sales-related work. 市场竞争非常激烈，人们越来越意识到不仅要重视销售，还要重视各种与销售相关的其他工作。

在本句中，注意 intensify 的意思是"加强，强化，变得更剧烈"，其词根是"intense"，添加了后缀"-fy"，类似的词语还有：purify（净化）、simplify（简化）、beautify（美化）、justify（辩解，认为……有理）、notify（通知）等。

在"… there seems to be a growing awareness that …"中使用了 that 引导的同位语从句，进一步解释说明"awareness"的内容。英语表达中常习惯用没有生命的物作主语（无生命主语），而汉语中则习惯用有生命的人作主语（有生命主语），因此这句话的意思是"人们越来越意识到……"。因此，在英语学习中要深刻体会到英、汉两种语言在表达上存在的差异。

3. Marketing is the process used to determine what products or services may be of interest to customers, and the strategy to use in sales, communications and business development. 市场营销这一过程用来确定顾客会对什么样的产品或者服务感兴趣，确定在销售、交流以及业务发展中采用什么样的策略。

本句中的"used to determine what products or services may be of interest to customers, and the strategy to use in sales, communications and business development"是过去分词短语作定语修饰"the process"，其中"what products or services may be of interest to customers"是宾语从句，作 determine 的宾语。短语"be of interest to customers"意思是"吸引客户，客户对……感兴趣"，类似的表达还有：be of great/first significance/importance（非常重要）、be of great/much help（非常有帮助）、be of high value（非常有价值）、be of the same age（年龄相当）等。

4. It is an integrated process through which companies build strong customer relationships and create value for their customers and for themselves. 这是一个整合的过程，各公司通过这一过程可以建立牢固的客户关系，为客户和自身创造价值。

本句是一个介词前置的定语从句，引导词 which 指代的是前面的先行词 process。

5. Marketing is founded in the belief that profitable sales and satisfactory returns on investment can only be achieved by identifying, anticipating and satisfying customer needs and desires. 坚信只有识别、预测以及满足顾客的诸多需求和愿望，投资才能获得销售利润和满意的回报，市场营销就是以此为基础的。

在本句中"in the belief that …"的意思是"坚信……"，其中 that 引导了同位语从句进一步解释说明 belief。此外，belief 还有其他常见的搭配，如：have belief in sth. 相信，信任；to the best of my belief 我坚信；beyond belief 难以置信等。

Unit 1 Marketing

I Answer the following questions according to the text.

1. What can we know about enterprises in the planned economy era?
2. What gave rise to the appearance of the marketing departments?
3. How can you understand the definition of marketing given by the Chartered Institute of Marketing?
4. What do the better definitions of marketing emphasize?
5. According to the writer, what is the basic belief of marketing?
6. In "Only with the joint efforts can an organization identify the needs and wants of the customer and deliver benefits …", what does the phrase "the joint efforts" refer to?
7. What does the sentence "Marketing involves an ongoing process." mean?
8. How can you understand "In other words, marketing begins and ends with the customer."?
9. Why are marketing activities numerous and varied?
10. What activities are included in the broad field of marketing?

II Decide whether the following statements are true or false.

1. In the planned economy era, the marketing concept was new to the public.
2. People used to attach more importance to sales rather than marketing.
3. The benefits that marketing brings to customers are more than those to organizations.
4. The definitions mentioned in the passage focus more on profits than on customers.
5. Marketing is so important that it should be left to managers and other senior members of the companies.
6. Companies are supposed to gear their products to the changing needs of customers.
7. Every aspect of business activities is involved in marketing.
8. Companies invest 80 percent of their money in marketing per year.
9. More profits are the basis of all marketing activities.
10. Market information management determines the best way to locate the products and services of an organization.

III Fill in each blank with the proper form of the word in the bracket.

1. The term *marketing concept* holds that _____ (achieve) organizational goals depends on knowing the needs and wants of target markets and delivering the _____ (desire) satisfactions.
2. It is reported that supermarkets intensively research and study consumer behavior, _____ (spend) millions of dollars.
3. Companies are always looking for marketing opportunities of filling _____ (satisfy) needs in areas in which they are likely to enjoy a differential advantage, due to their particular competence.
4. Marketing may be defined as a set of human activities _____ (direct) at facilitating exchanges.
5. Concern and _____ (responsible) for marketing must therefore permeate all areas of the enterprise.
6. Niche marketing is becoming an _____ (increase) popular concept in the field of marketing and advertising and is now one of the most _____ (prefer) methods of making a product known to consumers.
7. These technological wonders _____ (able) the marketing professionals to track the navigation of the users through the sites.
8. Companies in today's business environment often spend a lot of money _____ (conduct) marketing research before releasing new products or services.
9. The market needs to be studied and future trends _____ (forecast).
10. This customer _____ (focus) philosophy is known as the "marketing concept".

IV Fill in each blank with a proper preposition.

1. Their perceptions are built _____ culture, race, age or other personal opinions.
2. Companies will use test markets to determine the strength of consumer demand for goods or services prior _____ a national rollout of new products.
3. All resources need to be invested _____ the business and the staff needs to be motivated to adhere _____ the company's general objective.
4. The bankruptcy of that firm lies _____ the inefficiency of its marketing department.
5. Your new products are _____ great interest to us.
6. The company attaches importance _____ the customer satisfaction.
7. A businessman who is aware _____ the developments and increasing competition in the Internet knows that if a business entity owns only one website and promotes all of its

products there, then the website will most likely end _____ ranking low in the search results, thus not reaching its target audiences.
8. Simply stated, marketing is everything you do to place your product or service _____ the hands of potential customers.
9. Marketing is the social process _____ which individuals and groups obtain what they need and want through creating and exchanging products and value with others.
10. The philosophy of marketing needs to be owned by everyone _____ the organization.

V Fill in the blanks with the words and phrases given below. Change the form where necessary.

| lie in | potential | involve | perceived | stay profitable |
| available | focal | anticipate | identify | desire |

1. It _____ the customers by measuring the amount of time that they spend on each page, the links that they click on and therefore the products and options that they are interested in.
2. The marketing myopia _____ the concept of product.
3. Marketing _____ diverse disciplines like sales, public relations, pricing, packaging, and distribution.
4. In order to _____, companies are supposed to focus more on what consumers are willing to buy rather than on what the company can produce.
5. The most innovative ideas or the greatest products succeed only when you market within the context of people's _____.
6. A market can be defined as all the _____ customers sharing a particular need or want.
7. Marketers do not only identify consumer needs; they can _____ them by developing new products.
8. Marketing is your strategy for allocating resources (time and money) in order to achieve your _____ objectives.
9. The needs and wants of consumers should be regarded as the _____ point of all business activities.
10. The task of marketing research is to provide management with relevant, accurate, reliable, information _____ in the market.

VI Cloze.

Marketing is the process of teaching you 1_____ consumers should choose your product or service 2_____ your competitors; 3_____ you are not doing that you are not marketing. It's really 4_____ simple! The key is 5_____ the right method and defining the right message to use to educate and influence your consumers.

Companies make the mistake of thinking that marketing is just "one" thing, but marketing is 6_____ that the consumer encounters when it 7_____ to your business, from advertising, to 8_____ they hear, to the customer service that they 9_____, to the follow-up care that you provide. It's all marketing and creating the decision 10_____ the consumer whether or not to choose you initially or for 11_____ business.

If you work in a medium or large size organization, then 12_____ are that you would have heard the phrase "marketing communications". It is the department that deals 13_____ handling all 14_____ for the company. Marketing communications is nothing 15_____ the science and art of communicating information that the company wants to divulge 16_____ the public. The information could be 17_____ to the marketing of a product, talk about a new product launch or community initiatives 18_____ by the company. Even as just communicating may seem an easy task since that is 19_____ we do every day in our normal lives, there is a science behind what to communicate to whom and 20_____ what tone and manner.

1. A. what   B. why   C. which   D. how
2. A. over   B. rather   C. but   D. without
3. A. where   B. why   C. when   D. if
4. A. so   B. such   C. very   D. that
5. A. find   B. to find   C. finding   D. to finding
6. A. everything   B. nothing   C. something   D. /
7. A. refers   B. comes   C. relates   D. takes
8. A. that   B. what   C. which   D. how
9. A. have   B. offer   C. receive   D. own
10. A. in   B. beyond   C. for   D. within
11. A. daily   B. routine   C. repeat   D. usual
12. A. possibilities B. opportunities C. likelihood   D. chances
13. A. with   B. in   C. for   D. upon
14. A. communications B. transactions C. businesses   D. goods
15. A. beside   B. besides   C. for   D. but
16. A. for   B. on   C. to   D. at
17. A. subject   B. confined   C. accustomed   D. related
18. A. made   B. taken   C. undertaken   D. assumed
19. A. what   B. how   C. why   D. when
20. A. with   B. in   C. on   D. by

VII Translation.

1. Marketing communications is the science and art of communicating information that the company wants to divulge to the public.
2. This information is then delivered to the marketing department where it is analyzed and a specific customized communication is created for the users.
3. Yet the most brilliant strategy won't help you earn a profit or achieve your wildest dream if it isn't built around your potential customers.
4. Truly successful marketing understand the customer so well that the product or service satisfies the needs so perfectly that the customers are desperate to buy it.
5. The adoption of marketing strategies requires businesses to shift their focus from production to the perceived needs and wants of their customers as the means of staying profitable.

Extended Reading

Marketing and Selling

The end of both selling and marketing is to maximize profit by promoting sales. Both are necessities to the success of a business. You cannot do without either process. If marketing is done well, the products can sell themselves. By strategically combining both efforts you will experience a successful amount of business growth. So sales and marketing are closely interlinked and are aimed at increasing revenue. As they are closely intertwined, it becomes hard to realize the differences between them. Although there is a lot of confusion about the differences, it is important to realize that there is a fine line between them. The bigger firms have made clear distinction between marketing and sales and they have specialized people handling them independently.

In order to distinguish marketing from other related professional services, S.H. Simmons, author and humorist, relates this anecdote. "If a young man tells his date she's intelligent, looks lovely, and is a great conversationalist, he's saying the right things to the right person and that's marketing … "

In very simple words, sales can be termed as a process which targets individuals or small groups; marketing focuses on larger group or general public. As a matter of fact, marketing is much broader than selling. What's more, it is not a specialized activity at all. Instead, it encompasses the entire business and it is the whole business seen from the point of view of the final result, that is, from the customer's point of view. It covers a broad range of activities including monitoring market trends, conducting marketing research, demand forecasting, market segmentation, product development, branding, pricing, promotion, distributing the products and selling. Therefore, marketing is a comprehensive term, which includes selling, advertising and also the distribution of goods. In other words, marketing means generating leads or prospects. Selling is about closing a sale and turning a potential buyer into a customer, which is also called a conversion. Once the product is out in the market, it is the task of the salesperson to persuade the customer to buy the product. Well, selling means converting the leads or prospects into purchases and orders.

While marketing is aimed at longer terms, sales pertain to shorter goals. The former is concerned with a longer process of building a name for a brand and pursuing the customer to buy it even if they do not need it, while sales only involve a short term process of finding the target consumers. Marketing is not direct and it uses various methods like advertising, brand marketing, public relations, direct mails and viral marketing for creating an awareness of the product. Sales are really interpersonal actions. Sales involve one-on-one meetings, networking and calls.

It is of great help to define the two in that understanding the difference can highlight where your strengths and weaknesses lie and lead to improved results in that area.

Words and Expressions

necessity　*n.* 必需品	networking　*n.* 联网
strategically　*ad.* 从战略上来看	be termed as　被称为
interlink　*v.* 连锁，连环	market trend　市场趋势
intertwine　*v.* 纠缠，缠绕在一起	conduct market research　进行市场调查
confusion　*n.* 困惑	demand forecasting　需求预测
specialized　*a.* 专门的	market segmentation　市场细分
independently　*ad.* 独立地	product development　产品开发
distinguish　*v.* 区分，区别	close a sale　完成销售
anecdote　*n.* 轶事，趣闻	pertain to　适合
monitor　*v.* 检测，监督	build a name for …　为……赢得名声
branding　*n.* 品牌建设，品牌化	direct mail　直邮
comprehensive　*a.* 包罗广泛的，综合性的	viral marketing　病毒性营销
generate　*v.* 发生	interpersonal interaction　人际交互
lead　*n.* 领先地位	one-on-one meeting　一对一会议
prospect　*n.* 希望，期盼；前途，前景	in that　因为
conversion　*n.* 转变	highlight　*v.* 强调
convert　*v.* 转变	strength　*n.* 长处，优势

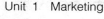
Unit 1   Marketing

Comprehension

I Answer the following questions according to the passage.

1. What is the ultimate goal of marketing and selling?
2. What are the relationships between marketing and sales?
3. What are the differences between marketing and selling?
4. Why is the awareness of the differences between sales and marketing important?
5. What does the writer mainly focus on in the passage?

II Write "T" for true, and "F" for false.

1. It's pointless to differentiate marketing and selling since they have the same goal.
2. Many people are confused about the differences between marketing and selling.
3. There may be no specialized people tacking the problems concerning marketing and sales.
4. Selling means saying the right thing to the right person.
5. Sales include advertising, marketing research, marketing and so on.
6. Marketing brings about leads or prospects, while selling converts them into purchases.
7. Marketing involves the entire business, so it is more important than selling.
8. Understanding what the company will produce is bound to bring about more profits to the marketers.
9. Marketing uses some indirect methods like advertising, brand marketing, networking, public relations and so on.
10. Sales involves the longer term process of finding the potential consumers.

Additional Terms

city marketing   城市营销
cultural marketing   文化营销
exhibition marketing   会展营销
green marketing   绿色营销
integrated marketing communication   整合营销传播
macro-environment   宏观环境
micro-environment   微观环境

market attractiveness   市场吸引力
market circumstance   市场环境
marketing concept   营销观念
marketing control   营销控制
marketing decision support system (MDSS)   营销决策支持系统
marketing environment audit   营销环境审计

marketing flow and function 营销过程和职能	marketing program 营销方案
marketing institution 营销机构	marketing relationship 营销关系
marketing management 营销管理	marketing research 营销研究
marketing message 营销信息	marketing strategy 营销战略
marketing mix 市场营销组合	market development 市场开发
marketing myopia 营销近视症	network marketing 网络营销
marketing organization 市场营销组织	product development 产品开发
marketing planning 市场营销计划	relationship marketing 关系营销
marketing policy 营销策略	

Unit 2
International Marketing

The days of isolated or shielded markets where businesses focus primarily on their domestic markets are no more.[1] Trade is becoming increasingly global throughout the world. In other words, a growing number of companies of all sizes can find sales opportunities abroad. They now operate in an international environment where customers may be from different countries. This gives rise to the mounting popularity of international marketing and presents an exciting but daunting challenge for those with responsibility for marketing.[2] No longer is international marketing an option, but a strategic imperative.[3] Businesses that cling to their domestic markets will be left far behind as their competitors gain "first mover advantage" in the international marketplace.[4] For those businesses choosing to explore foreign markets, all they need is the three "T's": *Time* to devote to building relationships and understanding regulations, *Tenacity* to follow up with contacts multiple times before the first sale, and *Tolerance* for differing business protocols and cultural expectations.

When it comes to the definition of international marketing, there are different versions.

- According to the American Marketing Association (AMA), "international marketing is the multinational process of planning and executing the conception, pricing, promotion and distribution of ideas, goods, and services to create exchanges that satisfy individual and organizational objectives."

- International marketing or global marketing refers to marketing carried out by companies overseas or across national borderlines.

- International marketing is the process of implementing marketing principles and practices to more than one country. It involves recognizing the truth that people from different countries have varying needs.

It works with the assumption that you cannot market products to one country the way you market to another country.[5] Usually, a company has to modify the marketing practices it's using in its home country to suit the needs of the foreign country. This strategy uses an extension of the techniques used in the home country of a firm. It refers to the firm-level marketing practices across the border including market identification and targeting, entry mode selection, marketing mix, and strategic decisions to compete in international markets. While the overall concept of marketing is the same worldwide, the environment within which the marketing plan is implemented can be drastically different. Many elements outside the control of managers, both at home and abroad, are likely to have a large impact on business decisions. The key to successful international marketing is the ability to adapt, manage, and coordinate a marketing plan in an unfamiliar and often unstable foreign environment.

International marketing has great significance for both the economic development of countries and the profitability of individual business firms. It can help to create and expand markets, increase profits, accumulate capital, balance international payments, extend production facilities, exchange primary products for machinery and equipment, and develop economic competence. As global economic growth occurs, understanding marketing in all cultures is increasingly important. International marketing tends to break down nationalistic and economic barriers and to encourage economic unity. People's horizons should not be confined to any specific nation or to the particular ways of doing business in a single country.[6] Therefore, curiosity about management practices of companies seeking market opportunities outside their home country has been stimulated. People come to view marketing management from a global perspective.

Companies choose to expand their markets into the international arena for a host of sound reasons which may fall into two categories, proactive and reactive reasons.[7] Sometimes, having taken the situations into consideration, companies come to realize the importance of international business and decide to export or import in order to be more competitive in the markets; sometimes they are forced into international selling just because of the increasingly competitive environment. So they have no choice but to react to some competitive, economic or technical pressure. Companies which are proactive in international business are, in most cases, better positioned than companies that simply react. If they simply react they might make a mistake and fail to do things properly because they are stressed for time, money or manpower.

The proactive reasons are listed as follows.

- **Growth**. This is the goal of international business. International markets help to expand the companies' customer base, sales and revenue.

- **Profit**. The main purpose of business is to make more profits for the people who own the business. All other objectives are secondary to achieving this goal.[8] The international business enables companies to increase the overall level of total profits.

- **Resource**. Some companies go international to take advantage of resources that are difficult to obtain in their home markets, or that can be obtained at a lower price. Thus they have ready access to lower costs of labor, production and energy.[9]

- **Tax advantage**. Sometimes the host government will offer special tax breaks to attract an investment. To enjoy the corporate tax advantages offered in overseas countries, some companies will choose the international market.

- **Idea**. Companies go international to broaden their work force and obtain new ideas. A work force comprised of different backgrounds and cultural differences can bring fresh ideas and concepts to help a company grow. For example, IBM actively recruits individuals from diverse backgrounds because it believes it's a competitive advantage that drives innovation and benefits customers.
- **Technology**. The growth of the technology has contributed to the increasing competition and opened up the doors to international business.[10] The technology of the Internet is a good case in point. More and more companies have developed a web presence to keep themselves ahead or in line with their competitors around the globe. The Internet has made it possible for companies, especially small businesses, to market themselves to a global market. Thus they can expand their business globally without having to set foot in another country. In other words, they can do everything right in the comforts of their homes, selling anything to anyone from anywhere in the world.

The reactive reasons include:
- **Market**. The home market may be saturated. In other words, in order to dispose of surplus production overseas, companies have to turn to other countries. In the meanwhile, the costs of production at home market increase, thus forcing the companies to find cheaper places to produce their products.
- **Competition**. Some companies may not feel the need to expand internationally; however, their marketplace may force them to move into international marketing to maintain competitive advantage.
- **Trade barrier**. In some countries, the government builds tariff barriers, or formulates "buy-local" policies and other regulations to block the export. Therefore, it's of great necessity for the companies to set up a local alliance or relationship.
- **Corporate risk**. Marketing abroad can also spread corporate risk and minimize the impact of undesirable domestic situations, such as recessions.

Countries in the last several decades have taken effective steps to promote global trade through agreements such as the General Treaty on Trade and Tariffs, and trade organizations such as the World Trade Organization (WTO), the North American Free Trade Agreement, the European Union (EU). It is at the WTO where the people in charge of global economy set the rules for what can be protected, what can be regulated, and what punishments can be imposed on whoever breaks the rules.[11]

Anyway, companies marketing abroad will be faced with many challenges which call for accurate and serious research and evaluation including language and cultural barriers, political and legal environments, and economic conditions.

Culture is that complex whole which includes knowledge, belief, art, morals, customs, and any other capabilities and habits acquired by a person as a member of society or group. It is a problematic issue for many marketers since it is often difficult to understand. Language is an important element of culture. Differences in cultural values result in different preferred methods of speech. For instance, in American English, where the individual is assumed to be more in control of his or her destiny than is the case in many other cultures, there is a preference for the active tense (e.g., "I wrote the marketing plan.") as opposed to the passive tense (e.g., "The marketing plan was written by me."). General Motors realized why it wasn't selling any Chevy Nova's in South America, when it figured out that "no va" means "it won't go." After the company figured out why it wasn't selling any cars, it renamed the car in its Spanish markets to the Caribe.

The political and legal influences carry great weight in international business. Politics can be a huge concern for companies marketing abroad. Unstable political situations tend to expose businesses to numerous risks that they would rarely face at their home markets.[12] When governments change regulations, there are usually new opportunities for both profits and losses, and firms must make modifications to existing marketing strategies in response. Legal systems vary from country to country in content and interpretation and will affect elements of marketing strategies.

Economic conditions exert great influence on the size and affluence of a particular target market. For example, many companies had to reevaluate international marketing strategies as international financial crises affected the economies of Southeast Asia, Russia, and Latin America in 1997.

Therefore, in order to get the most of international marketing, firms going abroad are supposed to learn the culture of the target markets. Of course, they don't have to learn everything. Just stick to those that may cause cultural barriers to their business. Have a good knowledge of regional laws, regulations and economic situations.

 Vocabulary

isolated	a. 孤立的	version	n. 版本
shielded	a. 受保护的	multinational	a. 多国的，跨国公司的
mounting	a. 不断增长的	execute	v. 执行
daunting	a. 勇敢的	borderline	n. 国界线
tenacity	n. 韧性，坚忍不拔	implement	v. 实施
tolerance	n. 容忍，忍耐	assumption	n. 假设
protocol	n. 草约，议定书	extension	n. 延伸，伸展

Unit 2 International Marketing

drastically ad. 剧烈的，急剧	alliance n. 同盟
coordinate v. 协调	minimize v. 最小化
profitability n. 利润，收益率	recession n. 萧条
perspective n. 视角	impose v. 施加
proactive a. 积极的，主动的	evaluation n. 评估
reactive a. 反应的	complex a. 复杂的
revenue n. 收入	problematic a. 麻烦的
saturate v. 使饱和	destiny n. 命运
tariff n. 关税	interpretation n. 解释，诠释
formulate v. 制定，明确地表达	affluence n. 丰富，大量

Phrases and Expressions

give rise to 使出现，产生	a host of 许多
cling to 坚持	fall into ... 分成……部分
be left far behind 远远落后于	have no choice but to do sth. 除了做某事之外别无选择
first mover advantage 先驱优势	be stressed for ... 急需……
devote to 致力于	customer base 顾客基础
follow up with 紧接着	be secondary to ... 次于……的
business protocol 商务礼仪	take advantage of 利用
when it comes to ... 当谈到……时	have access to 可以进入，可以使用
suit the need of ... 满足……的需求	tax break 减免税
market identification 市场鉴定	contribute to 有助于
entry mode selection 进入方式选择	web presence 网络存在，网络知名度
marketing mix 市场营销组合	in line with 与……保持一致
strategic decision 战略决策	dispose of 处理
marketing plan 营销计划	surplus production 剩余产品
accumulate capital 积累资本	competitive advantage 竞争优势
international payment 国际支付	tariff barrier 关税壁垒
production facility 生产设施，生产设备	local alliance 区域联盟机制
economic competence 经济能力	General Treaty on Trade and Tariffs 关税贸易总协定
break down 损坏	North American Free Trade Agreement (NAFTA) 北美自由贸易协定
economic unity 经济统一	
be confined to 局限于	
international arena 国际舞台	

World Trade Organization (WTO) 世界贸易组织	in response 作为回应
European Union (EU) 欧盟	exert great influence on 对……产生很大的影响
call for 需要，要求	get the most of 从……中获益最多；充分利用
carry great weight 非常有影响力	
make modification to 修改	stick to 坚持

1. The days of isolated or shielded markets where businesses focus primarily on their domestic markets are no more. 企业把主要的注意力都集中在国内市场上，使得市场之间孤立隔离，这样的日子一去不复返了。
   本句的主句是"The days are no more"，由于句中使用了 where 引导的限制性定语从句，整个句子显得很长。其中短语"no more"的意思是"不再"，例如，Troy is no more. 特洛伊现已不存在。
   No more will prisoners have to suffer the misery of being locked in their cells for 23 hours a day. 犯人们再也不必忍受每天被锁在地窖里长达 23 小时的痛苦了。

2. This gives rise to the mounting popularity of international marketing and presents an exciting but daunting challenge for those with responsibility for marketing. 这样一来，国际营销越来越受欢迎了，同时也给那些负责营销的人员带来了既兴奋又严峻的挑战。
   本句是简单句，其中使用了两个并列的谓语动词，"give"和"present"。give rise to sth. 意思是"使产生，带来"，例如：Delays could give rise to further problems. 延误会进一步引发其他问题。

3. No longer is international marketing an option, but a strategic imperative. 国际营销不再是一种选择，而是一项战略措施。
   本句句首是否定含义的短语"no longer"，因此要使用倒装语序，例如：
   No longer are they staying with us. 他们再也不会跟我们在一起了。
   此外，以 not、never、hardly、seldom、little、no sooner、in vain、not only、not until、by no means、under no circumstances 等含有否定意义的状语开头时，句子要使用倒装语序。例如：
   Never will I make that mistake again. 我不会再犯那个错误了。
   In vain did they try to persuade her to give up her plan. 试图说服她放弃计划是徒劳的。
   Not until all attempts at negotiation had failed did the men decide to go on strike. 所有谈判

的努力都失败了，人们才决定罢工。
No sooner had he arrived than he fell ill. 他刚刚来到这里就生病了。

4. Businesses that cling to their domestic markets will be left far behind as their competitors gain "first mover advantage" in the international marketplace. 死抓住国内市场不放的企业就会远远落后于竞争对手，因为后者在国际市场上获得了"先驱优势"。

先驱优势（first mover advantage）：先驱优势是设法使自己成为一个新开发市场或新产品的先驱者，以获取回报的一种战略。这种回报就是持久的、长期的市场控制力，令竞争对手无法或难以仿效，企业因此能够生存和发展，比如电子商务行业中的 Amazon 等公司。先驱优势理论在市场营销中多用来解释在市场竞争中，先进入市场者相比后进入市场者存在哪些竞争优势。

5. It works with the assumption that you cannot market products to one country the way you market to another country. 国际营销认为，人们向一个国家销售产品的方式与向另一个国家销售产品的方式应该是不同的。

本句中使用了 that 引导的同位语从句，解释说明"assumption"。一般在 fact、belief、suggestion、idea、assumption、news、hope、thought、doubt 等后面可以跟同位语从句，例如：

The fact that the new manager is incompetent is known to all of us. 新任经理工作能力差是众所周知的事实。

The news that the CEO is coming back tomorrow is not true. 首席执行官明天要回来的消息不属实。

6. People's horizons should not be confined to any specific nation or to the particular ways of doing business in a single country. 人们的视野不应该仅仅局限于某一个特定的国家，或者局限于在某一个国家以特定的方式做生意。

句中的"be confined to"的意思是"局限于"，例如：

The old lady was confined to bed because of the cold weather. 天气寒冷，老太太只能待在床上。

7. Companies choose to expand their markets into the international arena for a host of sound reasons which may fall into two categories, proactive and reactive reasons. 那些公司选择在国际舞台上拓展市场，有很多合理的原因，主要分为两类，即积极性的原因和反应性的原因。

句中的"a host of"的意思是"很多"，例如：

The hotel offers a host of leisure activities. 这家宾馆提供了各种各样的休闲活动。

fall into 的意思是"分成几类，分成几部分"，例如：

His report falls into three parts. 他的报告分为三个部分。

8. All other objectives are secondary to achieving this goal. 所有其他的目标都不如这个目标重要。

句中的短语"be secondary to"的意思是"不如……重要"，例如：
The color of the car is secondary to its quality and price. 汽车的颜色没有质量和价格重要。
英语中的比较结构一般来讲都使用 more … than，但是也存在一些特殊的情况，例如：be senior to（比……年长，比……有资历）、be junior to（比……年幼，比……资历浅）、be superior to（比……高级，优于，胜过）、be inferior to（比……次的，低劣的）。
He is ten years senior to me. 他比我大 10 岁。
This cloth is superior to that. 这块布料比那块质量好。

9. Thus they have ready access to lower costs of labor, production and energy. 于是他们可以获得廉价的劳动力、产品和能源。
短语"have access to"的意思是"可以使用，可以进入，可以得到"，例如：
Nowadays everyone has access to the Internet. 现在谁都可以上网。

10. The growth of the technology has contributed to the increasing competition and opened up the doors to international business. 技术的发展使得竞争更加激烈了，为国际贸易打开了大门。
句中短语"contribute to"的意思是"有助于，促进"，例如：
Unwillingness to understand foreign cultures contributed to the failure of the negotiation. 他们不愿意去了解外国文化，最终谈判失败了。

11. It is at the WTO where the people in charge of global economy set the rules for what can be protected, what can be regulated, and what punishments can be imposed on whoever breaks the rules. 在世界贸易组织中，全球经济的负责人制定一系列规章制度，确定应该保护什么，应该规定什么，如何惩罚违反规定的人。
本句中使用了 where 引导的定语从句，修饰限定 WTO。介词 for 后面跟了三个并列的宾语从句，均由 what 引导。其中，短语"impose on sb./sth."的意思是"施加……"，例如：
They have imposed restrictions on trade with foreign companies. 他们限制与外国公司进行贸易活动。

12. Unstable political situations tend to expose businesses to numerous risks that they would rarely face at their home markets. 不稳定的政治局势往往会使得企业面临各种风险，而这些风险是他们在国内市场很少碰到的。
句中短语"expose to"的意思是"揭露，使……暴露"，例如：
The repeated quality problems exposed the company to widespread criticism. 产品质量问题频发，引起了全社会对公司的批评。

Unit 2 International Marketing

I Answer the following questions according to the text.

1. How did companies do business in the past?
2. What are the three T's mentioned in the passage?
3. What is the key to successful international marketing?
4. How does international marketing influence the economic development of countries and the profitability of individual business firms?
5. Why do companies choose to expand their markets into the international arena?
6. What are the proactive reasons for international marketing?
7. What are the reactive reasons for international marketing?
8. What has been done to promote global trade?
9. What are the main challenges that trouble companies in the foreign markets?
10. Suppose your company will market abroad, what will you do to get the most of international marketing?

II Decide whether the following statements are true or false.

1. Only large companies can market their products in foreign countries.
2. Now international marketing is a strategic imperative rather than an option.
3. Companies are supposed to change their marketing practices in every aspect.
4. Companies choose to turn to international market for two reasons.
5. Companies can choose to either go international markets or focus on home markets as they like.
6. Those businesses that can find sales opportunities abroad in an active way have great advantage over those forced to enter the international market.
7. The main purpose of business is to make more money for people.
8. The Internet has contributed to the increasingly intense competition and quickened the pace of international business.
9. Companies, big or small, have ready access to the Internet.
10. International marketing enables companies to avoid the influence of undesirable domestic situations.

III. Fill in each blank with the proper form of the word in the bracket.

1. The _____ (mount) intensity of competition in global markets is a challenge facing companies at all stages of involvement in international markets.
2. A marketing _____ (confine) to the political boundaries of a country is called Domestic Marketing.
3. Internet marketing _____ (able) the marketers to reach consumers in a wide range of ways.
4. International marketing involves _____ (recognize) that people all over the world have different needs.
5. Since many of the products are targeted at a global audience, companies are _____ (suppose) to understand regional differences.
6. The most important factor spurring international marketing efforts is, of course, _____ (make) money.
7. With the increasing intensity of competition, some companies have no choice but _____ (go) international.
8. If _____ (misunderstand), social and cultural environment can do great harm to marketing efforts.
9. Some people claim that while a business that sells its products in the same way in every market may suffer losses in _____ (isolate) instances, it will reap compensatory savings elsewhere.
10. Analysts note that whereas large _____ (nation) companies can afford to take a hit on a poorly marketed product on occasion, most small businesses are not so strong.

IV. Fill in each blank with a proper preposition.

1. Sometimes companies buy firms in the foreign countries to take advantage _____ relationships, factories, and personnel already in place.
2. When it comes _____ global marketing strategies, the Internet plays a highly significant role.
3. Even the small businesses have access _____ the global market with the help of the Internet.
4. The potential market size, degree and type of competition, price, promotional differences, product differences as well as barriers to trade call _____ careful studies and analysis.
5. Global marketing refers _____ marketing carried out by companies overseas or across national borderlines.
6. When exporting into a foreign market, a company may be not in control _____ the

Unit 2 International Marketing

supply of the good within the foreign market.
7. Although firms marketing abroad are faced _____ many of the same challenges as firms marketing domestically, international environments present other uncertainties.
8. They cling _____ the belief that their plan will bear fruit.
9. Most complaints can be disposed _____ pretty quickly.
10. The scandal exposed the company _____ public criticism.

V Fill in the blanks with the words and phrases given below. Change the form where necessary.

implement	tariff	impose on	devote to	suit the needs of
assumption	a host of	give rise to	secondary to	carry great weight

1. The agreement was signed but its recommendations were never _____.
2. The law works on the _____ that it is preferable for children to be with their mother.
3. He _____ most of his time _____ advertisement.
4. The products are designed to _____ the local consumers.
5. In addition to gaining a competitive advantage, there are _____ additional reasons why a company's web presence is becoming an increasingly important tool to reach global markets.
6. The worldwide competition _____ greater awareness of international market opportunities and of the need to be internationally competitive.
7. Culture _____ in international marketing.
8. He maintains everything is _____ the growth of the business.
9. In order to protect home market, some governments _____ heavy taxes _____ foreign companies.
10. _____ have played different roles in trade policy and the nation's economic history.

VI Cloze.

Marketing is the efficient and effective management and utilization of a company's resources to 1_____ the consumers' demands. It involves 2_____ the company's products to satisfy the needs of consumers.

Marketing can be done within a local or domestic market or 3_____ national borders or in the international market. 4_____ marketing and international marketing are the same when it comes 5_____ the fundamental principle of marketing. With the world shrinking 6_____ a fast pace, the boundaries between nations 7_____ and companies are now progressing from 8_____ to local markets to reach out to customers in different parts of the world. 9_____ done at a local level or at the global level, the fundamental concepts of marketing remain the same.

Domestic marketing refers to the marketing plans and strategies that a company implements within its own 10_____. When marketing is done at the domestic 11_____ it is considered local and the business is not 12_____ with potential markets at the international level. This does not mean that the company is not competing 13_____ foreign businesses operating within the same country, as competition may be fierce; it simply means they are choosing to concentrate their marketing within the borders of their own country. All the products and services are produced 14_____ in mind local customers only.

When there are no 15_____ for a company and it targets customers overseas or in another country, it is said to be 16_____ in international marketing. It involves the targeting of consumers overseas. The strategies used in international marketing are often the same 17_____ in domestic marketing but the audience is 18_____. It is used when companies want to concentrate 19_____ exporting goods and services to multiple countries 20_____ just the country of residence.

1. A. give	B. meet	C. send	D. make
2. A. selling	B. sell	C. to sell	D. to selling
3. A. in	B. beyond	C. through	D. across
4. A. Domestic	B. National	C. Global	D. Multinational
5. A. from	B. towards	C. to	D. for
6. A. at	B. in	C. to	D. with
7. A. have melted	B. melt	C. melted	D. are melting
8. A. catering	B. sticking	C. referring	D. confining
9. A. If	B. Unless	C. Whether	D. Once
10. A. country	B. market	C. boundaries	D. objectives
11. A. part	B. aspect	C. respect	D. level
12. A. deal	B. concerned	C. in line	D. keep
13. A. for	B. with	C. to	D. against
14. A. keep	B. to keep	C. having kept	D. keeping
15. A. markets	B. products	C. boundaries	D. resources
16. A. engaged	B. involved	C. specialized	D. trapped
17. A. that	B. for	C. with	D. as
18. A. larger	B. more	C. bigger	D. smaller
19. A. towards	B. in	C. on	D. over
20. A. rather than	B. other than	C. no other than	D. more than

Unit 2   International Marketing

VII   Translation.

1. Whether a company hires international employees or searches for new markets abroad, an international strategy can help diversify and expand a business.
2. While it might be wonderful to stay the same size and just focus on quality, the problem is that the competitive environment creates situations where your competition continues to grow—so, if you do not grow and expand, you will lose customers.
3. If an exporting company finds that the government in the recipient country starts to build tariff or non-tariff barriers to block the export, then it might be a reason for the exporter to set up a manufacturing operation overseas in order to avoid the tariffs.
4. Therefore, international marketing needs to take into account the local culture of the country in which you wish to market.
5. There was a time when companies concentrated their marketing in the local area, however today they are using international marketing in hopes of reaching customers from all over the world.

Extended Reading

Cultural Differences and International Marketing

American ethnologist Ward H.Goodenough ever mentioned that culture, being what people have to learn as distinct from their biological heritage, must consist of the end product of learning: knowledge, in a most general, if relative, sense of the term ..., as such, the things people say and do, their social arrangements and events, are products or by-products of their culture as they apply it to the task of perceiving and dealing with their circumstances. Therefore, culture is of great significance in determining people's behavior.

It is true of business world. Respecting cultural differences has brought human beings close together and has tied them in a strong bond. The conquering of the cultural differences has also introduced people to global economy. The world has become a singular unit because the pace of economic development has accelerated due to an increase in marketing not only at a local level, but also at a global level. International marketing has conquered and crossed all the boundaries of cultural differences, and brought people together in a realistic global world. It has become a right hand tool of the global economy because it respects cultural differences, covers the barriers of cultural differences and boosts the global economy. International trade has existed from time immemorial and cultural differences were not given importance in the past, but today's world of global economy and global marketing cannot survive without paying heed to the most critical key of cultural differences because abiding by cultural differences is a sure way to a full-fledged success in any business. Culture is part of the external influences that impact the consumer. It is universally acknowledged that culture is the "silent language" in international business.

The aim of business is the same everywhere, but the way to do it varies from country to country. Similar business situations in different countries do not necessarily imply similar opportunities. The key reason lies in different cultures. Nowadays, companies that are going global with their products have to contend with local companies who are armed with vast knowledge on how the locals react to a certain cultural pulse. They had also established their presence much earlier—they were there first. Thus, the newcomers must make sure that their products and promotional techniques are sensitive to cultural values of the people to leave a good impression of their branding.

Cultural awareness should be applied in every aspect of marketing: in selling, label-printing, advertising and promotion of products. It covers language, education, religion and other aspects of the country of interest. In other words, the language a population speaks, the average level of education, the prevailing religion, and other social conditions exert great influences on the priorities people have and the different ways they react to the same events.

Language is an important element of culture. It is important to really understand how a language is used by the people in your target market. It should also be kept in mind that much information is carried in non-verbal communication. In some cultures, people nod to signify "yes" and shake head to signify "no"; in other cultures, the practice is reversed.

There are many differences in terms of the level and nature of education in each international market. This may impact the type of message or even the medium that companies employ. For example, in countries with low literacy levels, advertisers would avoid communications which depend upon written copy, and would favor radio advertising with an audio message or visual media such as billboards.

The nature and complexity of the different religions a company going international could encounter is pretty diverse. Therefore, it needs to make sure that their products and services are not offensive, unlawful or distasteful to the local nation. For instance, people from different cultures have different ideas about animals. The dog in western countries is regarded as man's best friends. *Love me, love my dog.* However, according to the Muslim culture, the dog is considered as dirty, so picturing it as man's best friend in an advertisement is counter-productive. In that case, the products will not become popular in that country. The marketing plan is a definite failure.

International marketing and cultural differences cannot be separated, they have become inter-linked and inter-dependent. International marketing is an answer to the demands of the modern world, and the understanding of cultural differences of different countries is the key to these demands. The success stories of some international companies have provided evidence that if any company wants to go global in the true sense, it cannot ignore cultural influences. Advertisements should be conceived after careful study of the cultural differences because the same thing may not appeal to the eyes of the consumers belonging to different cultures and countries. The international marketing mixes like price, product, distribution and promotion depend on the cultural differences and the underlying legal and technical laws of different countries. International marketing has realized this obvious nature of human beings, and this in turn has led it to the awareness of the importance of cultural differences for a successful business.

Since it is widely accepted that you are not born with a culture, and that it is learned. The international marketers are supposed to take into account the local culture and try to learn some basic and important points. It is of first importance to know that culture really counts in international business.

Words and Expressions

ethnologist n. 人种学家，民族学者，人类文化学者
distinct a. 明显的，有区别的
biological a. 生物的
heritage n. 遗产
perceive v. 想象
accelerate v. 加快，加速
boost v. 促进，提高，推动
full-fledged a. 完全的，完备的
drive v. 驱动
imply v. 暗示
priority n. 优先
non-verbal a. 非语言的
signify v. 表示，意思是
medium n. 媒介
reverse v. 颠倒
complexity n. 复杂
encounter v. 遇到
offensive a. 冒犯的
unlawful a. 不合法的
distasteful a. 使人不愉快的，令人反感的

consist of 由……组成
end product 最终产品
by-product 副产品
It is true of … 对于……来说也是这样的
from time immemorial 自古至今
pay heed to 注意，留心
abide by 遵守
be a sure way to 有效的方法
contend with 与……竞争
literacy level 文化水平
radio advertising 无线电广告
audio message 声讯信息
visual media 视觉媒体
billboard n. 广告牌
counter-productive a. 事与愿违的，适得其反的
in that case 如果那样的话
in the true sense 真正意义上
take into account 把……考虑在内
count v. 重要，起作用

Comprehension

I Answer the following questions according to the passage.

1. What is the main idea of the first paragraph?
2. What is the relationship between cultural differences and global economy?
3. How can you understand the last sentence in the second paragraph?
4. What can we know from the third paragraph?
5. What will impact people's perception and reaction in business?
6. How does language influence international marketing?
7. How does education exert great influence on international marketing?
8. What is the purpose of the writer to mention the example of "Love me, love my dog."?
9. What function does the last paragraph perform?

II Write "T" for true, and "F" for false.

1. According to American ethnologist Ward H.Goodenough, culture is the biological heritage of a given society.
2. People can apply culture to perceive and deal with their circumstances.
3. Culture influences people's behavior in daily life rather than in business world.
4. The awareness of cultural differences has contributed to the growth of global economy.
5. Culture is the "silent language" in international business, so it's not very important when people do businesses.
6. The goal and the way of doing business is not necessarily the same.
7. Language is the most important element in culture.
8. Non-verbal communication carries more information than verbal communication.
9. The nature of education may vary from country to country.
10. Since culture is learned, marketers are expected to learn every detail of foreign culture.

 Additional Terms

acculturation	文化适应，文化渗透	cultural borrowing	文化借鉴
assimilation	吸收，同化	cultural change	文化变迁，文化变革
absolute advantage	绝对优势	cultural norm	文化规范，文化标准
business ethic	商业伦理	cultural sensitivity	文化敏感性

Unit 2　International Marketing

cultural variability　文化变异，文化变化
cybersquatter　域名抢注者
domestic marketing　国内营销
enculturation　文化适应，同化
environmental sensitivity　环境敏感性
ethnocentrism　民族优越感，民族中心主义
geocentrism　地心说
global awareness　全球意识
global consumer culture　全球消费文化
global environmental scanning　全球环境扫描
global evolution　全球进化
global marketing involvement　国际营销参与
green marketing legislation　绿色市场营销立法
high-context culture　高语境文化
homogenization　同质化
inadequate protection　保护不足
international convention　国际惯例
international vision　国际视野
low-context culture　低语境文化
marketing law　市场营销法
marketing practice　营销活动
planned cultural change　计划文化变迁
planned domestication　计划本土化
polycentrism　多中心主义
product trade cycle　产品贸易周期
self-reference criterion　自我参照标准
service effectiveness　服务效能
standardization　标准化
time orientation　时间方向
unplanned cultural change　无计划文化变迁

Unit 3
Marketing Environment

Marketing is the process which involves identifying existing customer needs and requirements and anticipating future changes. It is therefore a dynamic discipline. In other words, marketing is not operating in a vacuum, but rather in a complex and changing marketplace environment. Marketing environment is the sum total of factors that affect the ability of a firm to build, maintain and control successful relationships with the whole database of its customers. It for most, if not all, products changes regularly.[1] The challenge facing the marketer is, therefore, to find out as much as possible about this changing environment so that the business can respond in an appropriate way. This remains true for any company regardless of the industry, from a bottle of car oil to a fast moving consumer goods such as a bar of chocolate or a packet of soap powder.

The marketing environment surrounds and influences the organization. There are three key elements to the marketing environment which are the internal environment, the micro-environment or task environment and the macro-environment which includes broader influences that have more intermittent impact on the business (such as social trends, politics, economics, technology or laws). Marketers build both internal and external relationships and aim to deliver value to customers, so we need to assess and evaluate our internal business/corporate environment and our external environment which is subdivided into micro and macro.

The internal environment consists of top management and other departments. The former is responsible for setting the organization's mission, objectives, strategies and policies to guide all the departments and employees. The success of the company is dependant on the competence of the top managers. Other departments must coordinate their efforts as to maximize potential and avoid conflicts. The smoother the departments work together the better the overall outcome is going to be. All employees should realize the importance of being market-orientated and of delivering customer satisfaction.

A useful tool for quickly auditing your internal environment is known as the five Ms which are men, money, machinery, materials and markets. Looking internally at men, British Airways employs pilots, engineers, cabin crew, marketing managers, etc. Money is invested in the business by shareholders and banks. Machinery would include its aircraft and access to air bridges and buses to ferry passengers from the terminal to the aircraft. Materials for a service business like British Airways would be aircraft fuel called kerosene. Finally, markets can be both internal and external. Some might include a sixth M, which is minutes, since time is a valuable internal resource.

The term micro-environment refers to those elements over which the marketing firm has control or which it can use in order to gain information to help it in its marketing operations.[2] In other words, these elements can be manipulated, or used to get information to provide fuller satisfaction to the company's customers. The objective of marketing philosophy is to make profits through satisfying customers. This is accomplished through the manipulation of the variables over which a company has control in such a way as to optimize this objective. Examples would include the day-to-day influences on a business such as customers, competitors, suppliers and distributors. It consists of certain forces that are part of an organization's marketing process, but remains external to the organization. This micro marketing environment that surrounds organizations can be complex by nature, however, the company has an element of control over how it operates within this environment. Marketing helps you to manage and make sense of this complexity.

Walmart's micro-environment would be focused on immediate local issues.[3] It would consider how to recruit, retain and extend products and services to customers. In addition, it would pay close attention to the actions and reactions of direct competitors. Walmart would build and nurture close relationships with key suppliers. The business would need to communicate with its publics such as neighbors who are close to its stores, or other road users. There will be other intermediaries as well including advertising agencies and trade unions amongst others.[4]

By and large, managers can control the four Ps of the marketing mix: they can decide which products to offer, what prices to charge for them, how to distribute them, and how to reach target audiences. Unfortunately, there are other forces at work in the marketing world—forces over which marketers have much less control. The macro marketing environment takes into account all factors that can influence an organization, but are outside of their control. It consists of much larger all-encompassing influences from the broader global society. Here we would consider social and cultural differences, political and legal issues, technological advances, economic factors amongst others. These factors—and changes in them—present both threats and opportunities that require shifts in marketing plans.

Again for Walmart, the wider global macro-environment will certainly impact its business, and many of these factors are pretty much uncontrollable. Walmart trades mainly in the United States but also in international markets. For example, in the United Kingdom, Walmart trades as Asda.[5] It would need to take into account local customs and practices in the United Kingdom such as bank holidays and other local festivals. The United States and Europe experience different economic cycles, so trading in terms of interest rates needs to be considered. Also remember that Walmart can sell firearms in the United States which are illegal under local English law. There are many other macroeconomic influences such as governments and other publics, economic indicators such as inflation and exchange rates. There are powerful influencers such as war and natural disasters which inevitably would influence the business and would be out of its control.

To summarize, all businesses operate within an environment of change. The controllable factors tend to be included in your internal environment and your micro-environment. On the other hand, less controllable factors tend to be in relation to your macro-environment.

Vocabulary

vacuum　　*n.* 真空
intermittent　　*a.* 间歇的，断断续续的
potential　　*n.* 潜力
machinery　　*n.* 机器，机械
ferry　　*v.* 运送，渡运，摆渡
terminal　　*n.* 终点
kerosene　　*n.* 煤油
manipulation　　*n.* 操控，控制
accomplish　　*v.* 完成，实现
manipulate　　*v.* 操控，控制
variable　　*n.* 可变因素，变量

optimize　　*v.* 使最优化，使最有效率
nurture　　*v.* 发展；养育；培育
intermediary　　*n.* 中间商
all-encompassing　　*a.* 包罗万象的，包括一切的
shift　　*n.* 变化，变动
uncontrollable　　*a.* 无法控制的，难以驾驭的
firearm　　*n.* 火器，枪炮
summarize　　*v.* 总结，概括

Phrases and Expressions

but rather　　而是，反而
sum total　　总数，总和
fast moving consumer goods　　快速消费品
internal environment　　内在环境，内部环境
micro-environment or task environment　　微观环境或者任务环境
macro-environment　　宏观环境
British Airways　　英国航空公司
cabin crew　　航空乘务人员

air bridge　　登机桥
have control over　　控制……
marketing philosophy　　营销理念
by nature　　就其本质而言，本性上
make sense of　　理解，明白
direct competitors　　直接竞争者
by and large　　大体而言
at work　　工作中
economic indicator　　经济指数，经济指标
be out of control　　难以控制，失控
be in relation to　　与……相关

Unit 3 Marketing Environment

1. It for most, if not all, products changes regularly. 即使不是对于所有产品来说，对于大部分产品来说，营销环境经常会发生变化。

   在本句中，句子的谓语动词是 change，中间使用了插入语 for most, if not all, products，这里可以理解为 for most products, if not for all products。

2. The term micro-environment refers to those elements over which the marketing firm has control or which it can use in order to gain information to help it in its marketing operations. 微观环境指的是营销公司可以控制的因素，或者是公司可以用来获得信息的因素，从而为营销活动提供帮助。

   在本句中使用了两个并列的定语从句，由并列连词 or 连接，在从句中关系代词 which 指代的是先行词 elements，短语 have control over 的意思是"控制……"，例如：

   People think human beings have control over the present and future, but we really don't. 人们认为人类能够控制现在和将来，但实际上，我们控制不了。

3. Walmart's micro-environment would be focused on immediate local issues. 沃尔玛的微观环境侧重于当地最紧迫的一些问题。

   沃尔玛公司由美国零售业的传奇人物山姆·沃尔顿先生于 1962 年在阿肯色州成立。经过 50 多年的发展，该公司已经成为美国最大的私人雇主和世界上最大的连锁零售企业。目前，沃尔玛在全球开设了 10 000 多家商场，员工总数达到 220 多万人，分布在全球 27 个国家和地区。沃尔玛提出"帮顾客节省每一分钱"的宗旨，实现了价格最便宜的承诺。沃尔玛还向顾客提供超一流服务的新享受，消费者可以体验"一站式"购物的新概念。在商品结构上，力求富有变化和特色，以满足顾客的各种喜好。经营项目繁多，包括食品、玩具、新款服装、化妆用品、家用电器、日用百货、肉类蔬菜等。

4. There will be other intermediaries as well including advertising agencies and trade unions amongst others. 除了其他中间商之外，还有包括广告代理和工会之类的中间商。

   在本句中，理解的重点和难点在于句尾的短语 amongst others，意思是"除了……之外，其中"，例如：

   Several persons are invited, and among others, Mr. Danglars, your banker. 我请了几个人，其中就有你们的银行家腾格拉尔先生。

   Why is Guangdong so rich? Historical links to the overseas Chinese, among other things, play an important role. 为什么广东这么富？除了其他方面的原因外，历史上形成的同海外华人的联系是一个重要因素。

5. For example, in the United Kingdom, Walmart trades as Asda. 例如，在英国沃尔玛就是以阿斯

达进行经营的。

阿斯达（Asda）是英国第一家在生产的食品和软饮料中禁止使用人工色素和香料的超市，致力于"无污染"食品的生产。1999年，沃尔玛收购了英国的阿斯达集团。这是一家实力强大、管理完善的连锁超级市场集团，是英国零售业的巨头之一。阿斯达与沃尔玛的风格非常接近。实际上，阿斯达集团很久以来一直在借鉴沃尔玛的经营宗旨与经营模式，因此几乎无须进行任何企业文化方面的改造。

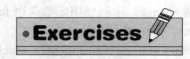

I Answer the following questions according to the text.

1. Why is marketing a dynamic discipline?
2. What is marketing environment?
3. How many types of marketing environment are mentioned? And what are they?
4. What are the responsibilities of top management?
5. How to quickly audit the internal environment?
6. What is micro-environment? And what are its characteristics?
7. What does macro marketing environment mainly concern?
8. What is paragraph 8 mainly about?
9. Suppose you are a marketing manager, then how can you deal with economic factors?

II Decide whether the following statements are true or false.

1. Marketing is not operating in a vacuum but in a complex marketing environment.
2. Marketing environment changes regularly for all products.
3. The challenge facing the marketers is not necessarily true for any industry.
4. There are three key elements to the marketing environment, namely, the internal environment, the micro-environment and task environment.
5. The success of the company depends upon the cooperation of top management and other departments.
6. In the tool for quickly auditing your internal environment, machinery refers to the machines used to produce desired products.
7. The objective of marketing philosophy is to make profits and satisfy customers.
8. Complex as the micro-environment is, the firm has control over it.

Unit 3 Marketing Environment

9. The micro-environment is no controllable than the macro-environment.
10. The macro-environment presents more opportunities than threats to firms.

III Fill in each blank with the proper form of the word in the bracket.

1. She uses her charm to _____ (manipulation) people.
2. It is difficult to convey the sheer _____ (complex) of the situation.
3. If political and ethnic problems are not resolved, the situation could become _____ (control).
4. Basically, the article can be _____ (summary) in three sentences.
5. No single document could _____ (encompassing) all the shades of interpretation.
6. By any standards, the _____ (accomplish) of the past year are extraordinary.
7. By changing its _____ (supply), the company saved thousands of pounds in import duty.
8. Industrialization _____ (inevitable) led to the expansion of the urban working class.
9. His job as a public relations director involves _____ (spend) quite a lot of time with other people.
10. They appointed a new manager to _____ (coordination) the work of the team.

IV Fill in each blank with a proper preposition.

1. Now is a good time to invest _____ the property market.
2. I have a lot to say in relation _____ that affair.
3. We had to take _____ account the strategic implications of these events.
4. Please make sense _____ these marks on paper immediately.
5. Unfortunately, the fire had been _____ of control before they arrived.
6. Sorry, Linda is _____ work right now, so please call her later.
7. He has no control _____ the current situation.
8. The process of learning a language does not take place _____ a vacuum.
9. Access _____ the papers is restricted to senior management.
10. Their target customers consists mainly _____ teenagers.

V Fill in the blanks with the words and phrases given below. Change the form where necessary.

| by and large | nurture | complexity | coordinate | but rather |
| sum total | optimize | potential | in relation to | make sense of |

1. They need to _____ the use of available resources.

2. He failed to _____ the report because it was too abstract.
3. We want to _____ the new project, not to destroy it.
4. We must _____ our efforts to conduct market research.
5. The product has even more _____ in export markets.
6. They discussed the latest development _____ online advertising.
7. This advertising campaign is not a success, _____ it brings a great loss to the firm.
8. Ten years was the _____ he worked as a shop assistant.
9. The _____ of economics are clearly and entertaininingly explained.
10. _____, how is your new business progressing?

VI Cloze.

The marketing environment is everything 1_____ your company must take into 2_____ when developing and presenting a new product. The elements of a marketing environment include, 3_____ are not limited to, the changing preferences of customers, your competition, the legal, political and regulatory environment, your own resources and budget, current trends and the overall economy. All these elements affect your marketing decisions—or 4_____ they should, because all of them 5_____ your prospects.

To be successful, a marketing plan should focus on 6_____ and current market trends. For example, many large retailers have decided to adapt to consumers' increasing 7_____ for social media by establishing corporate Twitter accounts and opening 8_____ storefronts in Facebook. Consumers 9_____ to visit a retailer's main website to buy; some platforms 10_____ them to make the purchase 11_____ ever leaving Facebook. Companies 12_____ fail to take major trends into account may find their sales lagging behind 13_____.

Your budget plainly has a role in your marketing decisions. It decides 14_____ advertising you buy and where you can afford to place it. The overall 15_____ also has a massive influence on your marketing decisions. If you're marketing in a down economy, your consumers won't be willing to pay a premium for your product, and your advertising should probably point out that the product saves your customers 16_____, costs less than your competitor's product, or lasts a 17_____ time and is therefore a good value. In a strong economy, your strategy probably will change.

If your competitors are able to offer their product for a much lower price than yours, your marketing strategy must stress the fact that your product is of a 18_____ quality, or that your product lasts longer. Changes in the political and legal environment can restrict or even end certain marketing activities. 19_____ offering a product, you should consider 20_____ it is a candidate for legal or regulatory trouble.

1. A. which   B. that   C. how   D. what

Unit 3 Marketing Environment

2. A. count   B. effect   C. practice   D. consideration
3. A. but   B. however   C. and   D. therefore
4. A. at least   B. at most   C. at best   D. at last
5. A. effect   B. change   C. influence   D. decide
6. A. marketing decisions B. consumer preferences C. websites   D. current economy
7. A. keen   B. care   C. enthusiasm   D. desire
8. A. real   B. online   C. big   D. small
9. A. don't need   B. needn't   C. needn't have   D. don't need have
10. A. make   B. let   C. allow   D. set
11. A. without   B. for   C. upon   D. with
12. A. /   B. that   C. who   D. whose
13. A. competitors   B. others   C. the others'   D. competitors'
14. A. how many   B. how much   C. how   D. what
15. A. growth   B. speed   C. economy   D. value
16. A. money   B. time   C. energy   D. space
17. A. shorter   B. long   C. short   D. longer
18. A. lower   B. higher   C. better   D. worse
19. A. After   B. When   C. Before   D. Since
20. A. whether   B. why   C. that   D. how

VII Translation.

1. Marketing planning works as a warning mechanism by making a company alert and sensitive to the environment.
2. The economic environment consists of all factors—such as salary levels, credit trends and pricing patterns that affect consumer spending habits and purchasing power.
3. The socio-cultural environment includes institutions and other forces that affect the basic values, behaviors, and preferences of the society—all of which have an effect on consumer marketing decisions.
4. It is also necessary to conduct marketing audit, which involves comprehensive, independent and periodic examination of marketing environment, objectives, strategies to determine problem areas and opportunities.
5. The technological environment consists of those forces that affect the technology with which can create new products, new markets and new marketing opportunities.

Extended Reading

Analyzing Web Marketing Environment

Successful companies take an outside-inside view of their business. They recognize that the marketing environment is constantly presenting new opportunities and threats. They also realize the importance of continuously monitoring and adapting to the environment. A company that has continuously re-invented one of its brands to keep up with changing marketing environment is "Mattel" with its "Barbie doll". Many companies fail to see change as an opportunity. They ignored or resisted changes until it is too late. Their strategies, structures, systems, and organizational culture grow increasingly obsolete. If marketing is indeed about understanding and responding to customers, then solid analysis of the environment is where great Web marketing plans begin. It is in the environment that we see the changes which indicate emerging segments.

When we speak of the marketing environment, we are referring to all of the things happening in our world that may have an impact on business. Web sites are unlike products. They can and do change frequently, with many major sites getting a substantial overhaul every six months. Web activity is "right here, right now" and people can react quickly. For instance, a well-publicized case of credit card fraud online would almost instantly affect buyer behavior. The site that had problem can fix that problem in an hour in many cases. This isn't like a lousy card that continues to be offered for years.

To some extent, demographic determines everything. On the web, though, it does not have the same importance as in conventional marketing. That's because visitors to a site are defined clearly by their interests more so than their demographics.

There are many sites which define themselves largely by age. Teens move towards sites for their favorite brands, while there are many sites geared to retired people. Women behave differently from men online and Europe is forecast to grow mightily online. Another issue is the number of people that will ultimately be regulars on the web. So far, higher levels of income and education are strong indicators of web participation. Consider how changing demographic trends, such as ageing Baby Boomers or a larger teenage cohort would affect the industry. Also, if there is a clear demographic profile for those who might visit sites in this industry, that will be helpful in reaching them.

The web has transformed the nature of competitive analysis. Web sites reveal much of the strategy and activity of firms, and they make it easy to assess strategies. Keep in mind that your competitors will be among the visitors to your web site. However, withholding information for this reason is counterproductive. Never forget that competition should always be broadly defined

Unit 3 Marketing Environment

(movies and bars compete for entertainment spending), so don't overlook the traditional businesses or catalogue operators. The web even has third parties that search out the lowest price for a given item, using robots to search sites. If they could take away some of your business, they're competitors.

Web technologies that allow faster file transfers, videoconferencing, interactive web pages are all progressing rapidly. If they could have an impact on the market under consideration, they must be tracked. Technology also makes it possible to create web sites that track visitor behavior and permit ongoing refinements so people stay longer. Those using such technologies can be more responsive to user trends. Database management is increasingly a part of most web marketing plans. Adoption of technologies also enhances some businesses. For instance, the adoption of extensible markup language will open new opportunities for supply chain management and effective administration.

The web may seem an area that would bear little fruit for political-legal matters. However, think of the impact taxation would have on the web. Consider the possibility of government regulation of web activity or commerce. Many are striving to "control" the web for their own interests.

For years, the idea of perfect competition, which requires perfect information, lived only in economic textbooks. Now, buyers can get huge amounts of information to make their decisions. The laws of supply and demand apply on the web as they do anywhere else. Don't jump to any conclusions about prices being driven down by the web. Consider how a recession would affect the web. In a recession, firms often shift to other activities to keep busy and the web opens new opportunities to do so.

For anyone considering retail sales on the web, the social-cultural area is crucial.

How will consumers react to bad experiences in the online world? If the order never comes, or is late, will they give up on web purchases? Some web sites are using the weak strategy of free shipping as a lure for business. Will consumers click on someone else's site? Consider social changes or trends that may work for or against growth in the category. For instance, if pet lovers are anxious to buy special presents for their animals, a site offering custom pet clothing might do well.

Words and Expressions

Mattel n. 美国美泰公司（全球最大的玩具公司）	overhaul n. 检修
resist v. 抵抗，抵制，抗拒	well-publicized a. 众所周知的
obsolete a. 过时的，陈旧的	fix v. 修理
emerging a. 新兴的	lousy a. 蹩脚的，糟糕的
	mightily ad. 非常，极其

regular n. 常客	competitive analysis 竞争分析
indicator n. 指标	entertainment spending 娱乐消费
cohort n. 一群人	file transfer 文件传输
withhold v. 拒绝给予	be responsive to sth. 对……反应快的
counterproductive a. 起反作用的，事与愿违的	database management 数据库管理
videoconference n. 视频会议	extensible markup language 可扩展标记语言
refinement n. 完善，改进	bear fruit 结出果实，奏效
credit card fraud 信用卡诈骗	jump to a conclusion 草草下结论，草率决定
web participation 网络参与	

Comprehension

I Answer the following questions according to the passage.

1. How can you understand "Successful companies take an outside-inside view of their business." in the first paragraph?
2. What will happen if businesses fail to keep up with changing marketing environment?
3. What are the differences between web sites and products?
4. Why does the writer say that web activity "right here, right now"?
5. Why doesn't demographic have the same importance on the web as in conventional marketing?
6. How has the web transformed the nature of competitive analysis?
7. What impacts do the web technologies have on businesses?
8. What is the relationship between the web and political-legal matters?
9. Why is the social-cultural area crucial for those considering retail sales on the web?
10. What does the writer mainly talk about in the passage?

II Write "T" for true, and "F" for false.

1. It's of great importance to continuously monitor and adapt to the marketing environment.
2. Mattel sets a good example for companies in terms of keeping up with changing marketing environment.
3. Demographic is more important on the web than in traditional marketing.
4. In most cases, sites are defined mainly by age.

5. Web participation has something to do with levels of income and education.
6. It's advisable for you to withhold some online information from your competitors.
7. Adoption of some technologies will contribute to the further growth of businesses.
8. The web is affected by political-legal matters.
9. The laws of supply and demand do not apply on the web as well we they do anywhere else.

Additional Terms

actor 参与者	marketing environment audit 市场营销环境审计
business market 生产者市场	marketing service agency 营销服务公司
citizen-action public 社团公众	natural environment 自然环境
competitive rivalry 竞争对手	non-profit organization market 非营利组织市场
cultural environment 文化环境	physical distribution firm 物流公司
customer market 消费者市场	potential entrant 潜在竞争者
demographic environment 人口环境	privacy concern 隐私问题
economic environment 经济环境	public 公众
Engle's coefficient 恩格尔系数	rank and priority 等级与优先
economic factors 经济要素	regional culture 区域文化
environment 环境因素	reseller market 中间商市场
financial intermediary 财务中介公司	reseller 中间商
financial public 融资公众	spending power 消费力
force 影响力	technological environment 技术环境
general public 一般公众	technological factor 科技要素
government public 政府公众	threat of entry 市场准入的威胁
identity theft 身份盗窃	threat of substitute 可替代产品的威胁
immediate environment 直接环境	time-poor society 时间短缺的社会
internal public 内部公众	
local public 社区公众	
media public 媒体公众	
marketing effort 市场效能,营销效能	

Unit 4
Marketing Information System

Information is king in the land of marketing. It can help even the smallest problem, by monitoring habits of buyers and looking at patterns in consumer buying. One company who stands out over all the others is AC Nielsen[1]. If you talk about marketing information systems, you can't discuss this without mentioning AC Nielsen, a leading global information and measurement company, which provides market research, insights and data about what people watch and what people buy.

Marketing activities are directed toward planning, promoting, and selling goods and services to satisfy the needs of customers; marketing information systems (MIS) support decision making regarding these activities. A good marketing information system balances the information users would like to have against what they really need and what is feasible to offer.[2]

Marketing information system is an efficient tool providing past, present and projected information relating to internal operations and external intelligence. It supports the planning, control, and operational function in an organization by furnishing uniform information in the proper time frame to assist the decision maker. Earlier generations of managers tended to adopt technology first and then try to figure out what to do with it; that approach is now grossly inadequate. Matching information technology to the organization in terms of its ability to shape the organization is central to success.[3] Part of that matching process rests with understanding the value of the collection, application and management of marketing information generated by information technology applications.[4] We speculate that under time pressure senior management in "second mover" firms are likely to make ad hoc adoption decisions without fully considering the match between the technology and the overall value orientation of their organization.

Marketing information system plays an important role in raising the efficiency of economic performance to the companies in highly competitive markets, through providing the necessary information for the various administrative levels. The success of the marketing process depends to a large extent on the marketing information system and the success in each element of this system. It has been needed by marketing management for the purpose of identifying, measuring, and forecasting marketing opportunities, besides, analyzing of market segments. It consists of people, facilities, and integrated procedures that can be used to provide management with accurate and regulated information about the environment-related marketing, which helps decision makers to hunt opportunities and build strategies and marketing plans.

Despite the fact that there are large and variety numbers of marketing information system definitions, but all of them are focused on one point: the marketing information system is a structure composed of personnel, equipment, thus ensuring the flow of internal and external information, which allows the spread and control of the organization's external environment, and the rationalization of marketing decisions.

The reasons for the need of marketing information system can be summarized as follows:

• Competitive pressures require the organizations to have the ability to compete, to produce, and to market developed products more quickly than before.

• The steady increase in consumer expectations and what they expect of products, in terms of its ability to satisfy their needs, and the consequences of less serious or inaccurate decision taking due to the lack or inaccuracy of the information upon which the decision will be built, and its impact on the organization's success and sustainability.

• The widespread production and distribution contributed to the emergence of large markets, and their requirements of a large number of intermediaries between producers and final consumers. These intermediaries become a barrier to the flow of data that can guide the development of marketing decisions related to the consumers' needs and desires, as a result, the widening gap between producers and final consumers reinforces the importance of marketing information system in bridging this gap.[5]

• Each organization has more than one source of information, but the problem lies in how to use and manage this information. With the development of computers and other operating data equipments, it has become quick and inexpensive for management to run and analyze vast amounts of marketing data and provide information necessary for effective decisions.

One aspect of the IT impact on the organization is the use of new organizational structures which leads to the reduction of the number of administrative levels, and expands the scope of supervision and control. Supervision in this way is based on staff confidence and less direct contact between supervisors and subordinates and relies on e-mail and software. In this way their coordination can be achieved between the individuals who perform common tasks, and decision-making responsibilities of managers can be increased, thus making the organization more responsive to its customers and its competitors.

With an increasingly competitive and expanding market, the amount of information needed daily by an organization is profound. Thus a marketing information system becomes a must. There are several advantages of marketing information systems.

- **Organized data collection**. Lots of data can be collected from the market. Organizing data is very important or else the data is meaningless.[6] Thus MIS helps you to organize your database thereby improving productivity.

- **A broad perspective**. With a proper MIS in place, the complete organization can be tracked to analyze independent processes. This helps to establish a broader perspective which enables us to know which steps can be taken to facilitate improvement.

- **Storage of important data**. Several times in pharmaceuticals, when one drug is being produced they may need data of another drug which was produced years back. Similarly in media, photographs are stored in archives. This storage of important data plays a crucial role in execution and thus proves again that MIS is not important only for information but also for execution.

- **Avoidance of crisis**. The best way to analyze a stock (share market) is to see its past performance. Top websites like moneycontrol thrive on MIS.[7] Similarly MIS helps you keep tracks of margins and profits. With an amazing information system established, you can know where your organization is moving and probably avert a crisis long before it has taken place. Ignoring hints received from MIS reports is foolhardy.

- **Co-ordination**. Consumer durables and FMCG companies have huge number of processes which needs to be coordinated. These companies depend completely on MIS for the proper running of the organization. There are dedicated people for marketing information systems in such organizations. This is mainly because of the speed required to access information and implement it.

- **Analysis and planning**. MIS is critical for planning. You cannot do planning without information. For planning, the first thing needed is the organizations' capabilities, then the business environment and finally competitor analysis. In a proper MIS, all these are present by default and are continuously updated. Thus MIS is very important for planning and analysis.

- **Control**. Just like MIS can help in a crisis, in normal times it provides control as you have information of the various processes going on and what is happening across the company. Thus it provides you with a sense of control.

The application of marketing information system in organizations faces some problems. The system depends basically on individuals in the supply, summary, generation, and dissemination, and interpretation of data. The possibility of bias of the system in terms of providing data that support preferred actions, rather than evaluating all possible actions has been raised. Analysts have drawn attention to the inaccuracy of the organization's research for the use of information, and the goals of individuals may be a particularly important factor for the objectiveness of marketing information system in managing the operation of providing the information to choose among alternatives, and making planning decisions.[8] Managers who use the marketing information system data may impose their private choice on the information, as well as on the ways of manipulating them. It should be noted that there are many obstacles that prevent the free flow of information, such as fear of the implementation, and personal reasons, mainly from the standpoint of self-protection within the organization.

In the stages of creation and development of the system, in addition to other problems related to planning and control, there is the problem of the degree of change resistance that can be directed to this change in different kinds of circumstances. Change is one of the main causes of organizational conflict in terms of creating tension and anxiety which lead to resistance and then the struggle to avoid or change the direction of change. Another important problem facing the use of marketing information system is the way in which institutional relations hinder the use of marketing information systems.

Vocabulary

feasible	*a.* 可行的	execution	*n.* 实行，贯彻，完成
furnish	*v.* 提供，供应	avoidance	*n.* 避免
assist	*v.* 帮助，援助	thrive	*v.* 兴盛，兴隆
grossly	*ad.* 大略，大约	margin	*n.* 利润，盈余
speculate	*v.* 猜测，推测	avert	*v.* 防止，避免
rationalization	*n.* 合理化	foolhardy	*a.* 莽撞的，有勇无谋的
sustainability	*n.* 持续性，永久性	dedicated	*a.* 专注的，投入的，献身的
reinforce	*v.* 加强	default	*n.* 默认
profound	*a.* 深远的	dissemination	*n.* 散播，宣传
must	*n.* 必须做的事情，必不可少的事情	standpoint	*n.* 立场，观点
pharmaceutical	*n.* 药物，药品	hinder	*v.* 阻碍，妨碍
archive	*n.* 档案，史料，记录		

Phrases and Expressions

external intelligence	外部情报	expect ... of sb.	对某人寄予……期待，指望某人……
time frame	期限	build upon	建立于
final consumers	最终消费者	in place	在适当的位置就绪
ad hoc	特定的，临时的，即席的	keep track of	记录，与……保持联系
value orientation	价值取向	consumer durable	耐用消费品
economic performance	经济表现，经济绩效	impose ... on	施加，强加
be composed of	由……组成		

1. AC Nielsen：AC 尼尔森公司是一家总部位于美国纽约的国际市场调查研究公司，北美地区的总部坐落于伊利诺伊州的绍姆堡。该公司是全球领先的市场研究、资讯和分析服务的提供者，服务对象包括消费产品和服务行业，以及政府和社会机构。在全球 100 多个国家有超过 9 000 家公司依靠 AC 尼尔森的专业人士监测竞争激烈的市场动态，分析消费者的态度和行为，获取促进销售和增加利润的高级分析报告。

2. A good marketing information system balances the information users would like to have against what they really need and what is feasible to offer.　良好的营销信息系统能够让消费者希望得到的信息与实际获得的信息以及能够提供的信息之间实现平衡。

   在本句中，the information 后面的"users would like to have"是定语从句，引导词在从句中作宾语，因此省略掉了。介词 against 后面是两个并列的宾语从句，由 what 来引导。

3. Matching information technology to the organization in terms of its ability to shape the organization is central to success.　信息技术要与机构相匹配，能够对机构产生一定的影响，这对于成功是至关重要的。

   在本句中"Matching information technology to the organization in terms of its ability to shape the organization"是句子的主语，-ing 短语作主语看作单数。match 的意思是"与……相称，与……匹配"，in terms of 的意思是"在……方面，就……而言"，例如：

   We will try to match you to employers with the vacancies you are looking for.　我们会争取为你找到提供你所需职位的用人单位。

   It can not be measured in terms of money.　这是不能用金钱衡量的。

4. Part of that matching process rests with understanding the value of the collection, application and management of marketing information generated by information technology applications.　一部分匹配过程取决于对营销信息收集、运用以及管理价值的理解程度，这种信息是运用类似于数据库营销这样的信息技术而产生的。

   在本句中，短语 rest with 的意思是"取决于，在于"，例如：

   It rests with the manager to decide which strategy to utilize.　全由经理来决定到底采用哪种策略。

5. These intermediaries become a barrier to the flow of data that can guide the development of marketing decisions related to the consumers' needs and desires, as a result, the widening gap between producers and final consumers reinforces the importance of marketing information system in bridging this gap.　数据可以引导领导者制定与消费者需求和愿望相关的营销决策，然而这些中介妨碍了数据的正常流动，因此，生产商与最终消费者之间的差距就会越

Unit 4　Marketing Information System

来越大,这样一来,营销信息系统在缩小差距方面所起到的重要作用就日益凸显出来了。
在本句中,barrier 的意思是"障碍,阻碍",例如:
Duties and taxes are the most obvious barrier to free trade.　关税和税收是自由贸易的最大壁垒。
Lack of confidence is the biggest barrier to investment in the region.　缺乏信心是在这一地区投资的最大障碍。
本句结构比较复杂,首先是 that 引导的定语从句用来修饰限定前面的 the flow of data,后面的分词短语 related to the consumers' needs and desires 用来修饰 marketing decisions。bridge this gap 的意思是"缩短差距",bridge 的意思是"弥合分歧,消除隔阂",例如:
It is unlikely that the two sides will be able to bridge their differences.　双方不太可能消除彼此之间的分歧。

6. Organizing data is very important or else the data is meaningless.　整理数据非常重要,否则的话数据就没有任何意义了。
在本句中 or else 的意思是"否则的话,要不然",例如:
He must be teasing, or else he's mad.　他一定是在开玩笑,不然他就是疯了。

7. Top websites like moneycontrol thrive on MIS.　像 moneycontrol 这样的顶级网站就是依靠营销信息系统而蓬勃发展起来的。
moneycontrol 是一个个人理财工具网站,成立于 1999 年 12 月 5 日,是印度最大的金融和商业门户网站,得到数以百万计的用户信任。使用 moneycontrol 应用程序,用户可以获得实时股票行情、全球市场指数,管理和跟踪你的投资组合,观看电视直播,并得到金融市场、经济和商业的深度报道和分析。

8. Analysts have drawn attention to the inaccuracy of the organization's research for the use of information, and the goals of individuals may be a particularly important factor for the objectiveness of marketing information system in managing the operation of providing the information to choose among alternatives, and making planning decisions.　分析家们已经注意到,公司针对信息使用而开展的研究不够精确,营销信息系统可以对提供的可供选择的信息进行管理,就其客观性而言,个人的目标也许是一个特别重要的因素。
本句看似结构复杂,实际上首先是由 and 连接的两个并列结构的句子,第二个句子的主要结构是 the goals of individuals may be a particularly important factor,后面跟 for 引导的介词短语,该短语中又包含了 in 引导的介词短语,在该介词短语中 and 连接并列的结构 managing the operation of providing the information 和 making planning decisions。

I Answer the following questions according to the text.

1. How do you understand the sentence "Information is king in the land of marketing."?
2. What is marketing information system?
3. What is the importance of marketing information system?
4. What do various marketing information definitions have in common?
5. Why is marketing information system needed?
6. How does the marketing information system affect organizations?
7. What are the merits of marketing information system?
8. What does the writer mean by "a broad perspective" in terms of advantages of MIS?
9. How can businesses avoid crisis with the help of MIS?
10. What are the problems facing the application of MIS?

II Decide whether the following statements are true or false.

1. Information is only of great help to some thorny problems.
2. The information users would like to have is not necessarily the same as what they really need and what is feasible to offer.
3. Managers used to ignore the impact of technology on the organizations.
4. The approach adopted by earlier managers was far from adequate.
5. The matching process rests with understanding the value of the collection, application and management of marketing information.
6. The success of the marketing process depends to a large degree on the marketing information system and the success in each element of this system.
7. Various as the definitions of marketing information system are, they have something in common.
8. Organizations can get some hints from the marketing information system to avoid crisis.
9. For analysis, the first thing needed is the organizations' capabilities, then the business environment and finally competitor analysis.
10. The system depends completely on individuals in the supply, summary, generation, and dissemination, and interpretation of data.

Unit 4 Marketing Information System

III Fill in each blank with the proper form of the word in the bracket.

1. He had managed to create the entirely misleading impression that the company was _____ (thrive).
2. The committee will study the _____ (feasible) of setting up a national computer network.
3. Julia was _____ (assist) him to prepare his speech at the next conference.
4. New business we have _____ (generate) should far exceed what's been lost.
5. The company is highly _____ (respond) to changes in demand.
6. His whole energies are _____ (dedicate) to improve the design.
7. He's speaking up and _____ (assertion) himself confidently.
8. For low-paid workers, the _____ (margin) tax rate is at least 75%.
9. The creation of an efficient and _____ (sustainability) transport system is critical to the long-term future of London.
10. One basic advantage of organization planning is _____ (avoid) of organizational inflexibility.

IV Fill in each blank with a proper preposition.

1. Firms have to be responsive _____ consumer demand.
2. The committee is composed mainly _____ skilled workers.
3. You are expecting too much _____ him; after all, he is a new comer in the company.
4. The proposal is not quite _____ place.
5. Whether the talks are successful or not rests _____ a small number of people.
6. New taxes were imposed _____ wines and spirits.
7. With eleven thousand employees, it's very difficult to keep track _____ them all.
8. His further plan is built _____ thorough market researches.
9. The company's attention needs to be directed _____ various tastes of customers.
10. The company is highly responsive _____ changes in demand.

V Fill in the blanks with the words and phrases given below. Change the form where necessary.

must	profound	generate	sustainable	reinforce
speculate	feasible	furnish	impose on	avert

1. They'll be able to _____ you with the rest of the details.
2. It's just not _____ to manage the business on a part-time basis.

3. We don't know all the circumstances, so it would be pointless to _____.
4. The company attaches more importance to _____ instead of blind pursuit of fast growth.
5. His theories had a _____ effect on the management of the firm.
6. I would do whatever I could to _____ that tragedy.
7. Your positive response will _____ her actions.
8. On the part of entrepreneurs, a market research is a _____ to determine if their ideas are viable.
9. The US could _____ punitive tariffs of up to 100% _____ some countries' exports.
10. He said the reforms would _____ new jobs, thus boosting the local economy.

VI Cloze.

In looking at the different marketing information systems, one can only 1_____ at the thoroughness of companies and the information it collects. A marketing information system (MIS) is a management information system 2_____ to support marketing decision making. It brings together many different kinds of data, people, equipment and procedures to help an organization make better 3_____. American academic Philip Kotler has 4_____ it more broadly as "people, equipment, and procedures to gather, 5_____, analyze, evaluate, and distribute needed, timely, and accurate information to marketing decision makers". This can optimize your sales, and if 6_____ right, can help monitor changes, patterns, and wants of consumers. Not to be confused for a management information system, marketing information systems are designed 7_____ for managing the marketing aspects of the business. Jobber defines it as a "system 8_____ marketing data is formally gathered, stored, analyzed and distributed to managers in 9_____ with their informational needs on a regular 10_____".

MIS 11_____ not only how things are going, but also why and where performance is failing to meet the plan. These reports include near real-time performance of cost centers and projects 12_____ details sufficient for individual accountability. MIS produces fixed, regularly scheduled reports to middle and operational level managers to 13_____ and inform structured and semi-structured decision problems.

A traditional marketing information system can provide endless benefits to any organization in the private or 14_____ sector, 15_____ its size or level of managerial sophistication. Some of these 16_____ include:

• It enables managers 17_____ information and work together virtually.

• It addresses operational needs through customer management systems that 18_____ on the day-to-day processing of customer transactions from the initial sale through customer service.

• The availability of the customer data and feedback can help the company align their business processes according to the needs of the customers. The 19_____ management of customer data can help the company perform direct marketing and promotional activities.

• Information is considered to be an important 20_____ for any company in the modern competitive world. The consumer buying trends and behaviors can be predicted by the analysis of sales and revenue reports from each operating region of the company.

1. A. shock	B. excite	C. dismay	D. marvel
2. A. designed	B. designing	C. designs	D. to be designed
3. A. promises	B. decisions	C. plans	D. judgment
4. A. defined	B. regarded	C. considered	D. thought of
5. A. collect	B. arrange	C. sort	D. organize
6. A. done	B. being done	C. doing	D. to be done
7. A. specially	B. especially	C. particularly	D. specifically
8. A. for which	B. that	C. in which	D. where
9. A. harmony	B. agreement	C. coordination	D. accordance
10. A. terms	B. basis	C. stage	D. foundation
11. A. indicates	B. tells	C. informs	D. implies
12. A. in	B. with	C. through	D. for
13. A. recognize	B. certify	C. identify	D. realize
14. A. public	B. individual	C. collective	D. social
15. A. despite of	B. despite	C. in spite	D. in despite of
16. A. disadvantages	B. sectors	C. benefits	D. organizations
17. A. share	B. sharing	C. being shared	D. to share
18. A. focus	B. touch	C. dwell	D. rely
19. A. efficient	B. effective	C. proficient	D. impressive
20. A. asset	B. wealth	C. property	D. heritage

VII Translation.

1. However, truly understanding customers involves not just collecting quantitative data (numbers) related to them but qualitative data, such as comments about what they think.
2. Sometimes companies hire professional spies to gather information about their competitors and their trade secrets or even bug their phones.
3. An obvious way to gain market intelligence is by examining your competitors' web sites as well as doing basic searches with search engines like Google.
4. Analytics software allows managers who are not computer experts to gather all kinds of different information from a company's databases—information not produced in reports regularly generated by the company.

5. An intranet looks like the web and operates like it, but only an organization's employees have access to the information.

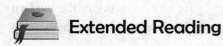

Extended Reading

Components of Marketing Information System

Marketing information is the lifeblood of marketing process, and marketing decision won't be taken in the absence of marketing information. Marketing decisions are affected by many internal and external environmental variables, so the marketing decision maker needs a great deal of information related to these variables, to predict their directions and their expected effects on the internal activities of the organization and the market, in order to make the rational marketing decisions in an uncertain environment facing the marketing administration. The marketing success in the organization depends basically on the availability and the accuracy of marketing information from its multiple sources. All marketing organizations try to find out and determine the nature of the markets and their trends, needs and changes that occur in these markets, as well as try to know the competitors, prices, options and other marketing information which is the key to success for any marketing decision.

To help managers to foresee the changes in markets or customer's preferences, you need sound information system, known as marketing information system (MIS). It collects the relevant data; organizes it into some thing meaningful, makes recommendations based on these figures and then stocks it up for future use. MIS is a computerized system that designed to provide an organized flow of information to enable and support the marketing activities of an organization. It consists of four integrated subsystems, which serves the company's marketing and other managers, begins and ends with information users. So companies must design effective marketing information systems that give managers the right information, in the right form, at the right time to help them make better marketing decisions.

MIS design is important since the quality of marketing information system has been shown to affect the effectiveness of decision-making. The MIS comprises the following four elements:

Internal records

Many companies build extensive internal data base, electronic collections of consumers and market information obtained from data source within the company network. Marketing managers can readily access and work with information in the data base to identify marketing opportunities and problems, plan programs, and evaluate performance. Internal records usually can be accessed more quickly and cheaply than other information sources.

Marketing intelligence

Marketing intelligence (MI) systems increasingly provide the data that drives both strategic and tactical decisions for enterprises. Many businesses have already invested heavily to aggregate data from diverse systems and applications in order to create a whole-enterprise view to fully reflect the daily state of business, as well as support more effective, informed decisions. A marketing intelligence system is a set of procedures and data sources used by marketing managers to sift information from the economic and business environment that they can use in their decision making.

Marketing research

Marketing research is a proactive search for information to solve a perceived marketing problem. It is the systematic and objective identification, collection, analysis, dissemination, and use of information and solution of problems and performance. N.K. Malhotra maintains that the reasons why organizations attach increasing importance to marketing research are listed as follows: to identify and to solve marketing problems. This distinction serves as a basis for classifying marketing research into two main parts. The first one is problem identification research; market potential research, market share research, image research, market characteristics research, sales analysis research, forecasting research, and business trends research. The second one is problem-solving research; segmentation research, product research, pricing research, promotion research, and distribution research.

Decision support system

A decision support system (DSS) is an integral set of computer tools allowing a decision maker to interact directly with computer to retrieve information useful in making semi-structured and unstructured decisions. It is an interactive computer system that is easily accessible to, and operated by non-computer specialists to assist them in planning and decision-making functions. While DSS may differ in their emphases on data-access and modeling functions, there is an overriding emphasis in all such systems on user accessibility to data for decision-making. This decision-making applicability permits managers to simulate problems using formal mathematical models and to test the outcomes of various alternatives for reaching the best possible decision.

Effective marketing information system helps in directly developing and improving the work service as a part of the product itself, or indirectly through increased responsiveness to the needs of the client. Organizations could benefit greatly from the analysis of customer data to determine their preferences to improve marketing support decision.

Words and Expressions

lifeblood   *n.* 生命线，命根子，命脉
rational   *a.* 合理的
multiple   *a.* 多重的，多个的，复杂的
sound   *a.* 合理的，明智的
computerized   *a.* 计算机化的
integrated   *a.* 完整的，整体的
effectiveness   *n.* 有效，有效性，效用
comprise   *v.* 包含，包括，由……组成
access   *v.* 使用，接近，获取
tactical   *a.* 战术的，策略上的
aggregate   *v.* 积聚
sift   *v.* 筛选，精选
systematic   *a.* 有系统的，有规则的，有条不紊的
integral   *a.* 基本的
retrieve   *v.* 取回，恢复，重新得到
semi-structured   *a.* 半结构化的
unstructured   *a.* 未组织的，非结构化的
accessible   *a.* 易接近的，能接近的
overriding   *a.* 最重要的，高于一切的
applicability   *n.* 适用性
simulate   *v.* 模仿，模拟

responsiveness   *n.* 响应性
marketing intelligence   市场情报
problem identification research   问题识别研究
market potential research   市场潜能研究
market share research   市场份额研究
image research   形象研究
market characteristics research   市场特征研究
sales analysis research   销售分析研究
forecasting research   预测研究
problem-solving research   问题解决型研究
segmentation research   市场细分研究
product research   产品研究
pricing research   定价研究
promotion research   促销研究
distribution research   分销研究
decision support system (DSS)   决策支持系统
modeling function   造型功能

 ## Comprehension

I   Answer the following questions according to the passage.

1. Why is the marketing information system so important?
2. What are the functions of the marketing information system?
3. What are the four elements of marketing information system?
4. How can the company benefit from the internal database?
5. What role does marketing intelligence play?

Unit 4 Marketing Information System

6. Why is marketing research so popular among companies?
7. What are the two main parts of marketing research?
8. According to the passage, what is a decision support system?
9. What is the main focus of the decision support system?
10. What is the main idea of this passage?

II Write "T" for true, and "F" for false.

1. Without marketing information system, it's impossible to make marketing decisions.
2. Marketing decision makers have access to marketing information from various sources.
3. Managers are responsible for collecting the relevant data; organizing it into some thing meaningful, making recommendations based on these figures and then stocking it up for future use.
4. The services of marketing information system are confined to marketing department.
5. Effective marketing information system enables managers to make better decisions.
6. Many companies build extensive internal data base, electronic collections of consumers and market information from the company network available.
7. Marketing managers can access internal data more quickly and cheaply than other managers.
8. Many enterprises spend a lot of money on gathering data to get insights into daily state of the business and support decision-making.
9. The marketing research can be randomly divided into two parts.
10. Even the non-computer specialists have access to the decision support system.

Additional Terms

accounting data　核算数据
back order　欠交订单
business operation　经营活动
clickstream data　点击流数据
consumer insight　消费者洞察
customer relationship management (CRM)
　客户关系管理
customer return　顾客退货
demographic data　人口数据
early-mover advantage　早动优势
industrial espionage　商业间谍

internal reporting system　内部报告系统
late-mover advantage　后动优势
management information system　管理
　信息系统
order-of-entry advantage　次序优势
outward market research　对外市场调查
pioneer advantage　先驱优势
second-mover advantage　次动优势
trade secret　商业机密
trade show　贸易展览

PART II

Consumer Analysis

Unit 5
Customer Value[1]

The goal of marketing is to create profitable customer relationships by delivering superior value to customers. Nike, the superb marketer, has built one of the world's most dominant brands. The power of its brand and logo speaks loudly of Nike's superb marketing skills. It spends hundreds of millions of dollars each year on big-name endorsements, splashy promotional events, and lots of attention-getting ads. Over the years, it has associated itself with some of the biggest names in sports. No matter what your sport, chances are that one of your favorite athletes wears the Nike swoosh. Nike gives its customers more than just good athletic gear. As the company notes on its web page (www.nike.com), "Nike has always known the truth—it's not so much the shoes but where they take you." Beyond shoes, apparel, and equipment, Nike markets a way of life, a sports culture, a "just do it" attitude.[2]

Driven by more demanding customers, global competition, and slow-growth economies and industries, many organizations search for new ways to achieve and retain a competitive advantage. Past attempts have largely looked internally within the organization for improvement, such as quality management, reengineering, downsizing, and restructuring. The next major source for competitive advantage will come from more outward orientation toward customers, as indicated by many calls for organizations to compete on superior customer value delivery. Although the reasons for these calls are sound, what are the implications for managing organizations in the next decade and beyond? Undoubtedly, customer value, customer value learning, and the related skills that managers will need to create and implement superior customer value strategies have become the focus of businesses.

The term *customer value* has many meanings, but two dominate—value for the customer (customer perceived value or customer received value) and value for the firm (value of the customer, now more commonly referred to as customer lifetime value). Our focus is on the former. Woodruff defines customer value as "a customer's perceived preference for, and evaluation of, those product attributes, attribute performances, and consequences arising from use that facilitates (or blocks) achieving the customer's goals and purposes in use situations", which can be evaluated pre-product or post-product use.[3] This broad conceptualization incorporating multiple contexts, multiple cognitive tasks, and multiple assessment criteria poses significant measurement issues and may not be operational.

The definition above suggests that there are two aspects to customer value: desired value and perceived value. Desired value refers to what customers desire in a product or service. Perceived value is the benefit that a customer believes he or she received from a product after it was purchased.

Consumers usually face a broad array of products and services that might satisfy a given need. Consumers make buying choices based on their perceptions of the value that various products and services deliver. Customer value is the difference between the values the customer gains from owning and using a product and the costs of obtaining the product. For example, FedEx customers gain a number of benefits. The most obvious is fast and reliable package delivery. However, when using FedEx, customers also may receive some status and image values. Using FedEx usually makes both the package sender and the receiver feel more important. When deciding whether to send a package via FedEx, customers will weigh these and other values against the money, effort, and psychic costs of using the service. Moreover, they will compare the value of using FedEx against the value of using other shippers—UPS, Airborne Express, the U.S. Postal Service—and select the one that gives them the greatest delivered value.[4]

Customers often do not judge product values and costs accurately or objectively. They act on *perceived* value. For example, does FedEx really provide faster, more reliable delivery? If so, is this better service worth the higher prices FedEx charges? The U.S. Postal Service argues that its express service is comparable, and its prices are much lower. However, judging by market share, most consumers perceive otherwise.[5] FedEx dominates with more than a 45 percent share of the U.S. express-delivery market, compared with the U.S. Postal Service's 8 percent. The U.S. Postal Service's challenge is to change these customer value perceptions.

Customer value can be examined at different levels. At a low level, it can be viewed as the attributes of a product that a customer perceives to receive value from. At a higher level, it can be regarded as the emotional payoff and achievement of a goal or desire. When customers derive value from a product, they derive value from the attributes of the product as well as from the attribute performance and the consequence of achieving desired goals from the use of the product.

Creation of value for customers is a critical task for marketers, particularly when developing new products and services or starting new businesses. From a customer's perspective, customer value is what they "get" relative to what they have to "give up" . The creation of customer value has long been recognized as a central concept in marketing and the fundamental basis for all marketing activities. It has been suggested as the purpose of organizations, a main key to success via differential positioning.

The emerging customer value paradigm and theory of the firm suggests that firms exist to create value for others where it is neither efficient nor effective for buyers to attempt to satisfy their own needs. From this perspective, the objective of marketing is to achieve personal, organizational, and societal objectives by creating superior customer value for one or more market segments with a sustainable strategy.

Drawing on, integrating, and extending previous conceptual foundations, a customer value framework is proposed that builds on the strengths of previous frameworks and mitigates their key weaknesses. This framework adopts a strategic orientation in that the focus is on identifying categories of value that could differentiate offerings and not on identifying all of the specific benefits and sacrifices that may be perceived by consumers or customers. It identifies four major types of value that can be created by organizations—functional/instrumental value, experiential/hedonic value, symbolic/expressive value, and cost/sacrifice value. The framework also identifies five major sources of value—information, products, interactions, environment, and ownership—that are associated with central value chain processes.

Each of the four major types of value has key facets or dimensions. These are discussed below with examples of specific benefits or sacrifices in that category and illustrative examples of firms that focus on creating that type of value.

Functional/instrumental value is concerned with the extent to which a product (good or service) has desired characteristics, or performs a desired function. As suggested by Woodruff, three key facets of functional/instrumental value are: ① correct, accurate, or appropriate features, functions, attributes, or characteristics (such as aesthetics, quality, customization, or creativity); ② appropriate performances (such as reliability, performance quality, or service-support outcomes); ③ appropriate outcomes or consequences (such as strategic value, effectiveness, operational benefits, or environmental benefits). The face validity of this conceptualization is seen in its application. Some firms, such as Rubbermaid, focus mainly on creating appropriate features and attributes that translate into customer benefits. Others, such as Ford, Sony, and McDonald's, focus on performance, while pharmaceutical companies such as Pfizer or Bayer focus on appropriate outcomes or consequences.[6]

Experiential/hedonic value is concerned with the extent to which a product creates appropriate experiences, feelings, and emotions for the customer. Some organizations, such as most restaurants and some retailers, focus on sensory value (such as aesthetics, ambiance, aromas, or feel/tone). Most organizations in the travel and entertainment industries focus on creating emotional value (such as pleasure/enjoyment, play/fun, excitement, adventure, or humor). Other organizations, such as toy or game companies, professional service organizations, and many business-to-business organizations, focus on social-relational value (such as relational or network benefits, bonding, personal interaction, developing trust or commitment, or responsiveness). Finally, some firms, such as Disney, America Online, and some travel and hotel companies, focus on epistemic value (such as curiosity, novelty, knowledge, or fantasy).

Symbolic/expressive value is concerned with the extent to which customers attach or associate psychological meaning to a product. Some products appeal to consumer's self-concepts and self-worth—that is, they make us feel good about ourselves—either in possession or in giving. Other products have personal meaning—associations with people or events that only have meaning to a particular consumer.

Products can also provide a means of self-expression—products such as Calvin Klein fragrances, Roots clothes, a Volkswagen Beetle, or The Body Shop lotions allow consumers to reflect or express their personalities, tastes, and values.[7] Still other products focus on social meaning—how others see us. Branded products such as BMW, Rolex, and Lee Valley Tools are purchased because of their prestige, status, or image. Finally, some products (such as roses on Valentine's Day) have conditional meaning—symbolism or meaning relating to sociocultural ethnic events and traditions. One might argue that personal meaning is a subset of conditional meaning. We see value in their separation. Conditional meaning is culturally based, and marketers can develop strategies to appeal to broad segments. Personal meaning is person specific, and although marketers often try to cultivate individual meaning, it is much more difficult to do so.

In addition, to try to maximize, or at least realize value benefits, customers also try to minimize the costs and other sacrifices that may be involved in the purchase, ownership, and use of a product.

Cost/sacrifice value is concerned with transaction costs. Some firms, such as Wal-Mart, Amazon.com, and most financial institutions, focus on minimizing economic costs, such as product price, operating costs, switching costs, and opportunity costs. Organizations such as auto malls, and retailers such as Sears focus on convenience and minimizing psychological or relational costs. Psychological-relational costs include cognitive difficulty/stress, conflict, search costs, learning costs, psychological switching costs, and psychological relationship costs, such as attachment. Firms such as 7-Eleven, Dell, and most Internet businesses try to minimize the personal investment of customers—the time, effort, and energy consumers devote to the purchase and consumption process. Finally, retailers such as Target, manufacturers such as Ford, hoteliers such as Marriot, among many others, attempt to reduce the risks (personal risk, operational risk, financial risk, or strategic risk) perceived by customers in buying, owning, and using a product, through the use guarantees, warranties, flexible return policies, and third-party endorsements.

Sources of value

Five key sources of customer value are captured—information, products, interactions, environment, ownership/possession transfer. These sources of value are created by a variety of "value chain" processes and activities within and between organizations.

Information is created by value chain activities associated with advertising, public relations, and brand management (such as through packaging, labeling, or instructions). It provides functional/instrumental value by informing and educating customers; experiential/hedonic value, such as sensory or emotion-based value, through advertising creatively; symbolic/expressive value by drawing associations and interpreting meaning; and cost/sacrifice value by helping consumers make more informed and faster decisions.

Products are created by value chain activities associated with new product development, market research, research and development, and production. They directly provide functional/instrumental value (such as safety features on a Volvo); experiential/hedonic value (such as the package of sensory, emotional, relational, and epistemic experiences offered by Club Med); symbolic/expressive value (such as Campbell's focus on developing personal meaning with the brand); and cost/sacrifice value (through the product price and augmented product considerations that reduce involvement, investment, and risk).

Interactions between customers and organizations' employees or systems are created, or enhanced, by value chain activities relating to recruitment and training, service quality, and operations. Such interactions provide functional/instrumental value, such as service timeliness; experiential/hedonic value, such as relational bonds; symbolic/expressive value, such as the prestige of privileged interactions; and cost/sacrifice value, such as reducing the personal investment required to purchase or use a product.

Environment is created by value chain activities such as facilities management, interior design, and merchandizing. The purchase or consumption environment can provide functional/instrumental value, such as lighting that makes it easier to read product labels; and experiential/hedonic value, such as music that makes shopping more enjoyable. It can also provide symbolic/ expressive value, such as holiday decorations that appeal to cultural traditions; and cost/sacrifice value, such as a shopping location that has ample and convenient parking.

Ownership/possession transfer is facilitated by value chain activities concerned with accounting (such as payment and billing), delivery (such as product picking, packing, shipping, and tracking), and transfer of ownership (such as contracts, copyright agreements, and titles). Processes involved with transfer of ownership and possession provide functional/instrumental value, such as timely delivery; experiential/hedonic value, such as customer satisfaction with the fulfillment process; symbolic/expressive value, such as enhanced product meaning by providing tasteful gift wrapping; and cost/sacrifice value, such as peace of mind provided by automated product tracking systems.

Being able to differentiate new products and services is at the heart of marketing. Without a unique position, businesses (and their associated products and services) struggle to survive let alone thrive. Being creative about creating customer value can enable marketers to be more successful in discovering opportunities.

Vocabulary

endorsement n. 担保，认可	perception n. 知觉，觉察
splashy a. 惹人注目的，颇受好评的	comparable a. 可比较的，比得上的
attention-getting a. 吸引人的注意力的，吸引眼球的	payoff n. 报酬；结清；发工资
demanding a. 要求高的，要求苛刻的	differential a. 差别的，不同的
retain vt. 保持，保留，保存	paradigm n. 范例，样式
reengineering n. 重组，再造	sustainable a. 可持续的
downsizing n. 缩小尺寸	mitigate vi. 减轻，缓和
restructuring n. 重建，改组	facet n. 方面
implication n. 暗示	pharmaceutical a. 制药的，配药的
conceptualization n. 概念化	ambiance n. 周围环境，气氛
incorporate vt. 合并，混合	aroma n. 芳香，香味；气派，风格
pose vt. 引起，导致	responsiveness n. 响应性，易起反应
weigh vt. 衡量，权衡	self-concept n. 自我概念
	self-worth n. 自我价值

Phrases and Expressions

quality management 质量管理	relative to 与……相关
customer delivered value 顾客让渡价值	functional/instrumental value 功能价值/工具性价值
customer perceived value 顾客感知价值	experiential/hedonic value 体验价值/享乐性价值
customer lifetime value 顾客终身价值	symbolic/expressive value 象征价值/表现价值
product attribute 产品属性	
attribute performance 性能属性	cost/sacrifice value 成本价值/牺牲价值
arise from 由于	operational benefit 运营收益，营业收益
assessment criteria 评价标准	environmental benefit 环境效益
desired value 期望值	face validity 表面效度
act on 对……起作用	sensory value 感性价值
express service 快递服务	
view ... as ... 把……看作……	

emotional value　情感价值
social-relational value　与社会相关的价值
epistemic value　新奇价值
value chain　价值链
comfort food　慰藉食物
operating cost　运营开支，营业成本
switching cost　转移成本，转换成本
opportunity cost　机会成本
third-party endorsement　第三方认可
be at the heart of　处于核心地位
let alone　更不用说

Notes

1. Customer value: 顾客价值。自从哈佛大学波特教授（Michael Eugene Porter）提出的竞争优势思想得到学术界和企业界的广泛认同后，人们开始为寻求可持续竞争优势进行了积极的尝试与探索。学者们从价值链管理、质量管理、组织与过程再造、企业文化、裁员等多方面阐述企业应当如何建立竞争优势，但是这些努力的根本都在于组织内部的改进，而当这些努力不能以市场为导向，其产品和服务不能被顾客所认同时，也就无法建立起企业真正的竞争优势。当企业家们指向企业内部改进的探索并没有获得想象中的成功时，人们开始转向企业外部的市场，即从顾客角度出发寻求竞争优势。Woodruff 提出，企业只有提供比其他竞争者更多的价值给客户，即优异的客户价值，才能保留并造就忠诚的客户，从而在竞争中立于不败之地。正因如此，客户价值已成为理论界和企业界共同关注的焦点，被视为竞争优势的新来源。早在 1954 年，Drucker 就指出，顾客购买和消费的绝不是产品，而是价值。Zaithaml 在 1988 年首先从顾客角度提出了顾客感知价值理论。她将顾客感知价值定义为：顾客所能感知到的利得与其在获取产品或服务中所付出的成本进行权衡后对产品或服务效用的整体评价。

2. As the company notes on its web page (www.nike.com), "Nike has always known the truth—it's not so much the shoes but where they take you." Beyond shoes, apparel, and equipment, Nike markets a way of life, a sports culture, a "just do it" attitude.　正如公司网站（www.nike.com）上所说的那样，"耐克一直了解事情的真相，那就是：与其说耐克公司推出了各种运动鞋，不如说耐克鞋带您周游世界。"除了运动鞋、服装和设备之外，耐克公司还推销了一种全新的生活方式，一种体育文化，一种"想做就做"的人生态度。

在本句中，as 引导的是非限制性定语从句，指代整个主句的意思，可以理解为"正如，正像"，例如：

As we had expected, all his efforts to promote products went to nothing.　正如我们所预料的那样，他为推销产品所做出的所有努力都白费了。

"just do it"这句广告语是广告中的经典，既简单、清楚又口语化，而且从不同人的角度看

都会有不同的意思。从消费者的角度是：我只选择它；就用这个。从商人的角度是：来试试。而将这句话用在日常的生活中就有了更丰富的含义，这要视语境而定。可以理解为：想做就做、坚持不懈等。这句广告词突出了年轻人的自我意识，强调运动本身，同时也是耐克公司体育精神的体现。

3. Woodruff defines customer value as "a customer's perceived preference for, and evaluation of, those product attributes, attribute performances, and consequences arising from use that facilitates (or blocks) achieving the customer's goals and purposes in use situations", which can be evaluated pre-product or post-product use. 伍德拉夫将顾客价值定义为："顾客价值是顾客对特定使用情境下有助于（有碍于）实现自己目标和目的的产品属性、性能属性，以及所感知的偏好与评价"，这可以在产品使用前或者使用后进行评价。

在本句中，which 引导的是非限制性定语从句，which 指代整个主语的意思。短语 define … as … 的意思是 "把……定义为，把……界定为"，例如：

The dictionary defines a workaholic as "a person obsessively addicted to work". 词典给 "工作狂" 一词下的定义是 "一个过分沉溺于工作中的人"。

facilitate 的意思是 "促进，使便利"，例如：

The new airport will facilitate the development of tourism. 新机场将促进旅游业的发展。

Both sides undertake to facilitate further cultural exchanges. 双方承诺为进一步开展文化交流创造便利条件。

4. Moreover, they will compare the value of using FedEx against the value of using other shippers—UPS, Airborne Express, the U.S. Postal Service—and select the one that gives them the greatest delivered value. 而且，他们会把使用联邦快递所带来的价值跟使用其他承运商，比如联合包裹速递服务公司、美国空运特快公司、美国邮政服务公司带来的价值进行对比，之后优先选择能够给自己带来最大让渡价值的公司。

联邦快递（FedEx）是一家国际性速递集团，提供隔夜快递、地面快递、重型货物运送、文件复印及物流服务，总部设于美国田纳西州。其品牌商标 FedEx 是由公司原来的英文名称 Federal Express 合并而成。其标志中的 "E" 和旁边的 "x" 刚好组成一个反白的箭头图案。

联合包裹速递服务公司（UPS）是世界上最大的快递承运商与包裹递送公司，1907年成立于美国，作为世界上最大的快递承运商与包裹递送公司，UPS 同时也是专业的运输、物流、资本与电子商务服务的提供者。每天都在世界上200多个国家和地区管理物流、资金流与信息流。

美国邮政服务公司（U.S. Postal Service）是一家独立的美国政府代理机构，前身是美国邮政部，1971年改为美国邮政服务公司，国会不再保留规定邮件资费的权力。尽管如此，公司的11个董事会成员中有9名要由美国总统任命。该公司负责全美的邮政服务，其业务范围包括邮件投递、包裹传送、货物运输、邮政服务等，并可提供网上服务。

顾客让渡价值是菲利普·科特勒在《营销管理》一书中提出来的，他认为，"顾客让渡价值"

是指顾客总价值（total customer value）与顾客总成本之间的差额。顾客总价值是指顾客购买某一产品与服务所期望获得的一组利益，它包括产品价值、服务价值、人员价值和形象价值等。顾客总成本是指顾客为购买某一产品所耗费的时间、精神、体力及所支付的货币资金等，因此，顾客总成本包括货币成本、时间成本、精神成本和体力成本等。顾客在购买产品时，总希望把有关成本包括货币、时间、精神和体力等降到最低限度，同时又希望从中获得更多的实际利益，以使自己的需求得到最大限度的满足，因此，顾客在选购产品时，往往从价值与成本两个方面进行比较分析，从中选择出价值最高、成本最低，即"顾客让渡价值"最大的产品作为优先选购的对象。企业为在竞争中战胜对手，吸引更多的潜在顾客，就必须向顾客提供比竞争对手具有更多"顾客让渡价值"的产品，这样，才能使自己的产品被消费者注意，进而购买本企业的产品。为此，企业可从两个方面改进自己的工作：一是通过改进产品、服务、人员与形象，提高产品的总价值；二是通过降低生产与销售成本，减少顾客购买产品的时间、精神与体力的耗费，从而降低货币与非货币成本。

5. However, judging by market share, most consumers perceive otherwise. 然而，大多数顾客通过分析市场份额，就会有不同的看法。
在本句中，otherwise 的意思是"不同的"，例如：
You evidently think otherwise. 你显然有不同的看法。
He should have been working but he was otherwise engaged. 他应该已经在工作了，但是他在忙别的事。

6. Some firms, such as Rubbermaid, focus mainly on creating appropriate features and attributes that translate into customer benefits. Others, such as Ford, Sony, and McDonald's, focus on performance, while pharmaceutical companies such as Pfizer or Bayer focus on appropriate outcomes or consequences. 有些公司，例如乐柏美，主要侧重于确定恰当的特征和属性，并将其转化为顾客利益。其他公司，比如福特、索尼、麦当劳则侧重绩效，而像辉瑞或者拜耳医药公司则侧重恰当的结果或者后果。
乐柏美（Rubbermaid）是美国家庭用品第一品牌，CURVER 系列保鲜盒是欧洲销量第一的保鲜盒品牌。1921 年开始制造耐用的家居用品，自从 1933 年获得第一个产品专利后，乐柏美不断创新并生产出更多的产品改变着我们的生活，包括家居收纳、车载保温箱、食物容器、洗衣/沐浴/清洁用品、壁橱、厨房用品等。它被 *Brand Marketing* 杂志评为 100 个"世纪品牌"之一。
辉瑞（Pfizer）是美国一家跨国制药公司，企业总部设在纽约，其畅销产品包括降胆固醇药立普妥、口服抗真菌药大扶康、抗生素希舒美等。
拜耳（Bayer）是一家化工跨国集团，德国股票指数 DAX 的成分公司，世界 500 强之一。拜耳集团是一家全球性企业，核心竞争力在于医疗保健、营养品及高科技材料。

7. Products can also provide a means of self-expression—products such as Calvin Klein fragrances, Roots clothes, a Volkswagen Beetle, or The Body Shop lotions allow consumers to reflect or express their personalities, tastes, and values. 各种产品可以提供一种表达自我的方式——卡尔

Unit 5 Customer Value

文·克雷恩香水、绿适服饰、大众甲壳虫汽车，或者美体小铺乳液，顾客可以反映或者张扬自己的个性、品位及价值观。

卡尔文·克雷恩（Calvin Klein）是美国时装品牌，于 1968 年成立，创始者为同名设计师卡尔文·克雷恩，他于 1942 年出生于美国纽约，就读于著名的美国纽约时装学院。"我要最纯粹、最简约、最时尚"是卡尔文·克雷恩的精神，其设计的灵感来源于人性中对于高贵的追求，并建立在对人类共同追求的价值：爱、永恒和分享的诠释上。

绿适服饰（Roots clothes）始于一个简单的理念——享受纯真、简朴的生活，爱护大自然环境。品牌发展至今，一直为实践该理念而努力。绿适服饰是由生于底特律的迈克尔·庞德曼（Michael Budman）及唐·格林（Don Green）所创立。1963 年，他们因参加加拿大阿尔贡金省立公园举办的一个夏季露营活动而相识，他们凭着自己对大自然及对阿尔贡金省立公园的钟爱，对纯真、俭朴生活的追求，以及共同拥有的价值观，于 1973 年在阿尔贡金省立公园的湖畔创立了绿适服饰。品牌商标中的动物海狸，是加拿大的象征之一，海狸性格非常温和，不会袭击其他生物，喜欢潜水、筑坝及搭巢，温和、勤奋和活力正好代表着绿适的精神，故绿适以海狸作为品牌商标并使用于产品设计中。

甲壳虫汽车（Volkswagen Beetle）是德国大众集团旗下的品牌，正式名称为大众 1 型（Volkswagen Type 1），是由大众汽车在 1938 年至 2003 年间生产的一款小型轿车。1998 年，在最初的甲壳虫下线许多年以后，大众汽车正式推出了外形与之非常相似的新甲壳虫（以大众高尔夫为平台），而甲壳虫则在墨西哥和其他一些国家一直生产到 2003 年。

美体小铺（The Body Shop）是高质量面部肌肤及身体护理产品零售商，由 Anita Roddick 于 1976 年在英国成立，其零售业务遍布全球 55 个国家，商店数目超过 2 200 家，产品全部不采用动物测试，并通过公平的贸易方式购买天然原材料。

I Answer the following questions according to the text.

1. What is the purpose of the writer to mention the example of Nike at the beginning of the text?
2. What are the driving forces for the companies to find new ways to retain their competitive advantage? And what is the new source of competitive advantage?
3. What are the two dominant meanings of the term "customer value"?
4. Why isn't Woodruff's definition of customer value operational?
5. What is the difference between desired value and perceived value?
6. How do customers make purchasing decision?

7. Why does the writer mention FedEx in paragraph 5?
8. What are the four main types and five major sources of value?
9. How can information provide different types of value?
10. What is the main idea of the text?

II   Decide whether the following statements are true or false.

1. Nike not only sells famous shoes but also offers people opportunities to travel a lot.
2. Because of slow-growth economies and industries, customers are becoming more and more demanding.
3. Past attempts to look internal factors like as quality management, reengineering, downsizing, and restructuring have proved to be a great success.
4. Woodruff's definition is too broad to be operational.
5. More often than not customers act on desired value while making purchase decisions.
6. In a sense, the goal of marketing is to achieve personal as well organizational objectives by creating superior customer value.
7. Such firms as Disney, America Online attach more importance to emotional values.
8. Sometimes some products are very popular because of their prestige, status, or image.
9. Firms such as 7-Eleven, Dell, and most Internet businesses try to minimize the organizational investment—the time, effort, and energy consumers.
10. Of the five key sources of customer value, information is the most important one.

III   Fill in each blank with the proper form of the word in the bracket.

1. This is a powerful _____ (endorse) for his softer style of government.
2. It seems almost inevitable that North African economies will still be primarily _____ (orientation) towards Europe.
3. He smiled, with the _____ (imply) that he didn't believe me.
4. The company will be retooled after the _____ (incorporate).
5. We do not have enough money to _____ (sustainable) our campaign for long.
6. In the contemporary western world, rapidly changing styles cater to a desire for _____ (novel) and individualism.
7. With the establishment of major new markets, the economy is _____ (thrive).
8. I plainly _____ (perception) some objections remain in terms of the promotion plan.
9. The manager spoke very slowly, _____ (weigh) what she would say.
10. The company chose to _____ (downsizing) and more fully utilize the remaining workers.

Unit 5 Customer Value

IV Fill in each blank with a proper preposition.

1. Such accidents often arise _____ carelessness.
2. We must not act _____ assumptions that our products will be popular among consumers.
3. They viewed his plan _____ infeasible although he had tried his best.
4. He asked me some questions relative _____ the subject.
5. We need to appeal _____ a wider customer base.
6. She gladly gave up her part-time job to devote herself entirely _____ her career.
7. Money lies _____ the heart of the debate over airline safety.
8. They have arrived at a solution _____ the market research.
9. The freighter carries a few passengers in addition _____ its cargo.
10. He is mainly concerned _____ the profits of the company without consideration of employees' well-being.

V Fill in the blanks with the words and phrases given below. Change the form where necessary.

| let alone | thrive | ambiance | sound | otherwise |
| chances are that | pose | retain | orientation | comparable |

1. This could _____ a threat to jobs in the coal industry.
2. In other _____ countries real wages increased much more rapidly.
3. The interior of the shop still _____ a nineteenth-century atmosphere.
4. His reasoning is perfectly _____, but he misses the point.
5. Their products are the best in the world, _____ in England.
6. I like the _____ of this restaurant, so I always eat there.
7. His company continues to _____ because of his effective marketing.
8. _____ their efforts may come to nothing because they fail to attach importance to customer value.
9. The rent is high, but _____ the house is satisfactory.
10. They are supposed to keep the _____ of creating superior customer value.

VI Cloze.

Understanding customer value is 1_____ the most important thing you can do to identify ways to grow your business. 2_____ you understand the value of your customers, you can determine which customers to invest 3_____, identify new customers and markets to

4_____, agree which products and service lines should be offered and promoted, and understand 5_____ to cut costs and investments that are not generating growth. In fact, a robust understanding of the lifetime value of each of your customers can provide an even clearer view of the value of your business, plus the potential opportunities 6_____ value going forward. Here's how we develop a detailed understanding of the lifetime value of our customers.

Step 1: Calculate the profit contribution of each customer in the current year

Determine revenue per customer minus any attributable costs to servicing that customer, including cost of goods, cost of services, etc. If you don't have customer-level financials in your accounting system, do your best to 7_____ up financials across product segments. If you are in a 8_____ with hundreds or thousands of small customers, develop a set of customer segments by rolling up product lines or estimating the buying patterns of various customer types.

Step 2: Develop a realistic estimate of how long you might retain each customer

The 9_____ duration of a customer relationship is more important than the absolute timeframe. Determine which customers are more loyal and which are 10_____ to be repeat buyers and 11_____ they buy.

Step 3: Estimate the cost to acquire or retain the customer

Some customers may require large 12_____ or heavy marketing investments up front, but little or no cost to retain. Others may require a costly reselling effort every month. Estimate the cost of this 13_____ a yearly basis.

Step 4: Do the math

Build a simple cash flow model 14_____ yearly contribution projections, costs to acquire or retain, and continue the cash flow for the projected life of the customer relationship. Be sure to subtract an "overhead charge" for your total operating costs and include any capital costs if customers require incremental capital investment. Discount future years 15_____ a reasonable cost of capital (8-10 percent is usually a good number to use—no reason to get too technical).

Most businesses are surprised by how many customers are 16_____ when they create a "fully loaded" 17_____ of customer profitability. Businesses are also likely to find drastic 18_____ in the value of various customers and segments.

This calculation of customer value may 19_____ you to question many of your previous investments and give you a better view of 20_____ to allocate future investments.

1. A. one of   B. /   C. the only   D. by far
2. A. If   B. When   C. As long as   D. Unless
3. A. on   B. in   C. into   D. with
4. A. favor   B. sell   C. target   D. enter
5. A. where   B. which   C. why   D. what
6. A. to increase   B. for increasing C. to decrease   D. for decreasing

Unit 5 Customer Value

7. A. line   B. roll   C. call   D. look
8. A. connection   B. relationship   C. transaction   D. business
9. A. absolute   B. short   C. relative   D. long
10. A. possibly   B. probably   C. certain   D. likely
11. A. how long   B. how often   C. when   D. why
12. A. discounts   B. coupons   C. bargain   D. quantities
13. A. in   B. on   C. with   D. for
14. A. combined   B. to combine   C. being combined D. combining
15. A. on   B. up   C. for   D. at
16. A. unprofitable B. profitable   C. different   D. similar
17. A. estimation B. estimator   C. estimate   D. guess
18. A. similarities B. changes   C. differences   D. varieties
19. A. make   B. cause   C. inspire   D. let
20. A. where   B. how   C. when   D. which

VII Translation.

1. Customer value is the benefit that a customer will get from a product or service in comparison with its cost.
2. Businesses of all sizes use customer value as part of a greater analysis to determine how well they are serving their customer base.
3. Businesses also look at the prices of their products in comparison with the value that customers receive from them, in order to price them competitively and to maximize profits.
4. Companies pinpoint the benefits that they believe customers will realize, and they display them in advertisements in the hope of attracting more customers.
5. Relative performance identifies how a company's product or service provides customer value in comparison with that of competitors' products or services.

 ## Extended Reading

Customer Value Proposition

Imagine a world where everyone is in sales. Well, the fact is, everyone is in sales, in some fashion. It's not just the salesman at the car lot or computer reseller who qualifies: maybe you are trying to sell your spouse your ideas for the next holiday; maybe you're pitching a new project to your boss; maybe you are headhunting someone to join your firm. It's all selling, and, whatever your offer (product, idea, project or job), it's important to have a really strong value proposition. A value proposition is a short statement that clearly communicates the benefits that your potential client gets by using your product, service or idea. It boils down all the complexity of your sales pitch into something that your client can easily grasp and remember.

In marketing, a customer value proposition (CVP) consists of the sum total of benefits that a vendor promises a customer will receive in return for the customer's associated payment (or other value-transfer).

Why CVP is important

A customer value proposition is an offering that helps customers do an important job more effectively, conveniently, or affordably than the alternatives. In addition to being "the heart of strategy", it is one of the four key components of a business model which include: customer value proposition, revenue/profit formula, resources and processes such as manufacturing.

Successful businesses that exist in a competitive industry environment know all too well about the need to gain and maintain sustainable points of differentiation in the form of a superior customer value proposition. They also understand the nature of customer value proposition.

A good customer value proposition will provide convincing reasons why a customer should buy a product, and also differentiate your product from competitors. Gaining a customer's attention and approval will help build sales faster and more profitably, as well as work to increase market share. Understanding customer needs is important because it helps promote the product. A brand is the perception of a product or service that is designed to stay in the minds of target consumers.

In all, there are three types of CVP.

All benefits. Most managers when asked to construct a customer value proposition, simply list all the benefits they believe that their offering might deliver to target customers. The more they can think of the better. This approach requires the least knowledge about customers and competitors and, thus, results in a weaker marketplace effort.

Favorable points of difference. The second type of value proposition explicitly recognizes that the customer has alternatives and focuses on how to differentiate one product or service from another. Knowing that an element of an offering is a point of difference relative to the next best alternative does not, however, convey the value of this difference to target customers. A product or service may have several points of difference, complicating the customer's understanding of which ones deliver the greatest value. Without a detailed understanding of customer's requirements and preferences, and what it is worth to fulfill them, suppliers may stress points of difference that deliver relatively little value to the target customer.

Resonating focus. The favorable points of difference value proposition is preferable to an all benefits proposition for companies crafting a customer value proposition. The resonating focus value proposition should be the gold standard. This approach acknowledges that the managers who make purchase decisions have major, ever-increasing levels of responsibility and often are pressed for time. They want to do business with suppliers that fully grasp critical issues in their business and deliver a customer value proposition that's simple yet powerfully captivating. Suppliers can provide a customer value proposition by making their offerings superior on the few attributes that are most important to target customers in demonstrating and documenting the value of this superior performance, and communicating it in a way that conveys a sophisticated understanding of the customer's business priorities.

A truly effective customer value proposition has the following 7 essential elements.

• The CVP is created by conducting a thorough needs analysis—starting with a complete understanding of the customer, determining what their needs, preferences and requirements of an improved solution would be (that meets or exceeds these needs and/or preferences). Again, determining how these identified needs are currently being satisfied, and applying the litmus test to an improved product or service in the areas of *effectiveness, affordability and convenience*.

• The CVP is truly customer experience driven. An effective value proposition is expressed in terms of real benefits, as defined by the customer, through their experience from the actual or expected consumption of the product and/or service. CVP must be integrated into all customer-facing activities, marketing materials and messaging.

• The CVP is simple, yet distinctive and all encompassing. It should reflect two aspects of what are called value elements: points of parity and points of difference. Points of parity are elements in common with the next best alternative whereas points of difference are elements that make your product better than the next best alternative. The third value element is called points of contention; they arise when you and the customer disagree as to how the elements compare to the next best alternative. To demonstrate value elements, you simply need to present clear proof of your product or service value versus the competition (to ensure an apples-to-apples comparison) by articulating the points of parity and differences between your product and the known alternatives.

• Your CVP is measurably better than the competition's customer value proposition. All customer value propositions should be based upon tangible points of difference, expressed in both qualitative, quantitative and ultimately, monetary terms. An effective CVP has a "resonating focus" on one or two points of parity and/or points of differences.

• To avoid being considered marketing puffery, your value proposition must be substantiated by actual case studies and/or testimonials. You need to demonstrate instances where the customer not only decided to purchase your product or service but did so from your company for reasons that you can substantiate. Customer testimonials are critical and must be expressed from a customer's viewpoint. They help to substantiate and authenticate the customer value proposition.

- The CVP is sustainable—not easily copied, substituted or subject to rapid obsolescence or, if it is, then the new and improved customer value proposition should be in the process of simultaneous development. To satisfy this requirement, you must be able to execute on this value proposition for a significant amount of time (which varies depending upon the intensity of your competitive environment). And, to avoid morale issues, you must constantly communicate to your people what the next value proposition is going to be, lest they think that you are "resting on your laurels".

- The CVP should be tied to business reviews and a performance evaluation program. A CVP review should be conducted in conjunction with monthly and/or quarterly business reviews. In addition to the typical business unit performance measures, a management performance review process should include an evaluation of each manager's performance in delivering the customer value proposition to each target segment and key clients they serve in their role within the company.

Words and Expressions

pitch　vt. 为……做宣传
headhunt　vt. 物色人才，挖走人才
value-transfer　n. 价值转移
differentiation　n. 区别，分化
differentiate　vt. 区分，区别，辨别
undertaking　n. 企业，事业
preferable　a. 更好的，更可取的
resonate　vt. 产生共鸣、共振
captivate　vt. 迷住，诱惑
sophisticated　a. 复杂的
exceed　vt. 超出，超过
articulate　vt. 清晰地发音，言语表达
monetary　a. 货币的，金钱的，财政的
substantiate　vt. 用事实证明，证实
authenticate　vt. 鉴定，证明是真实、可靠的
lest　conj. 以防，万一

customer value proposition (CVP)　顾客价值主张
car lot　停车场
litmus test　试金石，最后的检验
boil down　归结
customer-facing activities　面向客户的活动
apples-to-apples comparison　同类比较
marketing puffery　营销吹嘘
customer testimonial　客户见证
be subject to　易受……影响的
rest on your laurel　吃老本，不思进取
in conjunction with　与……协力
business review　业务回顾
resonating focus　突出共鸣点
customer validation　顾客验证

Unit 5 Customer Value

Comprehension

I Answer the following questions according to the passage.

1. What is a customer value proposition? Why is it so important?
2. What are the three types of CVP?
3. What are the main features of all benefits?
4. How can suppliers deliver the greatest value of points of difference?
5. How can you understand that "CVP is truly customer experience driven."?
6. Why is CVP simple, yet distinctive and all encompassing?
7. How can businesses avoid being considered marketing puffery?
8. Why is CVP sustainable? And how can businesses meet this requirement?

II Write "T" for true, and "F" for false.

1. The CVP is supposed to be easy to grasp and remember for your clients.
2. Of the four key components of a business model, CVP is the most important one.
3. All managers don't list all the benefits they believe that their offering might deliver to target customers.
4. With a detailed understanding of customer's requirements and preferences, and what it is worth to fulfill them, suppliers may deliver the greatest value to customers.
5. The resonating focus value proposition is much better than the other two types.
6. Points of difference are elements in common with the next best alternative whereas points of parity are elements that make your product better than the next best alternative.
7. Some CVPs are based on points of difference, while others are based on points of contention.
8. Actual case studies and/or testimonials are of great help to substantiate the CVP.
9. The CVP is closely related to business reviews and a performance evaluation program.

Additional Terms

customer account profitability 顾客获利贡献率	customer value model 顾客价值模型
	convergence 趋同
customer lifetime value 顾客终身价值	customer satisfaction 顾客满意度
customer profitability 顾客获利率	nonprofit marketing 非营利组织营销

product concept　产品概念
production concept　生产概念
selling concept　推销观念
social marketing concept　社会营销观念
symbolic value　象征价值
total customer cost　顾客总成本
total customer value　顾客总价值
total episode value　全情景价值
total quality management　全面质量管理
transaction marketing　交易营销
utilitarian value　实用性价值

Unit 6
Customer Demand

Demand is one of the most important decision-making variables in global and liberal economy. Under such type of an economy consumers and producers have wide choice. There is full freedom to both buyers and sellers in the market. Therefore, demand reflects the size and pattern of the market. The future of a producer depends upon the well-analyzed consumer's demand. That is also not possible without evaluating the consumer's tastes, preferences, choice, etc. All these things are directly built into the economic concept of demand.[1] The survival and the growth of any business enterprise depend upon the proper analysis of demand for its product in the market. Demand analysis has profound significance to management for the functioning and expansion of the business.[2] Thus the short term and long term decisions of the management are dependent upon the trends in demand for the product. Any reason for the rise or fall in demand has to be found out and production plan has to be revised accordingly.

The market system works in an orderly manner because it is governed by certain fundamental laws of market known as law of demand and supply.[3] The law of demand and supply is so important that it determines the price of goods and services in the market. It states that whenever the price of a product increases then the demand for that product decreases and vice versa provided other things remain constant. This is because under the economic theory price of a product is considered as the main determinant of demand in the short run period. Here these other things are income of the individual, price of related goods, tastes and preferences, population, advertisement and so on.

A demand schedule is the tabular presentation of the different levels of prices at corresponding levels of quantity demanded of that commodity. It shows the relationship between price and quantity demanded of a commodity, i.e., the law of demand.[4] Demand curve is the graphical representation of the demand schedule. It is obtained by plotting a demand schedule on a graph. It slopes downward from left to right, which shows there is inverse relationship between price and quantity demanded of a commodity.

Demand for goods and services constitute one side of the product market; supply of goods and services forms the other.[5] It is needless to say that if there is no demand for a good, there is no need to produce that good. Also, if the demand for a good exceeds its supply, there may be a need to expand its production. Further, production generally takes time, and so one has to plan its production properly to know the likely demand for a relevant product at future date. Thus, a clear understanding of the relevant demand is imperative for any producer worth his name.[6]

Demand analysis seeks to identify and analyze the factors that influence the demand. As we know, a firm is not a passive taker of the demand for its product. It has the capacity to create demand as well. Thus, a study of demand is necessary for a decision maker, for it has bearings on its production schedule, and influence on its profit, among other critical variables, is also subject to manipulation by the decision maker. Before we pursue this matter further, it is necessary to explain certain concepts.

There are four types of demand, namely, competitive demand, complementary or joint demand, derived demand and composite demand. Demand is the amount of a product buyers are willing and able to purchase at a given price over a particular period of time.

Competitive demand[7]

Commodities are substitutes if one can be used in place of the other. Substitute goods serve the same purpose and therefore compete for sales. Competitive demand is the demand for products that are competing for sales. People can substitute one competing product for another. If the demand for one product increases, the demand for its competitor will decrease. Examples of substitute goods are Milo and Bournvita, butter and margarine and so on. A change in the price of one affects the demand for the other. For instance, if there is an increase in the price of butter, demand for margarine will increase which will ultimately increase the price of margarine, provided the supply of margarine does not change. On the other hand, a decrease in the price of butter will lead to a decrease in the demand for margarine, and hence a fall in its price, given the supply.

Complementary or joint demand[8]

Complementary demand, also called joint demand, occurs when two products are necessary to meet one demand. Two or more goods are said to be jointly demanded when they must be consumed together to provide a given level of satisfaction. Some examples are cars and fuel, compact disc players and CD. There are perfect complementary goods and imperfect or poor complementary goods. For perfect complementary goods, the consumer practically cannot do without the other.[9] The example of cars and fuel is a good case in point. On the other hand, for imperfect complementary goods, a consumer can do without the other, so long as a substitute is obtained. For complementary demand, a change in the price of one good affects the demand for the other. If there should be an increase in the price of compact disc players, there will be a decrease in the demand for discs, other things being equal.[10]

Derived demand[11]

Derived demand refers to the relationship between the resources used to produce a good or service, called factors of production, and the finished product or service sold on the market. In other words, when the demand for a commodity is derived from the demand for the final commodity, that commodity is said to have derived demand. Wood may be demanded for the purpose of manufacturing furniture and not for its own sake. Here, the demand for wood is derived from the demand for furniture. Then demand for wood is therefore a derived demand.

Factors of production such as land, labor, and capital have derived demand. This is because an increase in the demand for a commodity will result in an increase in the factors of production used in producing the goods. The price of the factors of production will increase, other things being equal. Likewise, decreased demand for the final product reduces demand for the factors of production. For example, a rise in the demand for cars increases automobile manufacturers' demand for labor in assembly plants.

Composite demand[12]

Composite demand applies to commodities which have several uses and satisfy different needs or are demanded for several and different purposes. It influences how the market allocates goods with numerous uses. Wood as mentioned in the example above is used for furniture-tables, chairs, beds, windows, doors and so on. A change in demand for one of them will affect all others. An increase in demand for table will result in higher prices being paid for wood. The high price for wood will increase the cost of production of furniture like chairs, beds, windows and doors for which wood is used in manufacturing.

Small-business owners are often experts in the particular industries in which they operate, but there's a lot more to running a company than knowing the ins and outs of a single product or service.[13] A broad understanding of management and economics can help owners gain insight into what makes customers tick. Customer or consumer demand theory is an economic theory that attempts to explain how customers make choices at the individual level.

Supply and demand basics

The field of economics is divided into two broad categories: macroeconomics and microeconomics. Macroeconomics deals with looking at the economy and markets as a whole, while microeconomics focuses on issues facing individual businesses and consumers.[14] At the macro level, consumer demand and the supply of products and services provided by companies determine prices in competitive markets. Low supply and high demand tend to increase prices, while high supply and low demand tend to depress prices. As a result, industries with high demand or low supply may present the best opportunities for new businesses to enter the market.

Consumer utility

At the individual level, consumer demand theory states that consumers make choices based on utility: the value or benefit that is derived from an action. Utility gained from a specific action can vary from one person to the next based on their preferences. For example, someone who loves chocolate might get $5 worth of value from eating a candy bar, while a person who doesn't care for sweets might only value a candy bar at 50 cents. If a business can produce candy bars for 75 cents apiece, it stands to make a profit by selling to the consumer who likes chocolate, but it can't make a profit selling to the person who doesn't like candy.

Diminishing marginal utility

According to consumer demand theory, the utility an individual gains from consuming something decreases as he consumes more. For instance, someone who loves candy might get $5 worth of utility from eating one chocolate bar, but he might only get $3 of utility from eating a second bar and $1 for a third. The tendency of utility to decline as consumption increases is known as the law of diminishing marginal utility.

Applications of demand theory

Consumer demand theory is a framework for thinking about why people make the choices they do. The theory can potentially help business managers choose the types of products and services to offer and the prices to set to maximize profit. The concepts of utility and diminishing returns also apply human behaviors in other areas of life, such as the jobs workers choose to pursue, how much work people do around the house and how people choose to spend their leisure time.

When it comes to running a small business, customer demand is one of the things that are challenging to predict. Some companies are able to figure it out right away but many others have a smaller niche market and they do not always respond in the same way as larger audiences do. This means you will end up having peaks and valleys when it comes to sales. Selling more products can be done if you know how to market and to use effective copywriting when you are creating ads. It can be hard at certain times of the year as you will need to know when and why your customers may be locking up their money and why they aren't spending. Take a look at the economy to see what is happening. Gas prices can have a huge impact on a lot of other business industries as people start cutting back here and there to save money. The good news is that you can still make money; you just need to learn how to market to the customers in a different way. Here are some things that you can do in order to increase customer demand.

Know the competition

One of the best ways in which you can help to increase the product sales is by getting to know what you are up against. Small business owners do not have the same marketing budgets as the larger companies but you can still do a lot of competing with the right type of marketing strategy. You have to get to know the products that the competitors are selling and then take a good look at the way they market. Then you need to figure out how you can do it better. When you have a good strategy in mind, you can catch the attention of some customers that may be loyal to your competition.

Unit 6 Customer Demand

Maintain marketing promotions

It is hard when money is tight to continue paying for a lot of advertising. If you don't advertise, you don't earn. How else will customers get to know your company without effective advertising? You need to get your name out there some way. Look toward online marketing as it can be less expensive and might give you the benefits you need in order to attract new customers to your organization.

New packaging

If you buy a product over and over, pretty soon you stop looking at what you buy and you just buy it because you know it's useful. You need to be able to make your old products look new again. Start redesigning your packaging and look for different ways in which you can give your existing products and services some new life. This is one of the best ways to get your customers' attention again and it doesn't cost you hardly anything but a few hours of graphic design work.

Try incentives

This is a great way to get people to consider coming to your company as you have something different to give to them. Free products, even key chains, are enticing. People bite on the word free and it often doesn't matter what is free. You may even try a giveaway promotion where you have people put their names into a hat for a drawing of a free product. This is a great way to get a ton of new leads for marketing needs and it helps to get your name out there as well.

Vocabulary

accordingly *ad.* 相应地	margarine *n.* 人造奶油，人造黄油
determinant *n.* 决定物，决定性因素	provided *conj.* 假设，如果
tabular *a.* 表格形式的，表格的	likewise *ad.* 同样地
corresponding *a.* 相应的	allocate *v.* 分配
graphical *a.* 绘图的，绘画的	tick *v.* （某人的思想、愿望使其）做
plot *v.* 绘制	出……举动
graph *n.* 图表	macroeconomics *n.* 宏观经济学
slope *v.* 倾斜	microeconomics *n.* 微观经济学
inverse *a.* 相反的，逆向的，倒转的	depress *v.* 下跌
constitute *v.* 组成	framework *n.* 框架
imperative *a.* 势在必行的，必要的	tight *a.* （预算）紧张的，回旋余地不
pertinent *a.* 恰当的，中肯的，相关的	大的
Milo *n.* 美禄（一种巧克力饮料的名字）	incentive *n.* 动机
Bournvita *n.* 吉百利（一种可可麦精固体饮料的名称）	enticing *a.* 诱人的，迷人的

Phrases and Expressions

build into 使成为……一部分	补品
demand analysis 需求分析	imperfect or poor complementary goods 不完全互补品
law of demand and supply 供求规律	
vice versa 反过来，反之亦然	do without 没有……也行，将就，用不着
demand schedule 需求表	
worth one's name 名副其实	a good case in point 典型的例子
have bearings on … 与……有关，对……产生影响	factor of production 生产要素
	finished product 制成品，成品
production schedule 生产进度表	be derived from 起源于，从……获得
competitive demand 竞争需求	assembly plant 装配厂
complementary or joint demand 相辅需求	apply to 适用于
derived demand 派生需求，引申需求	consumer utility 消费者效用
composite demand 复合需求	marginal utility 边际效用
in place of 代替，取代	law of diminishing marginal utility 边际效用递减法则
compete for 为……而竞争	figure out 计算出，想出
substitute … for 代替，取代	lock up 锁起来
compact disc player 激光唱机，CD播放器	cut back 减少，缩减
	bite on 取得，尽力想
perfect complementary goods 完全互	giveaway promotion 赠品促销

 **Notes**

1. All these things are directly built into the economic concept of demand. 所有这些都会直接体现在需求的经济概念之中。
   在本句中短语 build into 的意思是 "使成为……一部分"，例如：
   You should build job rotation into your career planning. 你应该使工作轮换成为职业规划的一部分。

2. Demand analysis has profound significance to management for the functioning and expansion of the business. 需求分析会对公司的正常运转及业务扩展方面的管理产生深远的影响。

Unit 6 Customer Demand

市场需求分析主要是估计市场规模的大小及产品的潜在需求量，这种预测分析的操作步骤如下：第一，确定市场目标，在市场总人口数中确定某一细分市场的目标市场总人数，此总人数是潜在顾客人数的最大极限，可用来计算未来或潜在的需求量；第二，确定地理区域和目标市场，算出目标市场占总人口数的百分比，再将此百分比乘以地理区域的总人口数，就可以确定该区域目标市场数目的多寡；第三，考虑消费限制条件，考虑产品是否有某些限制条件足以减少目标市场的数量；第四，计算每位顾客每年的平均购买数量，从购买率和购买习惯中，即可算出每人每年的平均购买量；第五，计算同类产品每年购买的总数量，区域内的顾客人数乘以每人每年平均购买的数量就可算出总购买数量；第六，计算产品的平均价格；第七，计算购买的总金额，把第五项所求得的总购买数量，乘以第六项所求得的平均价格，即可算出购买的总金额；第八，计算企业的购买量，将企业的市场占有率乘以第七项的购买总金额，再根据最近 5 年来公司和竞争者市场占有率的变动情况，做适当的调整，就可以求出企业的购买量；第九，需要考虑的其他因素，例如：经济状况、人口变动、消费者偏好及生活方式等有所改变，则必须分析其对产品需求的影响。

3. The market system works in an orderly manner because it is governed by certain fundamental laws of market known as law of demand and supply.   市场体系是由市场的一些基本规律，即供求规律来调控的，因此，能够有条不紊地发挥着作用。
供求规律指商品的供求关系与价格变动之间相互制约的必然性，是商品经济的规律，商品的供给和需求之间存在一定的比例关系，其基础是生产某种商品的社会劳动量必须与社会对这种商品的需求量相适应。供求关系就是供给和需求的对立统一，这种对立统一是供求关系变化的基本法则。供求中的 4 种关系包括：供求竞争关系、供求数量关系、供求反应关系、供求时间关系。

4. It shows the relationship between price and quantity demanded of a commodity, i.e., the law of demand.   这表明了价格与所需要的商品数量之间的关系，即需求定律。
需求定律（law of demand）是一条经济学定律，假设其他因素不变，当一件物品价格增加，其需求量会下降，反之亦然。换言之，根据需求定律，若以竖线为价、横线为量，当中的需求曲线必定向右下倾斜。价格或代价与需求量是需求定律中的两个变量，这两个变量是反向函数。

5. Demand for goods and services constitute one side of the product market; supply of goods and services forms the other.   商品和服务的需求构成了产品市场的一方面，商品和服务的供应则构成了产品市场的另一方面。
在本句中，constitute 的意思是"构成，组成"，例如：
A whole consists of parts, and the parts constitute the whole.   整体由部分组成，部分构成整体。
Volunteers constitute more than 95% of the Center's workforce.   该中心 95%以上的工作人员是志愿者。

6. Thus, a clear understanding of the relevant demand is imperative for any producer worth his name. 因此，要对相关的需求有一个清晰的了解，这对于任何一个名副其实的生产商来说都是势在必行的事情。

   在本句中，短语 worth one's name 的意思是"名副其实"，相当于 worth one's salt，例如：After we saw how fast she straightened out our budget mess, we all agree she's certainly worth her name. 看到她那么快就把我们预算开支那笔糊涂账弄得一清二楚，我们一致认为她确实名副其实。

7. 竞争需求理论把人的需求分为生存需求与竞争需求两大类：生存需求与约束高度相关，竞争需求与激励高度相关。竞争需求是人类一切复杂的高层次活动产生的源泉，是指商品可以单独发挥功能、满足期望，且在同一时间内，只能择一进行，譬如穿西装或唐装，吃中餐或西餐。

8. 相辅需求是指消费者同时拥有两者才能发挥功能、满足需求。互补品如汽车需要汽油、听录音带需要有录音机，需两种以上相互补充才能满足消费者，又称为联合需求。

9. For perfect complementary goods, the consumer practically cannot do without the other. 对于完全互补品来说，消费者几乎离不开另一种产品。
   完全互补品是指必须以固定比例搭配起来才能满足消费者某种需求的两种或多种商品。
   在本句中，短语 do without 的意思是"没有……也行，将就，用不着"，例如：
   We can't do without the help of your organization. 我们不能没有你们机构的帮助。

10. If there should be an increase in the price of compact disc players, there will be a decrease in the demand for discs, other things being equal. 如果激光唱机的价格上涨，那么在其他因素不改变的情况下，消费者对于唱片的需求就会下降。
    在本句中，if 引导的条件状语从句，后面的 other things being equal 属于独立主格结构。

11. 派生需求是对一种生产要素的需求来自（派生自）对另一种产品的需求，其中该生产要素对这一最终产品做出贡献，如对轮胎的需求派生自对汽车的需求。

12. 复合需求是一种物品拥有不同的用途，这些来自不同市场的用途对物品的需求即是复合需求，因为不同的用途彼此竞争以求得到该物品。

13. Small-business owners are often experts in the particular industries in which they operate, but there's a lot more to running a company than knowing the ins and outs of a single product or service. 小公司的经营者在一些特定的行业是专家级人物，然而，经营一家公司，远不仅仅是了解某一产品或者服务的详细信息这么简单。
    在本句中，which 引导的定语从句用来修饰限定 industries，后面的 but 连接的是一个并列分句，表示转折。短语 more … than 的意思是"超过，不只是，不仅仅是"，ins and outs 的意思是"细节，详情"，例如：
    Do you know the ins and outs of the job? 你知道这份工作的详细内容吗？

14. Macroeconomics deals with looking at the economy and markets as a whole, while microeconomics focuses on issues facing individual businesses and consumers. 宏观经济学

Unit 6 Customer Demand

将经济和市场视为一个有机的整体，而微观经济学则侧重于单个的企业与消费者。

宏观经济学又称为总体经济学、大经济学，是微观经济学的对称。宏观经济学是现代经济学的一个分支，以整个国民经济为考察对象，研究经济中各有关总量的变动，以解决失业、通货膨胀、经济波动、国际收支等问题，实现长期、稳定的发展。

微观经济学主要以单个经济单位（单个生产者、单个消费者、单个市场经济活动）作为研究对象，分析单个生产者如何将有限的资源分配在各种商品的生产上以取得最大的利润；单个消费者如何将有限的收入分配在各种商品的消费上以获得最大的满足。同时，微观经济学还分析单个生产者的产量、成本、使用的生产要素数量和利润如何确定；生产要素供应者的收入如何确定；单个商品的效用、供给量、需求量和价格如何确定等。

I Answer the following questions according to the text.

1. What is the importance of demand analysis?
2. What are the main determinants of demand?
3. What is a demand schedule?
4. What are the four types of demand?
5. Why do factors of production have derived demand?
6. What are two broad categories of economics?
7. How can you understand consumer utility?
8. What is the law of diminishing marginal utility?
9. How can businesses increase customer demand?

II Decide whether the following statements are true or false.

1. Demand is regarded as the most important decision making variable in global and liberal economy.
2. The consumer's tastes, preferences, choice are closely related to the concept of demand.
3. The law of demand and supply makes it possible for the market to work smoothly.
4. According to the law of demand, whenever the price of a product increases then the demand for that product decreases and vice versa.
5. There is inverse relationship between price and quality demanded of a commodity.
6. As a passive taker of the demand, a firm hasn't the ability to create demand.

7. There are four types of demand, namely, competitive demand, complementary or joint demand, domestic demand and derived demand.
8. Knowing the ins and outs of a single product or service is far from enough in terms of running a business.
9. Consumers make purchases on the basis of values and benefits they will get from the products.
10. Consumers long for free products without consideration of the quality.

III Fill in each blank with the proper form of the word in the bracket.

1. The offer was too _____ (entice) to refuse, so finally he accepted it.
2. Economic _____ (global) brings not only opportunities for development but also challenges.
3. The treasurer was arrested for trying to _____ (manipulation) the company's financial records.
4. Free-market reforms have moved governments everywhere to downsize, deregulate, and _____ (private).
5. Other _____ (variable) in making forecasts for the industry include the weather and the general economic climate.
6. Only those homes offered for sale at _____ (compete) prices will secure interest from serious purchasers.
7. We _____ (complementary) one another perfectly at that time.
8. That salesman can _____ (derived) pleasure from helping others.
9. Economic policy is _____ (liberalization) to encourage initiatives in production.
10. She said she would go to London to _____ (pursuit) her career.

IV Fill in each blank with a proper preposition.

1. Could you help me figure _____ this problem?
2. These principles don't apply _____ out new products.
3. It is difficult for a small grocery store to compete _____ a supermarket.
4. Neither could theory do _____ practice, nor could practice do _____ theory.
5. In place _____ ordinary light bulbs, you could use fluorescent lamps.
6. The objective is to substitute the traditional ways of marketing _____ online marketing to reduce cost.
7. The plans are subject _____ change at short notice.
8. They specialize in products that are derived _____ animals.

Unit 6 Customer Demand

9. They have made a series of plans to cut _____ production cost.
10. Sometimes small firms can outdo big business when it comes _____ customer service.

V Fill in the blanks with the words and phrases given below. Change the form where necessary.

| accordingly | a good case in point | exceed | constitute | be subject to |
| provided | do without | likewise | apply to | ins and outs |

1. _____ you pay me back by Friday, I'll lend you the money.
2. Now that they have a regular income, they should be able to _____ any help from us.
3. He is so excellent that he knows the _____ of mechanical engineering.
4. They have broken the rules and will be punished _____.
5. The discount no longer _____ him because he's over eighteen.
6. These small nations _____ an important grouping within the EU.
7. All building firms _____ tight controls.
8. Shoppers tend to think that high prices mean high quality. Electrical goods are _____.
9. You will need to fill in a form for any claim _____ $500.
10. He voted for the change and he expected his colleagues to do _____.

VI Cloze.

Consumer choice is a microeconomic theory 1_____ preferences for consumption goods and services to consumption expenditures. It ultimately affects consumer demand curves. The link between personal preferences, consumptions, and demand curves is one of the most closely studied relations in economics. Consumer choice theory is a way of analyzing 2_____ consumers may achieve an equilibrium between their preferences and expenditures 3_____ maximizing utility as subject to consumer budget constraints.

Preferences represent individual desires for the consumption of goods and services, translating 4_____ consumer choices. These choices are based on income or wealth combined with the consumer's time to define consumption activities. Consumption is separated from production 5_____ two different actors are involved. In the first case, consumption is by the primary individual; in the second case, a producer might make something 6_____ he would not consume himself. 7_____, different motivations and abilities are involved. The models that 8_____ consumer theory are used to represent 9_____ demand patterns for an individual buyer 10_____ the hypothesis of constrained optimization. Prominent variables used to explain the rate 11_____ which the good is purchased (demanded) 12_____ the price per unit of that good, the prices of related goods, and the wealth of the consumer.

The fundamental theorem of demand states that the rate of consumption falls as the price of the good 13_____. This is called the substitution effect. No one can purchase an item they cannot afford, 14_____ their desire for it. As prices rise, consumers will 15_____ higher priced goods and services with less expensive alternatives. Subsequently, as the wealth of the individual rises, demand increases, shifting the demand curve 16_____ at all rates of consumption. This is called the income effect. As wealth rises, consumers will choose higher priced goods and services instead of lower priced alternatives. Preferences are assumed to be fairly constant 17_____ can change over time. This change in preferences 18_____ change the quantity demanded at a given price and shift the demand curve. The 19_____ of the shift in demand depends upon how 20_____ change.

1. A. connecting   B. connect   C. connected   D. connects
2. A. when   B. why   C. how   D. where
3. A. on   B. with   C. for   D. by
4. A. with   B. into   C. for   D. in
5. A. because   B. for   C. since   D. as
6. A. which   B. what   C. that   D. where
7. A. However   B. In addition   C. Accordingly   D. Therefore
8. A. compose   B. make up   C. consist of   D. comprise
9. A. observant   B. observatory   C. observed   D. observable
10. A. on   B. with   C. in   D. through
11. A. in   B. for   C. at   D. on
12. A. including   B. include   C. includes   D. included
13. A. raises   B. arises   C. rises   D. arouses
14. A. although   B. though   C. with   D. regardless of
15. A. substitute   B. change   C. exchange   D. vary
16. A. lower   B. larger   C. higher   D. smaller
17. A. but   B. and   C. while   D. /
18. A. should   B. will   C. may   D. can
19. A. situation   B. reason   C. direction   D. tendency
20. A. preferences   B. wealth   C. quantities   D. prices

VII Translation.

1. Businesses that reduce prices on all of their products or services in an attempt to woo new customers are likely to do more harm than good to their bottom line.
2. Focusing your energy on reaching these people may involve looking at your products and services from a new angle.

3. Introduce a customer rewards club to reward shoppers for repeat purchases.
4. Coupons are another effective way to catch the eye of a prospect. It is a great hook to get people to try your product or service.
5. If you have never spent as much time or money on your website as you would have liked, now is the time to start.

Extended Reading

In economics, demand is an economic principle that describes a consumer's desire, willingness and ability to pay a price for a specific good or service. It refers to how much (quantity) of a product or service is desired by buyers. The quantity demanded is the amount of a product people are willing to buy at a certain price; the relationship between price and quantity demanded is known as the demand relationship. The term demand signifies the ability or the willingness to buy a particular commodity at a given point of time.

Economists record demand on a demand schedule and plot it on a graph as a demand curve that is usually downward sloping. The downward slope reflects the negative or inverse relationship between price and quantity demanded: as price decreases, quantity demanded increases. The reasons behind the law of demand and the shape of demand curve are listed as follows.

- **Income effect**. When the price of a commodity falls, real income of a consumer increases in terms of that commodity. Such increase in demand due to increase in real income is called as income effect.
- **Substitution effect**. When the price of commodity falls, it becomes relatively cheaper compared to its other close substitutes. Rational consumer will definitely buy more units of relatively cheaper good than relatively dearer to maximize the satisfaction. This is known as substitution effect.
- **Diminishing marginal utility**. This is also responsible for the increase in demand for a commodity when its price falls. When a person buys a commodity he exchanges his money with the commodity in order to maximize his satisfaction. He continues to buy goods and services so long as marginal utility of money is less than marginal utility of commodity.

Therefore, the general shape of demand curve is negatively sloping downward from left to right. It positively slopes upward from left to right in the case of inferior, giffen or complimentary goods.

In principle, each consumer has a demand curve for any product that he or she is willing and able to buy, and the consumer's demand curve is equal to the marginal utility (benefit) curve. When the demand curves of all consumers are added up horizontally, the result is the market demand curve for that product which also indicates a negative or inverse relationship between the price and quantity demanded. If there are no externalities, the market demand curve is also equal to the social utility (benefit) curve.

Innumerable factors and circumstances could affect a buyer's willingness or ability to buy a good.

- **Good's own price**. The basic demand relationship is between potential prices of a good and the quantities that would be purchased at those prices. Generally the relationship is negative meaning that an increase in price will induce a decrease in the quantity demanded. This negative relationship is embodied in the downward slope of the consumer demand curve. The assumption of a negative relationship is reasonable and intuitive. If the price of a new novel is high, a person might decide to borrow the book from the public library rather than buy it.

- **Price of related goods**. The principal related goods are complements and substitutes. A complement is a good that is used with the primary good. Examples include hotdogs and mustard, beer and pretzels, automobiles and gasoline. Perfect complements behave as a single good. If the price of the complement goes up the quantity demanded of the other good goes down. Mathematically, the variable representing the price of the complementary good would have a negative coefficient in the demand function. Substitutes are goods that can be used in place of the primary good. The mathematical relationship between the price of the substitute and the demand for the good in question is positive. If the price of the substitute goes down, the demand for the good in question goes down.

- **Personal disposable income**. In most cases, the more disposable income (income after tax and receipt of benefits) a person has, the more likely that person is to buy.

- **Tastes or preferences**. The greater the desire to own a good, the more likely one is to buy the good. There is a basic distinction between desire and demand. Desire is a measure of the willingness to buy a good based on its intrinsic qualities. Demand is the willingness and ability to put one's desires into effect. It is assumed that tastes and preferences are relatively constant.

- **Consumer expectations**. If a consumer believes that the price of the good will be higher in the future, he is more likely to purchase the good now. If the consumer expects that his income will be higher in the future, the consumer may buy the good now.

- **Population**. If the population grows, it means that demand will also increase.

- **Nature of the good**. If the good is a basic commodity, it will lead to a higher demand.

This list is not exhaustive. All facts and circumstances that a buyer finds relevant to his willingness or ability to buy goods can affect demand.

The "voice of the customer" (VOC) is a phrase from Six Sigma that means the opinions and needs of your customers are being considered as you develop your products and services. In other words, the customer's desires are always foremost on your mind.

Customers are always looking for companies they can trust. They reward those that meet or exceed their expectations; they allow the others to fail. Everything about your business—advertising, cleanliness, return merchandise policy, courtesy and knowledge of employees, product selection, location, delivery time—is what matters to them. Your entire business is your product, and it must sparkle. When it does, you become the "best deal" to your target customer.

Each customer contact is a moment of truth, a time when a relationship is either made or broken. From the customer's point of view, certain things are "critical to quality" (CTQ). You must meet these customer CTQ specifications or expectations precisely, or you will lose your business.

In a previous life, I had a business that manufactured framed art. We also contracted with large companies like American Greetings to make small framed gift items. One time we shipped 5,000 plaques to a large distributor of religious books and gifts. To our shock, the customer called to report that the inspirational message on the plaque contained a misspelled word. The word "privilege" was printed as "priviledge". Neither our company nor theirs caught the mistake. They shipped the product back, and we remade the 5,000 plaques. From the customer's point of view, the product did not meet specifications.

At another time, we had a hot product—silhouetted trees printed on glass and set against recessed backgrounds. This item blew out the doors of our retail customers. We manufactured around the clock but could not keep up with the demand. Our shipments got further and further behind. Some customers canceled their orders. We failed to meet delivery expectations.

After you learn from the voice of the customer what is critical to quality in their minds, you must ensure that your business systems help you deliver on your promise. Nothing can be left to chance. All customers want four important things from your product or service.

● High quality: no defects; does what it is supposed to do; better than the competition.
● Speed: on schedule; meets deadline; no delay.
● Low cost: good value; competitively priced; occasional bargains.
● Pleasurable: good buying experience (clean store, knowledgeable sales people, etc.); killer customer care.

Please list what is critical to quality for your customers. Consider the four criteria above. Then find a way to enhance your business systems and elevate your product or service beyond your competition. Your customers will love you for it, and reward you handsomely.

Words and Expressions

willingness n. 自愿，乐意	induce v. 引起，引发
horizontally ad. 水平地	embody v. 体现，表现
externality n. 外部事物，外在效应	intuitive a. 直觉的，直观的
innumerable a. 不计其数的	complement n. 补足物

substitute *n.* 替代物	around the clock 昼夜不停
mustard *n.* 芥末	deliver on 履行，实行
pretzel *n.* 椒盐卷饼	killer customer care 非常棒的客户关怀
mathematically *ad.* 在数学方面，数学上地	specification *n.* 规格，具体要求
	plaque *n.* 匾
coefficient *n.* 程度，系数	inspirational *a.* 给予灵感的，鼓舞人心的
receipt *n.* 收入	
intrinsic *a.* 固有的，内在的，本质的	misspelled *a.* 拼写错误的
exhaustive *a.* 彻底的，详尽的	remake *v.* 再做，修改，翻新
courtesy *n.* 礼貌	silhouette *v.* 呈现影子，呈现轮廓
sparkle *v.* 闪光，闪耀	recessed *a.* 凹陷的，嵌入的
customer contact 顾客接触	defect *n.* 缺陷，不足
framed art 壁挂艺术品	handsomely *ad.* 慷慨地，大方地

Comprehension

I Answer the following questions according to the passage.

1. What is demand and what is demand relationship?
2. What factors will influence a buyer's willingness or ability to make a purchase?
3. How do prices of related goods affect a consumer's willingness to buy goods?
4. What is the basic distinction between desire and demand?
5. What is "voice of the customer"?
6. Why does the writer mention the example of plaques?
7. Can you exemplify the harm of failure to meet customer expectations?
8. What are the four important things customers want from your product or service?
9. How can you understand the last sentence "Your customers will love you for it, and reward you handsomely."?

II Write "T" for true, and "F" for false.

1. Demand refers to the price of a product or service desired by buyers.
2. The demand curve is usually downward sloping, which reflects the negative or inverse relationship between price and quantity demanded.
3. Substitution effect influences the shape of demand curve in the similar way as income

effect.
4. In the case of giffen or complimentary goods, the demand curve positively slopes upward from right to left.
5. The market demand curve is equal to marginal utility curve and social utility curve.
6. The basic demand relationship is between potential prices and qualities of goods.
7. The mathematical relationship between the price of the complement and the demand for the good in question is negative.
8. The relationship between population and demand is negative.
9. The most important factor that attracts consumers is low price.
10. Some customers are too particular about products, like misspelling of some words.

Additional Terms

choice theory 选择理论
behavioral assumption 行为假定
budget line 预算线
budget constraint 预算约束
competitive budget set 竞争性预算集
consumer choice theory 消费者选择理论
compensated demand curve 补偿需求曲线
conspicuous goods 炫耀性物品
consumer efficiency 消费者效率
consumer preference 消费者偏好，消费者喜好
consumer surplus 消费者剩余，消费者盈余
consumer welfare 消费者福利
consumption possibility 消费可能性
continuity assumption 持续假设
countervailing duty 倾销税
convexity assumption 凸性假设
direct demand 直接需求
demand equation 需求方程
effective demand 有效需求
elasticity of demand 需求弹性
Hicksian Demand Curve 希克斯需求曲线

Hicksian Demand Function 希克斯需求函数
income constraint 收入约束
indifference curve 无差异曲线
indirect demand 间接需求
individual demand 个别需求
individual supply 独立供给
inferior goods 劣质商品
latent demand 潜在需求
local content requirement 当地含量要求
long-term supply 长期供给
marginal utility theory 边际效用理论
Marshallian Demand Curve 马歇尔需求曲线
normal goods 正常品
nominal price 名义价格
open or global quota 双边或全球配额
optimal consumption 最优消费，最佳消费
optimal purchase mix 最佳购买组合
preference maximization 偏好最大化
quota 配额

revealed preference theory 显示性偏好理论
satisfier 满足者
short-term supply 短期供给
subsidy 补助金
total utility 总效用
utility function 效用函数
utility maximization 效用最大化
utility maximizing rule 效用最大化法则
utility theory 效用理论

Unit 7
Analysis of Consumer Buying Behavior

A consumer is the ultimate user of a product or service. The overall consumer market consists of all buyers of goods and services for personal or family use.[1] Consumers vary tremendously in age, income, education, tastes and other factors. In earlier times, marketers could understand consumers well enough through the daily experience of selling to them. But as companies and markets have increasingly grown in size and scope, those responsible for marketing decision making have lost direct and efficient contact with their consumers. Without better understanding of the secrets behind why people decide to pick one product or service over another, it's impossible to improve the sales.[2] Therefore, most of marketers have had to turn to consumer research. Every year they spend millions of money to uncover the secrets, trying to learn more information about them. The company that really understands how consumers will respond to different product features, prices, and advertising appeals has a great advantage over its competitors.[3] Accordingly, the research on the consumer behavior has been attached growing importance.

Basically speaking, consumer behavior refers to the study of when, why, how, and where people do or do not make the purchase decisions, that is to buy a product or service. It involves such elements as psychology, biology, sociology and economics. In a sense, consumer behavior means the psychological processes that consumers go through in recognizing needs, finding ways to solve these needs, making purchase decisions, interpreting information, making plans, and implementing these plans.[4] It attempts to understand the buyer decision making process, both individually and in groups. In the meanwhile, it also tries to understand people's wants and assess influences on the consumer from groups such as family, friends, reference groups, and society in general.[5]

Consumer behavior is of great importance since all marketing decisions are based on assumptions and knowledge of consumer behavior. Marketers strive to understand this behavior so they can better formulate appropriate marketing stimuli that will result in increased sales and brand loyalty.[6]

To understand consumer behavior, researchers examine consumer buying behavior, with the customer playing the three distinct roles of user, payer and buyer. Researching consumer behavior is a complex process, but understanding consumer behavior is critical to marketers because they can use it to: provide value and customer satisfaction; effectively target customers; enhance the value of the company; improve products and services; create a competitive advantage; understand how customers view their products versus their competitors' products; apply marketing strategies toward a positive effect on society.

Actually consumer behavior is strongly influenced by cultural, social, personal and psychological factors. Culture is the most basic cause of a person's wants and behaviors. Every group or society has a culture, and failure to adjust to cultural differences can result in ineffective marketing or embarrassing mistakes. International marketers must understand the culture in each international market and adapt their marketing strategies accordingly. Each culture contains smaller subcultures which include nationalities, religions, racial groups, and geographic regions. Consumer behavior is also influenced by such social factors as the consumer's small groups, family, and social roles and status. The personal factors include buyer's age and lifecycle stage, occupation, economic situation, lifestyle, and personality and self-concept. As for the psychological factors, there are motivation, perception, learning, and beliefs.

The marketers are supposed to get insights into consumer behavior in the hope of growing sales. Some tips are given as follows.

- Recent studies have shown that people buy products for emotional reasons. For example, the real reason they buy a car is how it makes them feel. Of course, there are some purchases based on logic, but most purchases start with an emotional intent to buy.

- When people engage with a product, the event is stored in short-term memory. But if a fact or event has emotional significance, it shifts from short-term memory to long-term memory. Once it is stored in long-term memory, you've taken the first critical step toward building a relationship with a customer. This is one of the secrets to selling more of your products to more customers for more money.

- You must know what your customers are really buying before you can sell it. For example, what makes people frequent a particular bookstore? What do people really want to buy in the bookstore? Only best-sellers with lower prices? Of course not. What really counts is the experience of buying a book. Do you feel at home while you browse? Can you flip through a couple of books while you curl up on a sofa? Does the coffee smell good? All of those experiences are critical to the success of any bookstore. When you understand that customers aren't buying your product as much as they're buying the experience of your product, you've unlocked one of the keys to increasing sales and revenue.[7]

- If you want to encourage consumers to buy your product, you need to create a dialogue with them over the entire lifecycle of their involvement with your brand. Social media is a terrific way to do this, but you have to understand social media before you can use social media.

● Keep in mind the internal and external factors influencing consumer behavior. The more you know about consumer behavior, the more likely it is that you'll be able to run a successful marketing campaign.

Vocabulary

overall *a.* 整体的	status *n.* 地位
scope *n.* 经营范围	occupation *n.* 职业
uncover *v.* 发现	self-concept *n.* 自我概念
sociology *n.* 社会学	logic *n.* 逻辑
interpret *v.* 解释	intent *n.* 意图
want *n.* 需求	frequent *v.* 光顾，常去
stimulus *n.* 激励（*pl.* stimuli）	browse *v.* 浏览
target *v.* 以……为目标	unlock *v.* 解开，揭开
ineffective *a.* 无效果的，不起作用的	involvement *n.* 参与，（投入的）感情，
embarrassing *a.* 令人尴尬的	（倾注的）热情
subculture *n.* 亚文化	

Phrases and Expressions

respond to 对……作出反应	in the hope of … 希望……
advertising appeal 广告诉求	engage with 适应，与……建立密切关系
psychological process 心理过程	short-term memory 短期记忆
in the meanwhile 同时	long-term memory 长期记忆
reference group 参照群体	feel at home 放松，自在
be based on … 以……为基础	flip through 浏览
brand loyalty 品牌忠诚	curl up 蜷缩
be critical to … 对……至关重要	social media 社会性媒体
get insight into … 深入了解……	

1. The overall consumer market consists of all buyers of goods and services for personal or family use. 整个消费者市场是由所有的产品或者服务购买者构成的，他们购买产品或者服务供个人或者家庭使用。
   本句中 consist of 的意思是"由……组成"，有类似含义的词或者短语还有：constitute、be composed of、make up of、comprise，但是用法略有不同。例如：
   They agreed to form a council composed of leaders of the rival factions. 他们同意成立一个由敌对派系的领袖组成的委员会。
   There are 5 stages that make up the process of every consumer's buying decision. 每位消费者做出购买决定都要经历 5 个不同的阶段。
   5 stages comprise the consumer buying decision process: problem recognition, information search, alternative evaluation, purchase decision and post-purchase behavior. 这 5 个阶段构成了消费者的决策过程：识别问题、搜索信息、评价其他产品、决定购买，以及购买后的行为。

2. Without better understanding of the secrets behind why people decide to pick one product or service over another, it's impossible to improve the sales. 人们决定购买一种产品或者服务而不是另一种产品或者服务，对其背后的原因如果了解得不够透彻的话，就不可能提高销售量。
   在本句中，without 引导的介词短语中使用了 why 引导的定语从句，用来修饰限定先行词 secrets，后面的 it's impossible to improve the sales 使用了形式主语 it，真正的主语是不定式 to improve the sales。

3. The company that really understands how consumers will respond to different product features, prices, and advertising appeals has a great advantage over its competitors. 公司若能真正理解消费者是如何对产品特征、价格和广告吸引力等作出反应的，那么就比竞争对手具有更大的优势。
   本句看似有些复杂，句子主语 the company 后面是 that 引导的定语从句，that 在从句中充当主语。该定语从句中又使用了 how 引导的宾语从句，作动词 understand 的宾语。have a great advantage over 的意思是"比……具有优势"，例如：
   The home team always has an advantage over it opponents. 主场队总是比竞争对手有优势。

4. In a sense, consumer behavior means the psychological processes that consumers go through in recognizing needs, finding ways to solve these needs, making purchase decisions, interpreting information, making plans, and implementing these plans. 从某种意义上来说，消费者行为指

Unit 7 Analysis of Consumer Buying Behavior

的是消费者的一系列心理过程，在这一过程中，消费者要识别需求、寻找解决方法、做出购买决定、解释信息、制订计划并实施这些计划。

本句比较长，主要是因为使用了 that 引导的定语从句，修饰限定先行词 psychological processes，that 在从句中充当宾语，也可以省略掉。定语从句中的介词 in 后面跟了几个并列的结构。

5. In the meanwhile, it also tries to understand people's wants and assess influences on the consumer from groups such as family, friends, reference groups, and society in general. 同时，消费者行为还试图了解人们的各种需求，评估各个群体对消费者产生的影响，一般来讲，这些群体包括家庭、朋友、参照群体及社团。

在本句中，reference groups 的意思是"参照群体"，指的是个体在形成其购买或消费决策时，用以作为参照、比较的个人或群体，其含义也随着时代的变化而变化。参照群体最初是指家庭、朋友等个体与之具有直接互动的群体，但现在它不仅包括了这些具有互动基础的群体，而且涵盖了与个体没有直接面对面接触但对个体行为产生影响的个人和群体。

6. Marketers strive to understand this behavior so they can better formulate appropriate marketing stimuli that will result in increased sales and brand loyalty. 市场经营者尽力去了解消费者行为，这样他们就能够更好地利用恰当的营销激励策略，提高销售量和品牌忠诚度。

在本句中，so that 引导目的状语从句，其中还包含 that 引导的定语从句，修饰限定先行词短语 marketing stimuli，that 在从句中充当主语。

7. When you understand that customers aren't buying your product as much as they're buying the experience of your product, you've unlocked one of the keys to increasing sales and revenue. 意识到与其说顾客购买的是产品本身，倒不如说是对产品的一种体验，你就已经找到了提高销售量、增加营业额的秘诀之一。

在本句中，when 引导时间状语从句，该从句中包含 that 引导的宾语从句，作状语从句中谓语动词 understand 的宾语，定语从句中使用了 not as ... as 同级比较的否定形式。在主句中，the key to 的意思是"……的秘诀"，其中 to 是介词。

I Answer the following questions according to the text.

1. How could marketers understand consumers in the past?
2. What makes it difficult for marketers to better understand their consumers?
3. What different roles do consumers play according to the passage?
4. Why is consumer behavior so important to marketers?

5. What are the factors influencing consumer behavior?
6. What can be called subcultures according to the passage?
7. What do consumers base their purchases on? Please illustrate it.
8. What are the consumers really buying?
9. What role does the dialogue play in the field of business?

II Decide whether the following statements are true or false.

1. Consumers are different in age, income, education, taste and other aspects.
2. Without better understanding of consumer behavior, marketers will have great difficulty improving sales.
3. All the marketers have not come to realize the importance of consumer research.
4. The better the company understands consumer behavior, the greater advantage it has over its competitors.
5. Culture plays the most basic role on a person's wants and behaviors.
6. Marketers are supposed to make marketing strategies according to different cultures of markets.
7. Consumer's purchase decision is based on logic rather than emotion.
8. When the event is stored in long-term memory, you're bound to be successful in building a relationship with a customer.
9. The consumers attach more importance to their experience of buying the product than the product itself.
10. Social media is the best way to create a dialogue with consumers.

III Fill in each blank with the proper form of the word in the bracket.

1. A person's buying choices are also influenced by four major _____ (psychology) factors—motivation, perception, learning, and beliefs.
2. The black box model considers the buyers _____ (respond) as a result of a conscious, rational decision process.
3. In addition, sensory _____ (stimulus) are important to marketing.
4. Indeed, evaluating all relevant marketing information can become time _____ (consumer) if it is done every time a person shops.
5. The company strives _____ (learn) more about its potential customers.
6. The new plan _____ (base) on his market research will bear fruit.
7. It's the key to _____ (develop) a friendly relationship with customers.
8. That is an _____ (effective) way to ease the situation for our products are becoming

Unit 7 Analysis of Consumer Buying Behavior

less popular in that region.
9. I wish she wouldn't ask such _____ (embarrass) questions.
10. The marketer needs to understand the role _____ (play) by the buyer's culture, subculture, and social class.

IV Fill in each blank with a proper preposition.

1. The firms that focus on consumer research have a great advantage _____ those fail to realize its importance.
2. This book enables us to get insights _____ people's minds.
3. The marketers are quick to respond _____ any change in the potential market.
4. Their failure to understand the subcultures resulted _____ great loss.
5. This department consists _____ five men and one woman.
6. What happens in the next few days is critical _____ our success.
7. The promoting plan is largely based _____ their market research.
8. It took her two months to adjust _____ the work in the new company.
9. The general manager attaches great importance _____ the quality of products.
10. _____ a sense, his knotted brow is a sign of disapproval of our promoting plan.

V Fill in the blanks with the words and phrases given below. Change the form where necessary.

| wants | brand loyalty | attach importance to | be critical to | complex |
| target | in general | feel at home | formulate | interpret |

1. One successful way an insurance company _____ this market was through its campaign.
2. Researchers _____ the consumer's motivation for buying products.
3. With soft music and comfortable sofa, consumers _____ in the supermarket.
4. _____ is the ultimate goal a company sets for a branded product.
5. Culture is the most basic cause of a person's _____ and behaviors.
6. _____, the standard of your work is very high.
7. Marketers are interested in the beliefs that people _____ about specific products and services.
8. Social media _____ turn communication into interactive dialogue.
9. This is a _____ and difficult task.
10. We need some help to _____ the data.

VI Cloze.

Social media has substantially changed the way organizations, communities, and individuals communicate. The best way to define social media is to break it 1_____. Media is an instrument of communication, 2_____ a newspaper or a radio, so social media would be a social instrument of communication. This would be a website that doesn't just give you 3_____, but interacts with you while 4_____ you that information. This interaction can be as 5_____ as asking for your comments 6_____ an article, or it can be as complex as Flixster recommending movies to you based on the ratings of other people with similar 7_____.

Think of regular media 8_____ a one-way street 9_____ you can read a newspaper or listen to a report on television, 10_____ you have very limited ability to give your thoughts on the matter. Social media, on the other hand, is a two-way street that gives you the 11_____ to communicate too. It is easy to confuse social media 12_____ social news because we often refer to members of the news as "the media". Adding to the 13_____ is the fact that a social news site is also a social media site because it 14_____ into that broader category. 15_____ social news is not the same thing as social media any more than a banana is the same thing as 16_____. A banana is a type of fruit, but fruit can also be grapes, strawberries, or lemons.

By analyzing identity, conversations, sharing, presence, relationships, reputation, and groups, firms can monitor and understand 17_____ social media activities vary in 18_____ of their function and impact, 19_____ develop social media strategy. Social media is not just a marketing discipline, 20_____ it has multiple touch-points in an organization such as customer service, sales, human resource management and R&D.

1. A. up   B. into   C. through   D. down
2. A. like   B. as   C. in   D. on
3. A. instrument   B. communication   C. information   D. media
4. A. giving   B. gave   C. being given   D. to give
5. A. effective   B. difficult   C. common   D. simple
6. A. on   B. for   C. with   D. in
7. A. comments   B. articles   C. interactions   D. interests
8. A. about   B. as   C. with   D. for
9. A. and   B. on which   C. where   D. that
10. A. and   B. so   C. because   D. but
11. A. ability   B. thoughts   C. matter   D. place
12. A. and   B. with   C. for   D. on
13. A. ability   B. news   C. media   D. confusion
14. A. breaks   B. falls   C. divides   D. include

Unit 7 Analysis of Consumer Buying Behavior

15. A. However   B. Therefore   C. So   D. But
16. A. apple   B. fruit   C. pear   D. food
17. A. what   B. when   C. how   D. why
18. A. forms   B. line   C. shape   D. terms
19. A. so that   B. so as that   C. so as to   D. so
20. A. but that   B. but also   C. but   D. except that

VII Translation.

1. A common thread running through all definitions of social media is a blending of technology and social interaction for the co-creation of value.
2. The purchase decision process is the stages a buyer passes through in making choices about which products and services to buy.
3. People can form different perceptions of the same stimulus because of three perceptual processes: selective attention, selective distortion, and selective retention.
4. Marketers need to focus on the entire buying process rather than on just the purchase decision.
5. Decision making is the cognitive process of selecting a course of action from among multiple alternatives.

Extended Reading

Consumer Buying Decision Process

Every consumer will inevitably undergo the stages of the buying decision process. Buyer decision processes are the decision making processes undertaken by consumers in regard to a potential market transaction before, during, and after the purchase of a product or service.

Consumers play five roles in a buying decision, namely, initiator (the person who first suggests the idea of buying the product or service), influences (the person whose view or advice influences the decision), decider (the person who decides on any component of a buying decision), buyer (the person who makes the actual purchase) and user (the person who consumes or uses the product or service).

Research suggests that customers go through a five-stage decision-making process in every purchase: problem recognition, information search, alternative evaluation, purchase decision and post-purchase behavior. With a good knowledge of the steps a customer goes through to make a purchase, marketers can influence a customer's purchase by providing targeted information, advertisements or guidance. In the meanwhile, it forces the marketer to consider the whole buying process rather than just the purchase decision. However, sometimes, the consumer does not pass through all the five stages before purchasing a product. In more routine purchases, customers often skip or reverse some of the stages. For example, a woman buying her favorite brand of lipstick will recognize the need and go right to the purchase decision, skipping information search and evaluation. Anyway we still use the model in that it shows all the considerations that arise when a consumer faces a new and complex purchase situation.

Problem recognition

The buying process begins with the problem recognition. In other words, the customer recognizes a problem or need. The need for a given product is triggered by internal and external stimuli. Internally, a consumer's normal needs like hunger, thirst, self-image rise to a level high enough to become a drive. By gathering information about consumers' needs, the marketer creates awareness for his product through sales promotion and advertisements.

Information search

If a consumer's drive is very strong and a satisfactory product is near at hand, the consumer is likely to buy it. If not, the consumer may look for information related to the need. The consumer can obtain information from any of several sources including personal sources (family, friends, neighbors, acquaintances), commercial sources (advertising, salespeople, dealers, websites), public sources (mass media, consumer-rating organizations), and experiential sources (handling, examining, using the product).

Generally speaking, the consumer receives the most information about a product from commercial sources—those controlled by the marketer. The most effective sources, however, tend to be personal. People often ask their friends, relatives, acquaintances for comments and recommendations concerning a product or service. Not only are satisfied customers repeat buyers, but they are also walking, talking billboards for your business. Thus marketer is supposed to keep in constant contact with them. In addition, marketers can help customers speed up their decision process by providing all the information needed for decision making as quickly as possible. Make sure that consumers do not have too much trouble to get the decision making information.

Alternative evaluation

In this stage, consumers arrive at attitudes toward different brands through some evaluation procedure. They are to select one alternative from the list of choices. The alternatives will be weighed to seek the best outcome. In some cases, consumers use careful calculations and logical thinking. At other times, consumers select a product without any evaluation; instead they buy on impulse. Sometimes consumers make buying decisions on their own; sometimes they turn to friends for advice. Marketers should study buyers to find out how they actually evaluate brand alternatives. If they know what evaluation procedure goes on, marketers can take steps to influence the buyer's decision.

Unit 7 Analysis of Consumer Buying Behavior

Purchase decision

This stage includes where to buy, when to buy and whether to buy. Generally, the consumer's purchase decision will be to buy the most preferred brand, but two factors can come between the purchase intention and the purchase decision. The first factor is the attitudes of others. The second one is unexpected situational factors. The consumer may form a purchase intention based on factors such as expected income, expected price, and expected product benefits. However, unexpected events may change the purchase intention. Thus, preferences and even purchase intentions do not necessarily result in actual purchase choice.

Post-purchase behavior

After the purchase, consumers may take further action based on their satisfaction or dissatisfaction with the product. If the product falls short of expectations, consumers are dissatisfied, which give rise to brand switching and negative communications with other consumers through word-of-mouth or through the web. Consumers happy with their purchases will become repeat customers and will tell others about their experience. Warranties, support, future discounts, and surveys can contribute to post-purchase behavior.

Taking the time to better understand all of the things that consumers need to do in order to buy often makes a great difference to marketers. Armed with a thorough understanding of the stages of consumers buying process, marketers can plan their work accordingly. Then every single step can be made with the specific intent of encouraging consumers to take the next step in order to make a purchase.

Words and Expressions

inevitably *ad.* 不可避免地	in regard to 关于
undergo *v.* 经历	decide on sth. 决定……
undertake *v.* 担任，承担；着手，开始	problem recognition 问题认知
transaction *n.* 交易	information search 信息搜集
namely *ad.* 即，就是	alternative evaluation 选择评估
initiator *n.* 发起者	purchase decision 购买决策
influence *n.* 有影响力的人	post-purchase behavior 购买后行为
routine *a.* 日常的，常规的	at hand 在手边
skip *v.* 略过，不做，不参加	keep in constant contact with … 与……经常保持联系
trigger *v.* 引起，造成	
acquaintance *n.* 熟人	in addition 此外
concerning *prep.* 关于	speed up 加速，加快
word-of-mouth *a.* 口头的，口述的	at other times 有时候

buy on impulse 凭一时冲动购物	brand switching 品牌转换
repeat buyer 回头客	make a great difference to … 对……来说是截然不同的
on one's own 靠自己	
fall short of 不足，不及，未达到（期望等）	armed with 全副武装的

Comprehension

I Answer the following questions according to the passage.

1. What are the five roles that consumers play in a buying decision?
2. What is the five-stage decision-making process?
3. In what cases will consumers skip or reverse some of the stages? Give some examples.
4. What is the importance of the research on the five-stage process?
5. Where can consumers obtain the information related to their need?
6. Why are the personal resources the most effective?
7. How can you understand "Not only are satisfied customers repeat buyers, but they are also walking, talking billboards for your business"?
8. What will happen if consumers are not satisfied with the product?
9. What plays a positive role on consumers' post-purchase behavior on the part of marketers?

II Write "T" for true, and "F" for false.

1. Buyer decision processes refer to the decision making processes undertaken by consumers before the purchase of a product or service.
2. Rather than just the purchase decision, the marketer should consider the whole buying process.
3. All the five stages are not necessary before consumers make a purchase.
4. Since consumers sometimes skip or reverse some stages, the research on the five-stage process becomes less important.
5. Consumers receive the most valuable information about a product from commercial sources controlled by the marketer.
6. Before making a purchase decision, the consumer must weigh the alternatives.
7. With purchase intention, actual purchase is bound to be made.
8. The marketer's job does not end when the product is bought.

9. If consumers are dissatisfied with the product, they may complain a lot on the Internet.
10. Marketers can do little to influence consumers' post-purchase behavior.

Additional Terms

adoption　采用
aspiration reference group　渴望群体
attribution　归因
awareness　知晓
brand personality　品牌个性
celebrity effect　名人效应
complex buying behavior　复杂的购买行为
dissociative reference group　规避群体，隔离群体
dissonance-reducing buying behavior　减少不协调购买行为
drive　驱力
economic risk　经济风险
extensive decision making　扩展型决策
external search　外部搜寻，外部查找
habitual buying behavior　习惯性购买行为
high involvement　高度介入
high involvement product　高介入产品
high involvement purchase　高介入购买
importance weight　权重
impulse buying　即兴购买

information input　信息输入
internal search　内部搜寻，内部查找
limited decision making　有限型决策
low involvement　低度介入
low involvement product　低介入产品
market recommendation　市场建议
marketing stimulus　营销刺激
membership group　成员群体
neutral reference group　中性群体
nominal decision making　习惯性购买决策
opinion leader　舆论领袖
personal risk　个人风险
psychological life cycle　心理生命周期
routine response　例行性反应
selective retention　选择性保留
selective distortion　选择性扭曲
selective exposure　选择性接触
self-reference criterion　自我参照准则
social risk　社会风险
trial　试用
variety-seeking buying behavior　寻求多样化的购买行为

PART III

Market Analysis

Unit 8

Market

What is a market? Almost all marketing and advertising executives could answer the question, and yet many could give different answers to the same question in that their particular jobs only require the use of limited definitions of a market. For instance, a media planner in an advertising agency might define a market either in terms of geographical places where purchasers live or with respect to the number of demographic characteristics of purchasers.[1] On the other hand, a marketing manager might think of a market in more comprehensive terms. He might include geographical places, demographic characteristics, and also social-psychological descriptions of purchasers; identifications of heavy-user groups; total number of units sold per year; or his brand share of total sales of a given product class. However, it still makes sense for all users of the term to have a fairly comprehensive understanding of its meaning if they are going to communicate with each other on the same semantic levels.[2]

A setup where two or more parties engage in exchange of goods, services and information is called a market. Ideally a market is a place where two or more parties are involved in buying and selling. The two parties involved in a transaction are called seller and buyer. Markets are dependent on two major participants-buyers and sellers. While parties may exchange goods and services by barter, most markets rely on sellers trading their goods or services (including labor), and/or information, directly or through intermediaries, in exchange for money from buyers. These interactions define demand and supply characteristics and are therefore fundamental to economies. It can be said that a market is the process by which the prices of goods and services are established. Historically, markets were physical meeting places where buyers and sellers gathered together to trade. Although physical markets are still vital, virtual marketplaces supported by IT networks such as the Internet have become the largest.

Some markets have low or no competition, particularly if the industry is protected by government legislation. Conversely, some markets are very competitive, with a number of vendors selling the same kinds of products or services.[3] For a market to be competitive, there must be more than a single buyer or seller. It has been suggested that two persons may trade, but it takes at least three persons to have a market, so that there is competition in at least one of its two sides. However, competitive markets, as understood in formal economic theory, rely on much larger numbers of both buyers and sellers. A market with single seller and multiple buyers is a monopoly.

A competitive market has many businesses trying to win the same customers. A monopoly exists when one firm has 25% or more of the market, thus reducing the competition. Competition in the market place can be good for customers. Governments encourage competition because it can help improve factors as follows.

- **Price**. If there are several retailers, each retailer will lower the price in an attempt to win customers. It is illegal for retailers to agree between themselves to fix a price. They must compete for business.
- **Product range**. In order to attract and satisfy customers, companies need to produce products that are superior to their competitors.
- **Customer service**. Retailers that provide customers with helpful and friendly services will win their loyalty.

The number of buyers and sellers involved will have a direct bearing on the price of the goods or services to be sold, and has become known as the law of supply and demand.[4] Where there are more sellers than buyers, the availability of supply will push down prices. If there are more buyers than sellers, the increased demand will push up prices.

Markets include mechanisms or means for determining price of the traded item; communicating the price information; facilitating deals and transactions; effecting distribution. The market for a particular item is made up of existing and potential customers who need it and have the ability and willingness to pay for it.

The simplest way to define a market is to think of it as consisting of all the people or organizations that may have an interest in purchasing a company's products or services. In other words, a market comprises all customers who have needs that may be fulfilled by an organization's offerings.[5] Yet just having a need is not enough to define a market. Many people may say they have a need for a California mansion that overlooks the Pacific Ocean, but most would not be considered potential customers of a real estate agent who is attempting to sell such a property.[6] So other factors come into play when defining a market.

The first factor is that markets consist of customers who are qualified to make a purchase. Qualified customers are defined as those who seek a solution to a need, and are eligible to make a purchase, and possess the financial ability to make the purchase, and have the authority to make the decision.

Note that a customer must meet all factors listed above, though for some markets the customer may have a surrogate who will handle some of these qualifications for a targeted customer. For instance, a market may consist of pre-teen customers who have a need for certain clothing items but the actual purchase may rest with the pre-teens' parents. So the parents could possibly assume one or more surrogate roles that will result in the pre-teen being a qualified customer.[7]

A second factor for defining a market rests with the company's ability to serve the market. To an organization a market can only exist if the solutions sought by customers are ones that the company can satisfy with their offerings. If a company identifies a group of customers who are qualified to make purchases they only become a market for the company once the company is in a position to execute marketing activities designed to service those customers.[8]

Thus, for the purposes of this tutorial, a market is defined as a group of customers who are qualified to make purchases of products or services that a marketer is able to offer. However, even if an organization can offer products and services to a market, not all markets will fit an organization's goals and objectives.[9]

Before delving too deep into the study of marketing, it is worth pausing to consider the different types of market that exist. Markets can be analyzed via the product itself, or end-consumer, or both. The most common distinction is between consumer and industrial markets.

- **Consumer markets**. Consumer markets are the markets for products and services bought by individuals for their own or family use. Goods bought in consumer markets can be categorized in several ways.

Fastmoving consumer goods: these are high volume, low unit value, fast repurchase, such as ready meals, baked beans and newspapers.

Consumer durables: these have low volume but high unit value. Consumer durables are often further divided into white goods (e.g., fridge-freezers, cookers, dishwashers, microwaves) and brown goods (e.g., DVD players, games consoles, personal computers).

Soft goods: soft goods are similar to consumer durables, except that they wear out more quickly and therefore have a shorter replacement cycle, such as clothes and shoes.

Services: hairdressing, dentists, childcare.

- **Industrial markets**. Industrial markets involve the sale of goods between businesses. These are goods that are not aimed directly at consumers. Industrial markets include: selling finished goods like office furniture, computer system and so on; selling raw materials or components like steel, coal, gas, timber and so on; selling services to businesses like waste disposal, security, accounting & legal services.

Industrial markets often require a slightly different marketing strategy and mix. In particular, a business may have to focus on a relatively small number of potential buyers. Whereas consumer marketing tends to be aimed at the mass market (in some cases, many millions of potential customers), industrial marketing tends to be focused.[10]

Unit 8 Market

Vocabulary

geographical	*a.* 地理的	mechanism	*n.* 机制
social-psychological	*a.* 社会心理学的	facilitate	*v.* 促进
semantic	*a.* 语义的	effect	*v.* 影响
setup	*n.* 组织，机构	fulfill	*v.* 完成
barter	*n.* 实物交易	offering	*n.* 待售品，出售品
historically	*ad.* 从历史的角度来看	surrogate	*n.* 代理，代表
legislation	*n.* 立法	pre-teen	*n.* 青春期前的儿童
conversely	*ad.* 相反地	tutorial	*n.* 说明，解释
monopoly	*n.* 垄断	via	*prep.* 通过，经过
availability	*n.* 可利用性	end-consumer	*n.* 最终消费者

Phrases and Expressions

brand share	品牌占有率		某事
product class	产品类别	delve into	钻研，深入研究
make sense	讲得通，有意义	consumer market	消费者市场
engage in	参与	white goods	白色货物，大型家用电器
in exchange for	交换	brown goods	棕色货物，指电视、录音机、音响等外壳为棕色的电子产品
physical market	现货市场		
virtual marketplace	虚拟市场	games console	游戏机
in an attempt to do sth.	试图做某事	soft goods	纺织品，非耐用品
compete for	为……而竞争	wear out	破损
push down	推倒，压倒	replacement cycle	重置周期
push up	提升，增长	industrial market	生产者市场，工业市场
think of ... as	把……看作		
come into play	积极活动，起作用	finished goods	制成品
be qualified to do sth.	有资格做某事	waste disposal	垃圾处理
be eligible to do sth.	有资格做某事	mass market	大众市场
have the authority to do sth.	有权力做		

1. For instance, a media planner in an advertising agency might define a market either in terms of geographical places where purchasers live or with respect to the number of demographic characteristics of purchasers.　例如，负责广告代理的媒体策划也许会按照购买者的地理位置，或者按照购买者的人口特征来界定市场。

本句看似很复杂，主要是因为句子中使用了两个并列的介词短语，分别是 in terms of （在……方面）和 with respect to（关于……），这样可以有效地避免重复。英语忌讳重复，喜欢使用替代的方法。第一个介词短语后面使用了 where 引导的定语从句，用来修饰限定 geographical places。在这里，需要注意两个介词短语的使用，例如：

The savings, in terms of time, could be considerable.　这些储蓄金从时间上来看是相当可观的。

In economic terms, this change is unlikely to affect many people.　这种变化不会在经济方面影响许多人的。

We must have a talk with respect to your market research.　我们必须就你的市场调查谈一谈了。

2. However, it still makes sense for all users of the term to have a fairly comprehensive understanding of its meaning if they are going to communicate with each other on the same semantic levels.　但是，如果所有的使用者想在意义层面进行相互沟通的话，他们还是可以很全面地理解市场的内涵的。

因为使用者采用的概念都不够全面，"市场"这一概念具有不同的解释，但是如果就词义本身来沟通的话，还是可以达成共识的。

3. Conversely, some markets are very competitive, with a number of vendors selling the same kinds of products or services.　相反，在有些市场上，很多卖方出售同样类型的产品或者服务，竞争是相当激烈的。

在本句中，注意 with 引导的复合结构的使用，即 "with + *n.* + *a./prep.*/past participle/present participle"，表示一种伴随的状态，例如：

They held the meeting with the window open.　他们开会的时候开着窗户。

He spoke with a book in his right hand.　他说话的时候右手拿着一本书。

With the prices soaring, they had to try every means to cut costs.　物价飞涨，他们只好想尽一切办法降低成本。

He sat in the conference room, with his eyes fixed on the ceiling.　他坐在会议室，眼睛盯着天花板。

Unit 8　Market

4. The number of buyers and sellers involved will have a direct bearing on the price of the goods or services to be sold, and has become known as the law of supply and demand.　参与其中的买卖双方的人数会直接影响产品或服务的价格，这就是供求规律。

供求规律指的是商品的供求关系与价格变动之间相互制约的必然性，这是商品经济的规律，商品的供给和需求之间存在一定的比例关系，其基础是生产某种商品的社会劳动量必须与社会对这种商品的需求量相适应。供求关系就是供给和需求的对立统一，供求规律就是供求关系变化的基本法则。供求变动引起价格变动——供不应求，价格上涨；供过于求，价格下降。价格变动引起供求的变动——价格上涨，需求减少；价格下跌，需求增加。

5. In other words, a market comprises all customers who have needs that may be fulfilled by an organization's offerings.　换句话说，市场是由所有具有需求的顾客组成的，某一组织所提供的产品或者服务可以满足这些顾客的需求。

本句使用了两个嵌套式的定语从句，首先是 who 引导的定语从句修饰限定 customers，之后是 that 引导的定语从句修饰限定 needs，因此句子结构显得有些复杂。另外，comprise 的意思是"组成"，例如：

Women comprise 44% of the employees in this company.　这家公司女职工占总职工人数的 44%。

6. Many people may say they have a need for a California mansion that overlooks the Pacific Ocean, but most would not be considered potential customers of a real estate agent who is attempting to sell such a property.　很多人可能会说他们想在加利福尼亚买套房子，可以俯瞰太平洋，但是他们中的大多数不会被看作负责销售那处房产的房地产代理商的潜在顾客。

本句使用了三个从句，结构有些复杂。首先是谓语动词 say 后面接宾语从句，引导词 that 省略掉了；that 引导的定语从句修饰限定 mansion，that 在从句中充当主语；最后是 who 引导的定语从句修饰限定 agent。另外，还要注意动词 overlook，除了"忽视"的意思之外，还有"俯瞰，俯视"的意思，例如：

This is a fact that we all tend to overlook.　这是我们所有人经常会忽视的事实。

Jack lived in a huge, two-storeyed house overlooking a flower-filled garden.　杰克住在一幢两层高的大房子里，可以俯瞰花团锦簇的花园。

7. So the parents could possibly assume one or more surrogate roles that will result in the pre-teen being a qualified customer.　因此，家长也许会扮演一个或者多个代理的角色，这样儿童也可以成为顾客了。

在本句中，that 引导定语从句修饰限定 roles。另外，注意动词 assume 的用法，例如：

Mr Cross will assume the role of chief executive with a team of four directors.　克劳斯先生将出任首席执行官，手下有 4 位经理。

8. If a company identifies a group of customers who are qualified to make purchases they only

become a market for the company once the company is in a position to execute marketing activities designed to service those customers. 如果公司确定了能够购买产品的顾客群，那么只有当公司能够完成旨在为这些顾客服务的营销活动时，他们才能成为公司的市场。在本句中，首先使用了 who 引导的定语从句修饰限定 customers，后面的 once 引导时间状语从句，意为"一旦……"。后面的"designed to service those customers"是过去分词短语作定语，用来修饰限定前面的 marketing activities。另外，注意短语"be in a position to do sth."，其意思是"能够做某事"，例如：

This company is in a position to meet the needs of the employees. 公司能够满足职工的需求。

9. However, even if an organization can offer products and services to a market, not all markets will fit an organization's goals and objectives. 但是，即使公司能够为市场提供产品和服务，也并不是所有的市场都能达到公司的目标和要求。

在本句中，要特别注意部分否定的使用。对3个或者3个以上的人或者物进行部分否定，就要使用 not all 或者 all not，例如：

Not all their products are very popular among children.（等同于 All their products are not very popular among children.）他们的产品并不是都受孩子的欢迎。

如果要对3个或者3个以上的人或者物进行全部否定，则要使用 none，例如：

None of their products are very popular among children. 他们的产品没有一种受到孩子们的欢迎。

10. Whereas consumer marketing tends to be aimed at the mass market (in some cases, many millions of potential customers), industrial marketing tends to be focused. 然而，消费者营销往往侧重大众市场（有些情况下，指的是数百万的潜在顾客），企业营销的侧重点则更集中。企业营销者面临的问题和消费者市场营销者面临的问题有很大的不同。当然，基本原理是相似的，那就是，所有营销者都必须考虑目标市场的选择，对这些市场进行细分，对产品、促销、定价和分销作出决策。不同的是这些决策的背景有时相去甚远，所以需要区别对待。企业营销指个人或组织，包括企业、政府和机构，采取将产品和服务销售给其他公司或者组织的方法。企业营销还被称为工业营销、企业对企业营销，或者简称为 B2B 营销。企业营销的分销渠道一般更短、更直接。消费者营销的目标是大量的人口统计群体，主要依靠大众传媒和零售商，而企业营销中买卖双方的谈判过程却更加私人化。

I Answer the following questions according to the text.

1. Why do people give different answers to the definition of market?

2. How do parties in the markets exchange goods and services?
3. What changes have happened to markets?
4. In terms of competitive markets, what can we learn from the third paragraph?
5. Is it good to have competition in the markets on the part of consumers? Why?
6. What is the law of supply and demand?
7. What factors do we need to define a market?
8. What consumers can be called qualified consumers?
9. What are the differences between consumer markets and industrial markets?

II Decide whether the following statements are true or false.

1. People give different answers to the definition of market solely because they have different comprehension of its meaning.
2. A marketing manager might have a better comprehension of market.
3. In most cases, sellers trade their goods or services, and/or information, either directly or indirectly, for money from buyers.
4. With the appearance of virtual markets, physical markets are becoming less vital.
5. All markets are not competitive according to the passage.
6. A market with a single buyer and multiple sellers is a monopoly.
7. When one firm has at least 25% of the market, there will be a monopoly.
8. Governments encourage competition because it can help improve the living standards of the people.
9. The more sellers in the markets than the buyers, the lower the prices will be.
10. Fast moving consumer goods refer to those that can be easily moved from one place to another.

III Fill in each blank with the proper form of the word in the bracket.

1. His report shows only a superficial understanding of the _____ (historically) context.
2. He was willing to face any hardship in _____ (fulfill) of his duty.
3. The _____ (available) of cheap long-term credit would help small business.
4. The hotel is _____ (ideal) placed for restaurants, bars and clubs.
5. He is glad to _____ (engage) in the group discussion about the promotion plan.
6. Running a shop _____ (involve) great experience and responsibility.
7. My remark is not _____ (aim) at you.
8. He is _____ (qualify) as a media planner.
9. It's _____ (legal) to employ teenagers to work in the factories.
10. If this was what his job required, then the job wasn't really worth _____ (have).

IV Fill in each blank with a proper preposition.

1. The firm will be _____ a position to provide employees with more opportunities for training.
2. The quality of the coffee in his company is superior _____ that of his competitors.
3. Woolen cloth and timber were sent to Egypt _____ exchange _____ linen or papyrus.
4. Whether the talks are successful or not rests _____ a small number of people.
5. We should not delve too deeply _____ this painful matter.
6. They think _____ this promotion campaign as a great success.
7. Two factories were closed _____ an attempt to cut costs.
8. The two companies compete _____ raw materials and customers.
9. He has never engaged _____ any illegal transactions.
10. Mr Baker will return home after the forum _____ Britain and France.

V Fill in the blanks with the words and phrases given below. Change the form where necessary.

| wear out | push down | with respect to | facilitate | consumer durables |
| come into play | make sense | in terms of | monopoly | have not the authority to |

1. He _____ sign such a contract without the permission of the manager.
2. His logic is too loose to _____.
3. A _____ exists when a specific person or enterprise is the only supplier of a particular commodity.
4. His contributions to the company cannot be measured _____ money.
5. Machines soon _____ under rough usage.
6. All your faculties have _____ in your work.
7. _____ the price of the new product, we'd better conduct a market research first.
8. He argued that the economic recovery had been _____ by his tough stance.
9. _____ involve any type of products purchased by consumers that are manufactured for long-term use.
10. When miners sell forward their production, they help _____ prices.

VI Cloze.

Organizations and individuals are similar 1_____ they both are someone's customer. Both need to purchase items to accomplish their daily tasks. Price is important in both markets. Both

Unit 8 Market

markets make judgments based on past 2_____ and expect service guarantees. There is a large difference, however, in how and 3_____ an organization and an individual purchase goods and services. Understanding these differences is important if you want to 4_____ into both an organizational market and a consumer market. In other words, it can determine business success.

Individuals purchase goods for their personal use. Individuals and families 5_____ the consumer market. While organizations tend to buy with the intent to purchase goods to use in their ongoing operations and to resell to consumers. Organizations also purchase more raw materials, such as wood, steel and other items used in manufacturing, 6_____ individuals who don't have the tools or knowledge to put those raw materials to use as a product. Organizational markets include corporations, governments, manufacturers and wholesalers and non-profit organizations. Organizations generally purchase goods 7_____ larger volumes than individuals and are 8_____ by customer demand and need for manufacturing materials. Consumers, on the other hand, are driven both by need and by want. It is possible to entice a consumer 9_____ something he does not need through effective marketing or peer pressure, but it is 10_____ to entice an organization to buy an un-needed product, especially 11_____ dealing with a purchasing department that is 12_____ for what it spends.

Organizations often purchase in bulk, 13_____ consumers typically do not. For example, a consumer 14_____ buy 3 gallons of white paint to paint his house, while an organization might need 3,000 gallons to paint shelving units for resale. The organizational market is thus more condensed—it is possible to have a business succeed 15_____ only to a small number of organizational clients—while businesses that typically focus on consumers sell smaller quantities to more people.

Consumers typically purchase goods for different reasons and have more 16_____ in choosing the items they want. A consumer may purchase a chair so people can sit comfortably in his home. He will be able to choose any chair within his 17_____ that he likes. An organization, on the other hand, may purchase a chair 18_____ an administrative assistant needs it to do his job. The organization may be restricted in a chair purchase, not only 19_____ the budget set by a purchasing manager, but also by guidelines 20_____ by the Occupational Safety and Health Administration (OSHA), and by company-wide guidelines on office furniture.

1. A. after   B. in which   C. at which   D. in that
2. A. experiences   B. memory   C. record   D. feelings
3. A. what   B. when   C. why   D. which
4. A. turn   B. tap   C. come   D. fall
5. A. consist of   B. compose of   C. make up   D. constitute of
6. A. and   B. but   C. while   D. than
7. A. in   B. with   C. at   D. for
8. A. forced   B. made   C. driven   D. compelled

9. A. to purchase   B. purchasing   C. to purchasing   D. being purchased
10. A. less hard   B. more harder   C. less harder   D. much harder
11. A. if   B. when   C. since   D. before
12. A. suitable   B. responsible   C. liable   D. passionate
13. A. however   B. in addition   C. whereas   D. and
14. A. must   B. should   C. could   D. might
15. A. catering   B. to cater   C. for catering   D. to catering
16. A. time   B. freedom   C. space   D. opportunity
17. A. power   B. knowledge   C. budget   D. limits
18. A. because   B. since   C. for   D. as
19. A. for   B. with   C. at   D. by
20. A. made   B. set   C. ordered   D. announced

VII Translation.

1. Marketing material is more technical and focuses on cost-effectiveness.
2. For example, a product producer will use physical retail stores, online retailers and trade shows to maximize the number of consumers who buy his products.
3. The exact number of buyers and sellers required for a competitive market is not specified, but a competitive market has enough buyers and sellers that no one buyer or seller can exert any significant influence on the dynamics of the market.
4. Markets vary in location, types, geographic range and size.
5. For example, a product that can be sold forever, like toilet paper or cooking oil, is better than one that is sold just once, like pet rocks.

Extended Reading

Market Systems

In market economies, there are a variety of different market systems that exist, depending on the industry and the companies within that industry. It is important for business owners to understand what type of market system they are operating in when making pricing and production decisions, or when determining whether to enter or leave a particular industry.

In the real world, firms operate in a large variety of environments. These different environments, based on different market conditions, influence the behavior of different firms in different ways. In order to analyze this real life behavior, economists have identified characteristics that make some firms similar to each other, and other firms different from one another. This has led to the study of firms based on five categories of market structure: perfect competition, monopoly, monopolistic competition, oligopoly, and monopsony.

  Perfect competition is a market system characterized by many different buyers and sellers. In the classic theoretical definition of perfect competition, there are an infinite number of buyers and sellers. With so many market players, it is impossible for any one participant to alter the prevailing price in the market. If they attempt to do so, buyers and sellers have infinite alternatives to pursue. In a perfectly competitive market, multiple suppliers have an insignificant market share; standardized or homogeneous products are supplied by each supplier; customers have full information on prices and trends; all industry participants (new and existing sellers) have equal access to technology and other resources; there are no barriers to exit and entry; and the market is open to external competition. A competitive market serves as a benchmark for other real-world markets.

  A monopoly or monopolistic market is one that has only one firm (or seller) that has the autonomy to raise and lower prices without affecting the demand for its services and products. To put it simply, it is just a market with only one seller and no close substitutes for that seller's products. Technically, the term "monopoly" is supposed to refer to the market itself, but it has become common for the single seller in the market to also be referred to as a monopoly. It's also fairly common for the single seller in a market to be referred to as a monopolist. Monopolies serve the needs of the sellers but are detrimental to customers. They are characterized by an absence of economic competition, technological superiority, no substitutes for goods sold and a seller having full control of market power (the ability to lower and raise the prices without losing clients or customers). Examples of monopolies include public utility companies (water, electricity and gas) and Internet service providers in remote areas. A monopoly is the exact opposite form of market system as perfect competition. In a pure monopoly, there is only one producer of a particular good or service, and generally no reasonable substitutes. In such a market system, the monopolist is able to charge whatever price they wish due to the absence of competition, but their overall revenue will be limited by the ability or willingness of customers to pay their price.

  Monopolistic competition, also called competitive market, is a type of market system combining elements of perfect competition and monopoly. Like a perfectly competitive market system, there are numerous competitors in the market. The difference is that each competitor is so sufficiently differentiated from the others that some can charge greater prices than a perfectly competitive firm. In addition, consumers look for those differences rather than price differences. An example of monopolistic competition is the market for music. While there are many artists, each artist is different and is not perfectly substitutable with another artist. Another example is the restaurant industry. Anyone can obtain the proper permits, licenses and open a restaurant offering any cuisine or food in the world. Whether the restaurant is successful or not depends upon whether or not consumers like the food, service, location, and all the other factors that make restaurants successful.

Oligopoly is a market structure involving a relatively small number of sellers on the market who can control the price of their goods. When an oligopoly results in collusion, or secret deals, among the participating companies, the result can be control of prices. An example of a well-known oligopoly would be the gasoline industry, in which only a few companies dominate the market and have the opportunity to collude to control prices. An oligopoly usually forms either because the cost of getting into a business is high or because rich competitors dominate the market with a big product promotion budget. An oligopoly market is characterized by a limited number of competing sellers who sell similar or different products. Sellers compete with each other by aggressive advertising and improved service delivery. An oligopoly sets barriers to entry and makes it difficult for new sellers to enter the market. Barriers include patent rights, financial requirements and legal barriers. Tobacco companies and airlines are oligopolies.

Market systems are not only differentiated according to the number of suppliers in the market. They may also be differentiated according to the number of buyers. Whereas a perfectly competitive market theoretically has an infinite number of buyers and sellers, a monopsony has only one buyer for a particular good or service, giving that buyer significant power in determining the price of the products produced. In other words, it is a type of market in which a single powerful buyer controls and affects market prices. Multiple sellers offer goods and services, but there is only a single buyer who has exclusive control of market power and can bring the prices of goods/services down. According to the textbook *Microeconomics: Principles and Applications*, a pure monopsony is rare. An example of monopsony is a coal company in a small town.

Managers define market structure with the understanding that market structure is fluid. What the market looks like today, and what it looks like tomorrow, may be two completely different pictures. Changes in technology and business can transform the market structure of an industry. The oligarchic market that houses the record industry has seen a transformation with the advent of home computers bearing simple recording technology combined with the development of the Internet. With new, cheaper technology, an Internet-savvy recording hobbyist with some extra money can now build a fan base and get money without the help of a record company or contract.

Words and Expressions

oligopoly *n.* 寡头垄断	benchmark *n.* 基准，参照
infinite *a.* 无限的	autonomy *n.* 自治
prevailing *a.* 主要的，普遍的，盛行的	technically *ad.* 在技术方面
insignificant *a.* 不重要的，微不足道的	monopolist *n.* 垄断者
standardized *a.* 标准的	superiority *n.* 优越，优等
homogeneous *a.* 同性质的，同类的	substitutable *a.* 可替代的，可替换的

Unit 8 Market

permit *n.* 许可，准许；许可证，执照
cuisine *n.* 菜肴
collusion *n.* 共谋，串通
dominate *v.* 控制
aggressive *a.* 侵略性的
tobacco *n.* 烟草
theoretically *ad.* 从理论上来看
monopsony *n.* 买主垄断，买主独家垄断
exclusive *a.* 排外的，独家的
fluid *a.* 易变的，不固定的
house *v.* 给……提供住房
advent *n.* 到来
Internet-savvy *a.* 熟悉网络的
hobbyist *n.* 沉溺于某种癖好者
perfect competition   完全竞争
market structure   市场结构
monopolistic competition   垄断竞争
to put it simply   简单地说

be detrimental to sb.   对某人有害
have a full control of ...   完全控制……
market power   市场控制力
public utility   公用事业
pure monopoly   纯粹的垄断
due to   由于
overall revenue   总收入
be differentiated from   不同于
price difference   价格差异
service delivery   提供服务
set barrier to   设置壁垒
patent right   专利权
financial requirement   财政需求，资金需要
legal barrier   法律方面的障碍
bring down   降低
record industry   唱片行业
home computer   家用电脑
fan base   粉丝团

Comprehension

I Answer the following questions according to the passage.

1. What is the importance of market structure to business owners?
2. How many categories of market structure are mentioned in the passage? What are they?
3. What are the characteristics of a perfectly competitive market?
4. What are the disadvantages of a monopoly or monopolistic market?
5. What are the differences between monopolistic competition, perfect competition and monopoly?
6. What has caused the appearance of oligopolies?
7. What are the main characteristics of oligopolies?
8. What is a monopsony according to the passage?
9. What is the main idea of the last paragraph?
10. What does the writer mainly talk about in this passage?

II Write "T" for true, and "F" for false.

1. Market structure is important for business owners to understand pricing and production decisions, or determine whether to enter or leave a particular industry.
2. There are five categories of market structure: imperfect competition, monopoly, monopolistic competition, oligopoly, and monopsony.
3. It's rather difficult for any buyer or seller to change the prevailing price in the market because of the existence of many different buyers and sellers.
4. In a monopolistic market, one seller has the autonomy to raise and lower prices, which will definitely affect the demand for its services and products.
5. Monopolies are very popular among both sellers and customers.
6. Monopolistic competition is an exact opposite of perfect competition.
7. The market for music is a typical example of pure monopoly.
8. A monopsony sets barriers to entry and makes it difficult for new sellers to enter the market.
9. Tobacco companies and restaurants are oligopolies.
10. The market structure will change with the development of science and technology.

Additional Terms

adoption rate 采购率，采纳率	financial strength 财务优势
barrier to entry 进入壁垒	free entry and exit 自由进出
black market 黑市	free market 自由市场
blue ocean strategy 蓝海战略	future market 期货市场
bond market 债券市场	growth rate 增长率
bulk purchase 成批采购	internet market 网络市场
clone market 组装市场	liquid asset 流动资产
competitive spectrum 竞争图谱	market anarchism 市场无政府主义
currency market 货币市场	market cap 市场资本
desk research 案头调研	market characteristic 市场特性
dominant market share 压倒性的市场份额	market culture 市场文化
	market equilibrium 市场均衡
excess capacity 超额能力	market failure 市场失灵
existing market 现存市场	market forecast 市场预测
field research 现场调查	market growth 市场增长
financial market 金融市场	market inclusion 市场纳入

market intelligence　市场情报
market leader　市场领导者
market measurement　市场测量
market price　市场价
market pull　市场拉动
market size　市场规模
market symmetry　市场对称性
market value　市场价值
money market　货币市场
niche strategy　利基战略
organizational market　组织市场

physical retail market　实物零售市场
prediction market　预测市场
price taker　价格接受者
primary market　初级市场
product differentiation　产品差异化，产品特色化
regulatory barrier　监管障碍，监管壁垒
stock market　股票市场
upfront investment　启动投资
up-sell　追加销售，提升销售

Unit 9

Market Research

When developing your marketing plan, chances are that you will not get it right the first time.[1] That is to say, you need time to learn about the demographics, geography, and psychographics of your customers before your marketing can really be effective. Anyway, if you hate making mistakes and want to get it right the first time, there is a way, and that is market research. Market research is a continuous process of systematic gathering, recording and analyzing information about particular market a company operates in or a product/service the company offers for selling in that market, and also about potential and existing competitors and the past, present and potential customers who purchase and consume the offered product/service to help identify and define marketing opportunities and problems, as well as generate sales. Through it you can create a business plan, refine and evaluate all your marketing activities, monitor your marketing performance, gain competitive advantages and continuously improve your marketing processes and efforts.

It is said that the early 1820s saw the first recorded market research when newspapers in the United States carried out simple street surveys to see how the political winds were blowing.[2] However, at that time most companies would keep track of their own sales figures and accounting figures, but were not always aware of their competitors' place in the market. By the early 1900s a fledgling market research industry had started in the U.S. focusing on advertising testing in one form or another. In 1920 market research began to come across to the UK. It's believed that in the 1950s, Dial America Marketing, Inc.[3] became the first company completely dedicated to inbound and outbound telephone sales and services. In 1995 first commercial online market research was conducted. Only in a short period of time the Internet grew from something believed to be inferior to the most dominant way of conducting market research. In 2010, crowdsourcing began to become popular with business turning to customers for ideas.[4]

The importance of market research is often overlooked and underestimated by entrepreneurs when starting a business. Some maintain that taking action and getting started is far greater than doing market research, and others argue that market research is expensive and small businesses cannot afford it, but light end market research is possible. Basically, you just have to look at the demographic of your competitors and make your demographic. It's not that easy, though.[5] Demographics may vary between businesses of the same nature, and that is where testing comes in. You need to test if that demographic works for you, and if it does not, you need to test another demographic. Through surveys, literature research, internet research, and other information gathering techniques, you can learn the trends in your industry, as well as individual preferences of your potential customers. Market research has a direct link with the success of your marketing, advertising and branding campaigns. Without market research, you'll be running your business in blind-mode; luckily, it's quite easy to obtain much of your research through very common reports, analytics and freely available tools online. Market research is important for your business because it provides you with the following opportunities.

- **Better understanding of potential customers**. Without knowing who your potential customers are and what they want, it's impossible for you to entice users to conduct business with you. So it's important to spend time and money to develop an image of your true customer down to the finest detail (age, sex, location, income). While conducting market research, you can use tools of marketing campaigns (questionnaires, meetings, discussions, messaging) to reach a wide audience of customers, investigate current and future needs and expectations of the customers, and achieve higher customer satisfaction.

- **Reduced costs and increased sales**. Nowadays competition is becoming increasingly intense, which will raise your costs and stretch budgets thin. Anyway, market research will enable your team to find hidden marketing platforms with very little competition but with a very high return on investment.

- **Planning for the future**. Market research is often important to find future trends that will help drive the success of the firms. Although business is conducted in real-time, knowing what the future holds for your market will help set you on the right path to catch the wave.

- **Business growth**. Because of market research, your sales tends to be on the increase, your customer management gets better, and your company gains an opportunity for further business growth and development.

Not doing market research will place marketers in a space where the majority of their success will be dependent on luck rather than market strategy. It's claimed that there are some dangers to be associated with not doing market research: potential investors will not invest if the marketer fails to provide adequate research and facts about their industry; the cost of the company will be raised; marketers fail to attend to the needs of potential customers; marketers are troubled by a shortage of information as to the future trends of the market.

In summary, before you invest in business and spend your hard-earned money on a new venture, consider conducting market research first. Running or starting a business without conducting regular, relevant market research is a serious management mistake. It's like packing for a holiday without checking the weather conditions at your holiday destination. Make sure to base your business plan on relevant and accurate market research.

Generally speaking, there are six steps to follow.

1. Determine the goal of your research

Do you need to improve customer service or increase sales? Are you looking for the right market for a new product? This is a crucial step and should not be rushed. Time and money spent on determining the exact goal of the research often saves time and money in the long run.

2. Determine your target market

A target market is the group or groups of people you will be promoting, advertising, and ultimately selling your product to. To find your market, you should begin by answering some simple questions: What are the demographics of the area you are competing in? Who will buy you products based on price? What is the age range? What kind of lifestyle does your product relate to? Is it everyday use, specific to times of the year or to specific activities?

3. Decide the ways to conduct research

Once you figure out your target market, make an effort to reach out to this group and find out what they think about your product. This is the heart of market research, and there are many ways to do it.

Qualitative research is a good way to find out the kinds of feelings and needs people have about your product or service. It involves a fewer number of people and is not statistically representative. Methods include focus groups and in-depth interviews.

Quantitative research gets you solid statistics you can base your financial plans on. It involves a large number of respondents, such as surveys and questionnaires. Surveys can be conducted by phone, in person by mail or on-line. The key to getting good research is to get a truly representative, random sample of your target market.

4. Gather information

Conduct mail and telephone surveys using randomly selected addresses and telephone numbers in your local area. Collect information from existing customers. Use questionnaires, personal interviews to get feedback on your products and services. If you have a web site, start a chat room or message board and encourage customers to participate.

5. Interpret the data

After doing the research, the findings have to be analyzed and interpreted. The findings can be interpreted in charts and tables.

6. Reach a conclusion

A conclusion can be drawn on what is to be done next once the data has been interpreted. However, in some cases, reaching a conclusion may not be so easy because of gaps in the information. A valid conclusion might be that you need further information to be able to make a decision.

Vocabulary

systematic	a. 系统性的	blind-mode	n. 黑场模式
evaluate	v. 评估	analytic	a. 分析的
fledgling	a. 没经验的	real-time	a. 实时的
inbound	a. 回内地的，入境的	shortage	n. 短缺，缺乏，缺少
outbound	a. 开往外地的，开往外国的	respondent	n. 回答者，答卷人
crowdsourcing	n. 众包	finding	n. 结果
overlook	v. 忽视，忽略	hard-earned	a. 辛苦得到的
underestimate	v. 低估	random	a. 任意的，随机的

Phrases and Expressions

keep track of ... 与……保持联系，了解	attend to the need of ... 满足……的需求
advertising testing 广告测试	consider doing sth. 考虑做某事
dedicated to ... 致力于……	figure out 计算出，断定
be inferior to ... 比……差的，比……次的	qualitative research 定性研究
individual preference 个人偏好	quantitative research 定量研究
set sb. on the right path 让某人走上正路	in-depth interview 深度访谈
on the increase 增长，增加	message board 留言板
be dependent on 依赖，依靠	be representative of ... 代表……
be associated with ... 与……相关	

1. When developing your marketing plan, chances are that you will not get it right the first time.
   在制订营销计划时，第一次你可能会失败。
   主句中使用了 that 引导的表语从句。chance 的意思是"可能性"，例如：
   He has a poor chance of winning the game. 他赢这场比赛的可能性很小。

What are the chances that we shall succeed? 我们赢的可能性有多大？
The chances are that the company will lose its market share. 公司可能会失去其市场份额。

2. It is said that the early 1820s saw the first recorded market research when newspapers in the United States carried out simple street surveys to see how the political winds were blowing. 据说19世纪20年代早期第一次出现了有记载的市场调查，当时美国的各大报纸开始进行简单的街头调查，想从中了解人们的政治倾向。

在本句中，it 是形式主语，真正的主语是后面的 that 从句。在从句中，see 的意思是"体验，经历，见证"，例如：

The next ten years saw the family constantly on the move between England and Ireland. 在接下来的10年里，这家人奔波于英格兰与爱尔兰之间。

The company has seen great changes in the recent years. 近几年公司发生了很大的变化。

英语句子中常常使用没有生命的物作主语，这样可以显得更加客观，例如：

Such a chance denied me. 我没有得到这样一个机会。

Her name escaped me. 我想不起她的名字了。

3. Dial America Marketing, Inc.: 这是一家美国公司，位于加利福尼亚州的圣地亚哥，属于管理咨询服务行业。

4. In 2010, crowdsourcing began to become popular with business turning to customers for ideas. 2010年，众包开始受到那些愿意了解顾客想法的企业的欢迎。

crowdsourcing 的意思是"众包"，指的是一个公司或机构把过去由员工执行的工作任务外包给非特定的（而且通常是大型的）大众网络。众包的任务通常是由个人承担的，但如果涉及需要多人协作完成的任务，也有可能以依靠开源的个体生产的形式出现。众包与外包的不同在于前者的任务和问题是外派给不确定的群体，而后者是外派给确定的个体。

5. It's not that easy, though. 但是，那可不是容易的事情。

句中 that 的意思是"very"，常常用在否定句或者疑问句中，例如：

I know some people left before the end, but was it really that bad?

It isn't that cold.

I've done only that much.

句中 though 的意思是"然而，不过"，例如：

He will probably agree; you never know, though.

He said he would come; he didn't, though.

Unit 9 Market Research

I Answer the following questions according to the text.

1. What is market research?
2. Give a brief account of the history of market research.
3. What is the importance of market research?
4. What opportunities will market research bring to companies?
5. What are the dangers to be associated with not doing market research?
6. What are the six steps of conducting a market research?

II Decide whether the following statements are true or false.

1. When you develop marketing strategy, your efforts may end in total failure.
2. It was in the early 1820s that the first recorded market research appeared in the United States.
3. With the appearance of market research, companies attached importance to their competitors' place in the market.
4. The Internet used to be considered as an ineffective way of conducting market research.
5. All entrepreneurs are not in favor of market research.
6. Demographics are not necessarily the same even between businesses of the same nature.
7. The more detailed information about potential customers, the easier to understand them.
8. Without market research, marketers will rely on more luck than market strategy.
9. An acquaintance with future trends of the market will enable companies to keep with the times.
10. Qualitative research is a good way to get a truly representative, random sample of your target market.

III Fill in each blank with the proper form of the word in the bracket.

1. It was built in a year, which seems absolutely _____ (incredibly).
2. This report is a _____ (system) study of the potential customers.
3. Their big mistake was to _____ (estimate) their opponents' skill in handling the news media.

4. Her _____ (invest) was mainly in technology stocks.
5. The project's success _____ (dependent) on the support of everyone concerned.
6. He had been a _____ (dominant) figure in this field.
7. The company seems to have ignored the _____ (find) of the report.
8. They are facing a _____ (short) of raw materials.
9. They try to do everything in their power to avoid _____ (offend) their customers.
10. They claimed that the group _____ (representative) the interests of the workers in the company.

IV Fill in each blank with a proper preposition.

1. This design is inferior _____ the one the German company proposed.
2. You can turn to him _____ advice if necessary.
3. _____ the long run, this strategy will do a world of good to the company.
4. Proper planning is the key _____ success.
5. I couldn't figure _____ what the manager was talking about.
6. She reached _____ to touch the beautiful vase in exhibition.
7. The Dow Jones Index is not necessarily representative _____ the whole of corporate America.
8. It took me several hours to fill _____ the application form.
9. We need a system to keep track _____ all our expenses.
10. The goal of the plan is to attend _____ the needs of potential customers.

V Fill in the blanks with the words and phrases given below. Change the form where necessary.

| incredibly | dedicate | that | in-depth interview | as to |
| evaluate | consider | say | chances | random |

1. The performance of each employee is _____ once a year.
2. He is _____ buying a new car.
3. There is some doubt _____ whether the information is totally accurate.
4. If I want to get a job in advertising, what do you think my _____ would be?
5. He has an _____ good eye for details.
6. He _____ himself to academic work.
7. There is no need to rush around—it's not _____ urgent.
8. This is only a _____ sample of customers.
9. _____ are useful when you want detailed information about a person's thoughts and

behaviors or want to explore new issues in depth.

10. Why don't we have a break until, _____, 10:20?

VI Cloze.

Market research is about finding out answers 1_____ questions that deal with 2_____ or not there is a local or national market for your product or service. It doesn't mean that you're supposed 3_____ if some customers will buy your products or services, but 4_____ in your target market there is a continuous need for your products or services. Market research enables you to obtain new, up-to-date information that guide you break 5_____ a market or take market to a higher level. Competitors 6_____ not be able to match the knowledge you have gathered or improved product features, so in the short term it could give you enough of an early and powerful 7_____ to grab, or consolidate a share of the market. The minimum way to approach market research is to look in local libraries for commercial information, newspapers and businesses 8_____ to the one you intend to start and decide how much 9_____ there is for another similar business. What's more, with the help of market research, you will get to know more about your target market including the market leader, market challengers and market followers. In most markets, there is a market leader, with the 10_____ market share. In most cases, it's the first company to have entered the field, or at least the first to have 11_____ in it. Besides, there is a market challenger or challengers, 12_____ the second largest market share. They either attempt to attack the market leader, or 13_____ their market share by attacking market followers. Most companies in the market are market followers which present 14_____ threat to the leader. They concentrate on market division, and try to find a profitable place in the market that is not 15_____ by other products or services.

1. A. with   B. of   C. for   D. to
2. A. whether   B. if   C. that   D. why
3. A. to look for   B. to find out   C. looking for   D. finding out
4. A. if   B. whether   C. that   D. /
5. A. up   B. into   C. in   D. into
6. A. may   B. can   C. must   D. might
7. A. opportunity   B. chance   C. advantage   D. way
8. A. attached   B. similar   C. devoted   D. relative
9. A. room   B. money   C. opportunity   D. chance
10. A. most   B. less   C. larger   D. largest
11. A. engaged   B. engrossed   C. succeeded   D. won
12. A. with   B. /   C. have   D. has
13. A. to increase B. increase   C. increased   D. increasing

14. A. much   B. little   C. many   D. no
15. A. occupied   B. satisfied   C. taken   D. designated

VII Translation.

1. Some of your marketing campaigns will fail, but instead of getting discouraged, analyze what went wrong.
2. For your company it is also important to organize regular market research to get insight into the market, investigate spending habits of your customers, identify existing and potential competitors, develop solutions for product promotion and advertising, improve your business reputation, and so on.
3. Obviously the marketing department of your organization can optimize its marketing campaigns through planning and conducting market research activities.
4. Market research will not only save you months of headache but will help structure your business plan.
5. Market research is absolutely necessary because we all have different tastes, different ideas about what is important in our lives, and different ability (or willingness) to pay a particular price for what we want.

Extended Reading

Market Research Methods

Market research can be classified as either primary or secondary research. The difference is quite simple, yet there is often confusion around this topic.

The term primary research is widely used in academic research, market research and competitive intelligence. When marketers conduct research to collect original data for their own needs, it is called primary research. Primary research consists of a collection of original primary data collected by the researcher. It is often undertaken after the researcher has gained some insight into the issue by reviewing secondary research or by analyzing previously collected primary data. It can be accomplished through various methods, including surveys, questionnaires and telephone interviews in market research, or experiments and direct observations in the physical sciences, amongst others. In the case of primary research, you are generating your own data from scratch as opposed to finding other people's data.

While not as frequently used as secondary research, primary research still represents a significant part of overall marketing research. For many organizations, especially large consumer products firms, spending on primary research far exceeds spending on secondary research.

The primary research consists of marketers carrying out their own research and an extensive group of companies offering their services to marketers.

- **Full-service market research firms**. These companies develop and carry out the full research plan for their clients.
- **Partial-service market research firms**. These companies offer expertise that address a specific part of the research plan, such as developing methods to collect data, locating research participants or undertaking data analysis.
- **Research tools suppliers**. These firms provide tools used by researchers and include data collection tools, data analysis software and report presentation products.

Primary data collection offers advantages and disadvantages for the marketers. Marketers often turn to primary data collection because of the benefits it offers.

Addresses specific research issues

Carrying out their own research allows the marketing organization to address issues specific to their own situation. Primary research is designed to collect the information the marketer wants to know and report it in ways that benefit the marketer. For example, while information reported with secondary research may not fit the marketer's needs, no such problem exists with primary research since the marketer controls the research design.

Greater control

Not only does primary research enable the marketer to focus on specific issues, it also enables the marketer to have a higher level of control over how the information is collected. In this way the marketer can decide on such issues as size of project, location of research (e.g., geographic area) and time frame for completing the project.

Efficient spending for information

Unlike secondary research where the marketer may spend for information that is not needed, primary data collections focus on issues specific to the researcher, thus improving the chances that research funds will be spent efficiently.

Proprietary information

Information collected by the marketer using primary research is their own and is generally not shared with others. Thus, information can be kept hidden from competitors and potentially offer an "information advantage" to the company that undertook the primary research.

On one hand, primary data collection is a powerful method for acquiring information, and on the other hand, it does pose several significant problems.

Cost

Compared to secondary research, primary data may be very expensive since there is a great deal of marketer involvement and the expense in preparing and carrying out research can be high.

Time consuming

To be done correctly primary data collection requires the development and execution of a research plan. Going from the start-point of deciding to undertake a research project to the end-point of having results is often much longer than the time it takes to acquire secondary data.

Not always feasible

Some research projects, while potentially offering information that could prove quite valuable, are not within the reach of a marketer. Many are just too large to be carried out by all companies except the largest ones and some are infeasible at all. For instance, it would not be practical for McDonald's to attempt to interview every customer who visits their stores on a certain day since doing so would require hiring a huge number of researchers, an unrealistic expense. Fortunately, as we will see in a later tutorial there are ways for McDonald's to use other methods (e.g., sampling) to meet their needs without the need to talk with all customers.

Sometimes secondary research is called "desk research" because it can be done from behind a desk. This technique involves research and analysis of existing research and data; hence the name, "secondary research." Conducting secondary research may not be so glamorous, but it often makes a lot of sense. First, secondary research is often free. Second, thanks to the Internet, data is increasingly available and comes in all sorts of shapes and sizes. Internal company data like customer details, sales figures can also be considered as secondary data. Published articles, including peer-reviewed journals, newspapers, magazines, and even blog postings count as secondary data sources. Don't forget legal documents like patents and company annual filings. Social media data is a new source of secondary data. Your job as a secondary researcher is to seek out these sources, organize and apply the data to your specific project, and then summarize/visualize it in a way that makes sense to you and your audiences. So, that's what secondary research is all about. The downside, of course, is that you may not be able to find secondary research information specific enough (or recent enough) for your objectives. If that's the case, you'll need to conduct your own primary research.

In a nutshell, primary research is original research conducted by you (or someone you hire) to collect data specifically for your current objective. Conversely, secondary research involves searching for existing data that was originally collected by someone else. You might look in journals, libraries, or go to online sources. You will apply what you find to your personal research problem, but the data you are finding was not originally collected by you, nor was it obtained for the purpose you are using it for.

English

Unit 9　Market Research

Words and Expressions

primary research　初步研究，基础研究	data collection tool　数据收集工具
secondary research　间接研究，二手研究	proprietary information　专有信息
academic research　学术研究	information advantage　信息优势
competitive intelligence　竞争情报	desk research　案头研究
in the case of ...　至于……，就……而言	peer-reviewed journal　同行评审期刊
from scratch　从头做起，从零开始	blog posting　博客布告
as opposed to ...　与……形成对照	count as　当作，看成，视为
full-service market research firm　完全服务市场调查公司	in a nutshell　简而言之
	patent　n. 专利
partial-service market research firm　不完全服务市场调查公司	filing　n. 整理成档案，文件归档
	visualize　v. 设想，想象

Comprehension

I Answer the following questions according to the passage.

1. In what cases is primary research widely used?
2. How can we accomplish primary research?
3. What companies are more likely to conduct primary research?
4. What tools do the research tools suppliers provide?
5. What are the advantages of primary data collection?
6. What are the disadvantages of primary data collection?
7. What can be called secondary research according to the passage?
8. Why is conducting secondary research said to make a lot of sense?
9. What are considered as sources of secondary data?
10. What are the differences between primary research and secondary research?

II Write "T" for true, and "F" for false.

1. Simple as it is, there is always confusion concerning the difference between primary research and secondary research.
2. Secondary research is widely used in academic research, market research and competitive intelligence.

3. Primary research is no more frequently used than secondary research.
4. Spending on primary research far exceeds spending on secondary research in most companies.
5. Secondary research enables the marketer to focus on specific issues and to have a higher level of control over the way the information is collected.
6. Different from secondary research, primary research focuses on specific issues to improve the efficiency of spending.
7. Internal company data like customer details, sales figures can also be considered as secondary data.
8. The advantages of secondary research outweigh its disadvantages.
9. Secondary research is less expensive since it needs no expense in preparing and carrying out research.
10. In secondary research, you have to search for existing data, say, in journals, libraries, or go to online sources.

Additional Terms

above the line　线上活动	market information　市场信息
below the line　线下活动	marketing effectiveness　营销效果
blind test　盲测	media analysis　媒体分析
business strategy　经营战略	motivation research　动机研究
cascading　阶式渗透	multi-dimensional scaling　多方面衡量
causal research　因果性调研	observation study　观察调研法
choice modeling　选择模型法	off the research　间接调研
consumer surplus　消费者剩余	omnibus research　混合调研，混合调查
coverage　覆盖率	online research　在线调研，在线调查
depth interview　深度访谈	paired comparison　成对比较法
desk research　案头调研	pilot study　前导性研究
duplication　重叠率	qualitative research　定性研究
exploratory　探索性调研	quantitative research　定量研究
feasibility study　可行性研究	quota sampling　配额抽样
financial performance　财务绩效	red goods　红色商品
frequency distribution　频率分布	reference group　相关群体
gap analysis　缝隙分析	risk analysis　风险分析
habit buying　习惯性购买	sales territory　销售领域
heavy user　重度消费者	simulated test marketing　模拟试销
inertia selling　惰性销售	sampling　抽样
interviewer　访问员	

Unit 10
Market Segmentation

It's universally acknowledged that segmentation is a major element of marketing.[1] Market segmentation is the process of defining and subdividing a large homogenous market into clearly identifiable segments having similar needs, wants, or demand characteristics. The differences between customers within each segment are as small as possible. Its objective is to target specific products and services for each group or segment and design a marketing mix that precisely matches the expectations of customers in the targeted segment. By tailoring the offering (communication, product, channel, price) to different groups companies are in a good position to more precisely meet the needs of more customers and consequently to gain a higher overall level of share or profit from a market. The key elements of a market segment include: must have unique requirements, attributes, or behavior; must be reasonably stable over time; must be able to be reached efficiently through specifically targeted distribution and communication initiatives; must be measurable.

The importance of market segmentation arises from the fact that all customers of a product or a service don't share the same interests.[2] Most companies come to the realization that every customer has individual needs, preferences, resources and behaviors. Since no two people are exactly alike, it is virtually impossible that they will be able to meet the needs of all customers in a market with a single product or service. Besides, they also realize that it is almost infeasible to create a distinct product for every customer. Therefore, most businesses attempt to divide the overall market into segments, then try to match their product and marketing mix more closely to the needs of one or more segments.

Theoretically speaking, a number of customer characteristics, known as segmentation bases, can be used to define market segments. Some commonly used bases include geographic segmentation, demographic segmentation, psychographic segmentation and behavioral segmentation.[3] Marketers divide the markets according to geographic units, such as nations, states, regions, counties, cities, or neighborhoods. They study the population density or regional climate as factors of geographic segmentation. Demographic segmentation, such as age, gender, income, has been widely used. That works well when demographics are highly associated with needs and wants. Psychographic segmentation has become more popular as it reflects people's lifestyles, attitudes and aspirations. It can be very useful in strengthening brand identity and creating an emotional connection with the brand, but may not necessarily result in sales. Behavioral segmentation is based on product consumption-related behaviors and can include frequency, volume and type of product usage. This type of segmentation can be very powerful for firms that have a membership-type relationship with customers. A drawback is that firms typically can only observe the behaviors with regard to their own products, but not those of their competitors.

A business must analyze the needs and wants of different market segments before determining their own niche. The segmented markets must meet the following criteria, namely, measurable, relevant, accessible, distinguishable and feasible.

• **Measurable**. Can you measure the size and growth of the segment? It has to be possible to determine the values of the variables used for segmentation with justifiable efforts. This is important especially for demographic and geographic variables.

• **Relevant**. The size and profit potential of a market segment have to be large enough to economically justify separate marketing activities for this segment.

• **Accessible**. Is it easy for you to target and reach your segment? Can they be reached with basic communication tools such as radio and TV advertising? If you cannot target your segment effectively with marketing communication then it is not viable. So the segment has to be accessible and servable for the company. That means, for instance, that there are target-group specific advertising media, like magazines or websites the target audience likes to use.

• **Distinguishable**. The market segments have to be that diverse that they show different reactions to different marketing mixes.

• **Feasible**. It has to be possible to approach each segment with a particular marketing program and to draw advantages from that.

Market segmentation helps the marketers to bring together individuals with similar choices and interests on a common platform. There are several important reasons why businesses should attempt to segment their markets carefully. These are summarized as follows.

Market segmentation helps the companies to target the right product to the right customers at the right time. Geographical segmentation classifies consumers according to their locations. A grocery store in colder states of the country would stock coffee all through the year as compared to places which have defined winter and summer seasons.

Segmentation helps better match customers' needs. In other words, segmentations enable the companies to know and understand their customers better. Organizations can now reach a wider audience and promote their products more effectively. It helps the organizations to concentrate their hard work on the target audiences and get suitable results. By marketing products that appeal to customers at different stages of their life (life-cycle), a business can retain customers who might otherwise switch to competing products and brands.

Market segmentation also offers the customers opportunities to get a clearer view of what to buy and what not to buy. A Rado or Omega watch would have no takers amongst the lower income group as they cater to the premium segment. College students seldom go to a Zodiac or Van Heusen store as the merchandise offered by these stores are meant mostly for the professionals. Individuals from the lower income group never use a Blackberry. In simpler words, the segmentation process influences the buying decision of the consumers.

Market segmentation helps the marketers understand the needs of the target audiences and adopt specific marketing plans, devise appropriate marketing strategies and promotional schemes accordingly. By segmenting markets, businesses can raise average prices and subsequently enhance profits.

Market segmentation helps the marketers gain larger market share. Unless a business has a strong or leading share of a market, it is unlikely to be maximizing its profitability. Minor brands suffer from lack of scale economies in production and marketing, pressures from distributors and limited space on the shelves. Through careful segmentation and targeting, businesses can often achieve competitive production and marketing costs and become the preferred choice of customers and distributors. In other words, segmentation offers the opportunity for smaller firms to compete with bigger ones.

Vocabulary

subdivide v. 再分，细分	powerful a. 有力的
homogenous a. 相同的	context n. 环境
identifiable a. 可辨别的	niche n. 产品或服务的特殊领域
tailor v. 适应，适合	measurable a. 可测量的，可衡量的
stable a. 稳定的	distinguishable a. 区别得出的，辨认得出的
initiative n. 主动权	
alike a. 相同的	justifiable a. 合理的
virtually ad. 几乎	viable a. 切实可行的，有望实现的
infeasible a. 不可行的	professional n. 专业人士
gender n. 性别	enhance v. 提高，增长
aspiration n. 愿望，抱负	

Phrases and Expressions

come to the realization　逐渐意识到
theoretically speaking　从理论上说
geographic segmentation　地理细分
population density　人口密度
demographic segmentation　人口细分
psychographic segmentation　心理细分
behavioral segmentation　行为细分
segmentation base　细分基础
brand identity　品牌识别

1. It's universally acknowledged that segmentation is a major element of marketing.　众所周知，市场细分是营销的主要因素之一。
   本句中句型 It's universally acknowledged that ... 的意思是"众所周知……"，例如：
   It's universally acknowledged that the concept of market segmentation was put forward by Wendell R. Smith in the 1950s.　众所周知，市场细分的概念是温德尔·R.史密斯在20世纪50年代提出来的。

2. The importance of market segmentation arises from the fact that all customers of a product or a service don't share the same interests.　某一产品或者服务的顾客并不是都具有相同的兴趣爱好，这使得市场细分变得非常重要了。
   本句的理解主要在于"all ... not"部分否定的理解上，意思是"并不是所有的……都……"，相当于"not all ..."，例如：
   All of the proposals were not accepted. 等同于 Not all of the proposals were accepted.　并不是所有的建议都被采纳了。

3. Some commonly used bases include geographic segmentation, demographic segmentation, psychographic segmentation and behavioral segmentation.　常用的细分基础包括：地理细分、人口细分、心理细分、行为细分等。
   地理细分：总体市场由不同地域的消费需求构成。不同地域的消费者基于当地的自然条件、经济发展水平、文化和生活方式，以及消费观念，在消费和购买行为上存在较大的差别。
   人口细分：总体市场以不同消费者和家庭需求为载体，因年龄、性别、职业、收入、宗教信仰及国籍、民族的差别，形成一个个有差别的消费群体。消费群的偏好、购买力和需求重点不同，同一消费群中的不同消费者，既有共性，又有特性，但其共性大于特性。
   心理细分：心理细分是比人口细分更加深入的市场细分方法，社会阶层、个性和消费观念，以及生活方式都可作为细分的标准。在大城市，青年消费者中"白领"和"蓝领"的购买动机有明显差别，独生子女和多子女、核心家庭和三代同堂家庭的子女，他们的个性差别比较明显。

行为细分：依据消费者购买行为的分类，可以从购买时机、利益要点、使用状况、更新频率及态度、忠诚度等具体标准出发，将总体市场逐一分解。

I Answer the following questions according to the text.

1. What is market segmentation?
2. What is the goal of segmenting markets?
3. What are the key elements of a market segment?
4. What are popular segmentation bases among marketers?
5. What are the criteria the segmented market must meet?
6. How can you understand the accessibility of the market segments?
7. What are the reasons for segmenting markets?
8. What is the purpose of the writer to mention the example of Rado and Omega watch?
9. How can segmentation help the marketers to gain larger market share?

II Decide whether the following statements are true or false.

1. Segmentation is of first importance in marketing.
2. The differences between customers in segments are as small as possible.
3. Not all customers of a product or a service share the same interests.
4. The key elements of a market segment include geographic segmentation, demographic segmentation, psychographic segmentation, and behavioral segmentation.
5. Only segmentation bases can be used to define market segments.
6. Demographic segmentation works well under any circumstance.
7. Since psychographic segmentation is more popular, it is bound to improve sales.
8. The research on the population density or regional climate is concerned with demographic segmentation.
9. Market segmentation enables marketers to earn more money.
10. Smaller businesses are troubled with lack of scale economies in production and marketing,

pressures from distributors and limited space on the shelves.

III Fill in each blank with the proper form of the word in the bracket.

1. The market is segmented according to _____ (geography) criteria—nations, states, regions, counties, cities, neighborhoods, or zip codes.
2. Market segmenting is dividing the market into groups of individual markets with similar _____ (want) or needs.
3. Improved segmentation can lead to _____ (improve) marketing effectiveness.
4. Once a market segment has been identified and targeted, the segment is then subject to _____ (position).
5. A niche is a more narrowly defined customer group _____ (seek) a distinct set of benefits.
6. Where a monopoly exists, the price of a product is likely to be _____ (high) than in a competitive market.
7. Every _____ (experience) marketer knows that different customers buy for different reasons.
8. Demographic segmentation consists of dividing the market into groups based on _____ (vary) such as age, gender family size, income, occupation, education, religion, race and nationality.
9. He touched upon the _____ (feasible) of the plan by pointing out the main drawback.
10. Their goal was to make their product more _____ (access).

IV Fill in each blank with a proper preposition.

1. In behavioral segmentation, consumers are divided into groups according to their knowledge of, attitude _____, use _____ or response to a product.
2. Marketing programs tailored _____ the needs of local customer groups.
3. It provides insight _____ how, why, where, and when a customer gets value out of a product.
4. Firms vary widely in their abilities _____ serve different types of customers.
5. The economic loss arose _____ his carelessness in segmenting the markets.
6. With regard _____ the marketing strategy, I'd like to hear Mr Smith.
7. New market segmentation strategies are often required for a company to create a strategic advantage _____ its competition.
8. A new market segment must respond differently _____ variations in the product.
9. The process of segmentation starts _____ research and market analysis.

Unit 10 Market Segmentation

10. A key factor _____ success in today's market place is finding subtle differences to give a business the marketing edge.

V Fill in the blanks with the words and phrases given below. Change the form where necessary.

| homogenous | tailor | drawback | enhance | in a position to |
| brand identity | classify | justifiable | distinguishable | with regard to |

1. In the study, families are _____ according to their incomes.
2. The main _____ of the scheme is its expense.
3. All of our courses can be _____ to the needs of individuals.
4. The outward expression of a brand—including its name, trademark, communications, and visual appearance—is _____.
5. Market segmentation allows a small business to develop a product and a marketing mix that fit a relatively _____ part of the total market.
6. I side with you _____ the final decision.
7. The measures taken should considerably _____ the sales of the products.
8. It allows you to achieve results _____ from those achieved by professional publishers.
9. It is also important to determine who does not use the product in order to determine whether a target marketing program would be _____.
10. I'm not _____ say who my sources are.

VI Cloze.

First of all, is your product international or 1_____ in scope? Or is it more likely that you will sell it primarily in your own region or community? 2_____ our charter business, our primary market is actually national or international-tourists who come to this area from all over the world. Our 3_____ market is local-people who have a special event to celebrate, a company meeting or a company coming from out of town.

Let's say that your primary market is local or regional, and 4_____ you live in a community with 5_____ of 20,000 people. The first thing is to research the demographics of your community, and divide it 6_____ market segments. This information is 7_____ great importance and the 8_____ detail you can get, the better. Next, you need to segment the market as 9_____ as possible 10_____ psychographics as your guide: lifestyle, social class, opinion, activities and interests, attitudes and beliefs.

If you are a B2B company, you'll also need to consider the types of industries 11_____ to you, and their number of employees, annual sales volume, location, and company stability.

12_____, you might want to find out how they purchase: seasonally, locally, only in volume, who makes the decisions? It is important to note that businesses, 13_____ individuals, buy products or services for three reasons: to increase revenue, to maintain the status quo, or to 14_____ expenses. If you fill one or more of these corporate 15_____, you will find a target market.

By now you should have a picture emerging of who you think your ideal customer is or who you want it to be. 16_____ on the nature of your business, you might even be able to write a 17_____ of your customer. "My target customer is a middle-class woman in 18_____ 30s or 40s who is married and has children, and is environmentally conscious and physically fit." Based on the 19_____ you uncovered in your research, you may even know, 20_____, that there are approximately 9,000 of those potential customers in your area. It may well be that 3,000 of them are already loyal to a competitor, but that still leaves 6,000 who are not, or who have not yet purchased the product from anyone.

1. A. multinational   B. local   C. global   D. national
2. A. In the case of   B. In case of   C. In case   D. In no case
3. A. main   B. secondary   C. second   D. important
4. A. that   B. where   C. which   D. then
5. A. population   B. populations   C. the number of   D. a population
6. A. among   B. into   C. to   D. with
7. A. with   B. /   C. of   D. along
8. A. many   B. much   C. more   D. fewer
9. A. many   B. much   C. few   D. soon
10. A. to use   B. being used   C. to be used   D. using
11. A. important   B. available   C. worthy   D. ideal
12. A. In addition   B. Therefore   C. Hence   D. accordingly
13. A. dislike   B. likes   C. unlike   D. like
14. A. fall   B. deduce   C. increase   D. decrease
15. A. needs   B. reasons   C. expenses   D. forms
16. A. Depending   B. To depend   C. Based   D. To base
17. A. report   B. description   C. research   D. wish
18. A. hers   B. their   C. her   D. the
19. A. customer   B. woman   C. child   D. numbers
20. A. however   B. for example   C. such as   D. in addition

VII Translation.

1. Market segmentation and the identification of target markets, an important element of each

marketing strategy, are the basis for determining any particular marketing mix.
2. Such varied marketing activities in the diverse segments could confuse customers and would lead to cannibalization effects.
3. Organizations that serve different segments can guide their customers from stage to stage by always offering them a special solution for their particular needs.
4. If a product meets and exceeds a customer's expectations by adding superior value, the customer normally is willing to pay a higher price for that product.
5. Thus if the principles of market segmentations are not applied, the firms ignore the differing customer needs and another firm would likely enter the market with a product that serves a specific group, and the incumbent firms would lose the customers.

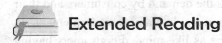

Extended Reading

Mass Marketing

Mass marketing is one of the success stories of the 20 century. The mass market companies provide the bulk of the goods and services we consume. Though mass marketing cannot fully satisfy the needs of every customer in a market, many companies still adopt this strategy. It is commonly used in the marketing of standardized goods and services—including sugar, gasoline, or dry cleaning services—when a lot of people have similar needs and they regard the products or service as largely the same regardless of the provider. Mass marketing offers some advantages to businesses, such as reduced production and marketing costs through economies of scale. Due to the efficiency of large production and a single marketing program, businesses may be able to provide consumers with more value for their money.

Mass marketing has some limitations. For example, markets consist of buyers, and buyers have many different characteristics which are important in determining their willingness to purchase products and services. Few companies are big enough to supply the needs of an entire market; most must breakdown the total demand into segments and choose those that the company is best equipped to handle.

Applying a market segmentation strategy is most effective when an overall market consists of many smaller segments whose members have certain characteristics or needs in common. Through segmentation, businesses can divide such a market into several homogeneous groups and develop a separate product and marketing program to more exactly fit the needs of one or more segments.

Maximizing sales, which eventually leads to increase in profit, is the key objective of any marketer. For the sake of sales maximization, marketers employ marketing, a process of commercially promoting, distributing and advertising a given product or service. Market segmentation process is one such technique that has been developed by marketing professionals. The five step process of market segmentation goes as follows.

The first step is to establish the market and targeted consumers. It involves tremendous paperwork and surveys. Economic and demographic factors are also analyzed in the process. In addition, this step might also include advertising about the product.

The second step is often termed as market mapping and involves structuring the entire marketing procedures based upon the needs of the given market. Logistic costs, retail and wholesale costs are some important parameters that are set up during this stage. Another very important factor involved in this step is the targeting of consumers who are also known as decision makers. The remaining three steps are derived on the basis of this step.

The third step is entirely dependent upon the consumers as the demand by consumers and their suggestions are largely viewed, surveyed, taken into consideration and in many cases implemented.

In the fourth step, the actual segment begins to take shape as like-minded consumers having same demands are placed together and are analyzed as a group. Launching of a parallel or a totally new product is viewed in this situation. This segregation is often based upon economic indexes, demographic and geographic situations.

The last step is catering to the needs of existing consumers and finding new markets. This step is purely the first step towards a new 5-step-cycle that begins with finding a new market.

In a word, market segmentation is by no means an easy task, as you need to consider several factors including current fashion, economic conditions, demographics and even simple logic used by consumers.

Words and Expressions

mass marketing 大众营销	retail n. 零售
mass market 大众市场	wholesale n. 批发
regardless of 不管，不顾	parameter n. 参数，决定因素
for the sake of 为了	derive v. 得到
bulk n. 大批，散装	take shape 成形，具体化
paperwork n. 文书工作	like-minded a. 具有相似意向的
procedure n. 步骤	economic index 经济指数
logistic n. 物流	cater to 适应，迎合

Unit 10 Market Segmentation

Comprehension

I Answer the following questions according to the passage.

1. What are merits and demerits of mass marketing?
2. Under what circumstance is mass marketing commonly used?
3. In terms of the cost advantages, what are the limitations of mass marketing?
4. When is market segmentation strategy most effective?
5. What is the five step process of market segmentation?
6. What is the relationship between the five steps?
7. What factors are to be considered in the first step?
8. What factors are involved in the second step?
9. What is the fourth step based on according to the passage?
10. Why is market segmentation considered as a hard job?

II Write "T" for true, and "F" for false.

1. The advantages of mass marketing outweigh its disadvantages.
2. Different characteristics of customers are the most important factors determining their willingness to purchase products and services.
3. Quite a few companies are big enough to supply the needs of an entire market.
4. Segmentation enables companies to develop a separate marketing program to more exactly fit the needs of a single segment.
5. The only objective of any marketer is to maximize sales, which eventually leads to increase in profit.
6. In the first step, marketers are supposed to analyze economic and demographic factors as well as advertisements.
7. The important factors involved in the second step include logistic costs, retail and wholesale costs, the targeting of consumers and so on.
8. Actually the segment begins from the fourth step.
9. Marketers will take into account the economic, demographic, geographic situations and even logic of consumers during segmenting markets.
10. The fourth step also functions as the beginning of next five step process.

Additional Terms

market coverage strategy 市场覆盖策略	consumer market 消费者市场
market targeting 目标市场选择	business market 商业市场
life cycle 生命周期	cohort effect 世代效应
family life cycle 家庭生命周期	income and expenditure pattern 收入和消费模式
occasion 购买时机	few financial burden 极少经济负担
user status 用户状况	fashion opinion leader 领导时尚者
non-user 非用户	recreation-orientation 娱乐导向
potential user 潜在用户	primary motivation 根本动机
ex-user 以前的用户	striver 奋斗者
first-time user 初次用户	maker 制造者
regular user 经常用户	macrosegmentation 宏观细分
light product user 少量使用者	microsegmentation 微观细分
medium user 中等使用者	inter-market segmentation 市场间细分
heavy product user 大量使用者	global market standardization 全球市场标准化
usage rate 使用率	multisegment targeting strategy 多元细分策略
usage rate segmentation 使用频率细分	cannibalization 品牌替换
loyalty status 忠诚度	setup time 启动时间
market survey 市场调研	homogenous preference 同质偏好
segment size 目标市场规模	diffused preference 分散偏好
segment growth 目标市场的增长潜力	clustered preference 集群偏好
company resource 企业实力	
product variability 产品差异性	
market variability 市场差异性	

Unit 11

Market Positioning

As individuals, we continually position ourselves, which allows us to create an image, and image is the outward representation of being who you want to be, doing what you want to do, and having what you want to have. Therefore, positioning ourselves can give rise to a sense of personal fulfillment. Nowadays we live in a world where the competition is becoming increasingly intense for almost every product or service. If we don't know who our intended customers are and what they want from us, it can be like shooting in the dark. Hence, after the company has selected its target market, the next stage is to decide how it wants to position itself within that chosen segment. In other words, it needs to find its position in the market in hope of getting any chance of success. More often than not, a product fails because of wrong positioning.

Positioning is a concept in marketing which was first introduced by Jack Trout and then popularized by Al Ries and Jack Trout in their bestseller book *Positioning—The Battle for Your Mind*.[1] There are many definitions for market positioning.

- Market positioning is about how you want consumers to perceive your products and services and what strategies you would adopt to reach this perceptual goal.
- Market positioning is the manipulation of a brand or family of brands to create a positive perception in the eyes of the public.
- Market positioning is all about finding a way to get customers to develop a positive view of a product. It is all about branding and marketing a product in such a way as it appeals to those people most likely to buy the product.
- Market positioning refers to the process by which marketers try to create an image or identity in the minds of their target market for its product, brand, or organization.

From the definitions mentioned above, we can see that positioning actually starts with a product or service. It is not what you do to a product or service, but what you do to the mind of the prospect. That is, you position your product or service in the mind of the prospect. Market positioning is the final, and perhaps the most important step of a marketing strategy. Once the market has been segmented and an appropriate segment has been targeted, the firm needs to position itself in the minds of the customer. If a product is well positioned, it will bring about strong sales, and it may become the go-to brand for people who need that particular product.[2] So correct positioning is extremely crucial for the success of the marketing strategy and eventually the product or service. Poor positioning, on the other hand, can lead to bad sales and a dubious reputation. Therefore, a business has to think hard about the effects of any change they make while positioning its product or service; it can trigger losses as well as gains.

Generally speaking, there are three types of positioning concepts.

- Functional positions: solve problems, provide benefits for customers, and get a favorable perception by potential investors and lenders.
- Symbolic positions: self image enhancement, ego identification, belongingness and social meaningfulness, and affective fulfillment.
- Experiential positions: provide sensory and cognitive stimulation.

Periodically, companies may reposition, trying to adjust their perception among the public. It involves changing the identity of a product, relative to the identity of competing products, in the collective minds of the target market. Repositioning a company involves more than a marketing challenge.[3] It involves making hard decisions about how a market is shifting and how a firm's competitors will react. For example, a company may redesign product packaging, start a new ad campaign, or engage in similar activities to capture a new share of the market. Often these decisions must be made without the benefit of sufficient information, simply because change becomes difficult or impossible to predict.

Anyway, a company can positively influence the perceptions through strategic actions. Developing a market positioning strategy is an important part of the research and development process. The marketing department may provide notes during product development which are designed to enhance the product's position, and they also determine the price, where the product should be sold, and how it should be advertised. Every aspect of the product's presentation will be carefully calculated to maximize its position.

There are seven market positioning strategies.

Monosegment positioning

As the name suggests, monosegment positioning involves developing a program tailored to the preferences of a single market segment. Successful implementation of this strategy would give the brand an obvious advantage within the target segment, but would not generate many sales from customers in other segments. This strategy is best used with mass marketing.

Multisegment positioning

It involves positioning a product so as to attract consumers from different segments. This is an attractive strategy since it provides higher economies of scale, requires smaller investments, and avoids reduction of managerial attention. It is particularly appropriate when individual segments are small, as is generally the case in the early stages of the product's life cycle.[4]

Standby positioning

It may not be in the best economic interest of a firm to switch from a multisegment positioning strategy to a monosegment strategy (assuming the use of several brands, each positioned to serve the needs of only one segment) even if it increases total market share. In such a case, the firm may decide to implement a monosegment positioning strategy only when forced to do so. In order to minimize response time, the firm prepares a standby plan specifying the products and their attributes as well as details of the marketing programs that would be used to position the new product.

Imitative positioning

This is essentially the same as a head-on strategy where a new brand targets a position similar to that of an existing successful brand. It may be an appropriate strategy if the imitative firm has a distinctive advantage beyond positioning, such as better access to channels of distribution, a more effective salesforce, or substantially more money to spend on promotion, including price deals.

Anticipatory positioning

A firm may position a new brand in anticipation of the evolution of a segment's needs. This is particularly appropriate when the new brand is not expected to have a fast acceptance, and market share will build as the needs of consumers become more and more aligned with the benefits being offered. At its best, this strategy enables a firm to establish a market position that may have a substantial long-term potential. At its worst, it may cause the firm to face a difficult economic situation for an extended period if the needs of a segment do not evolve as expected.

Adaptive positioning

Adaptive positioning consists of periodically repositioning a brand to follow the evolution of the segment's needs.

Defensive positioning

When a firm occupies a strong position in a market segment with a single brand, it is vulnerable to imitative positioning strategies. The firm may adopt competitive strategies by introducing an additional brand in a similar position for the same segment. This will reduce immediate profitability, but it may allow the firm to better protect itself against competitors in the long term. For example, Procter & Gamble has seven brands of laundry detergents, such as Tide and Bold, several of which occupy similar positions in consumers' minds.

Positioning is all about finding the right path to create a significant and unique place amidst a crowd of different competing brands, and the marketer can adopt different strategies according to the specific situation.

Vocabulary

representation n. 表现，陈述
popularize v. 流行，普及
dubious a. 可疑的
belongingness n. 归属感
sensory a. 感觉的，感官的
cognitive a. 认知的
periodically ad. 定期地
capture v. 抓住
managerial a. 管理上的

standby n. 备用的人或物
specify v. 详述，具体说明
imitative a. 模仿的，仿效的
salesforce n. 销售人员
evolution n. 发展，变化
vulnerable a. 脆弱的，敏感的；易受攻击的
admist prep. 在……中

Phrases and Expressions

personal fulfillment 个人价值的实现
in hope of 希望
more often than not 经常，常常
family of brand 品牌系列
bring about 产生，引起
ego identification 自我认同
in the interest of 为了……的利益
response time 反应时间，回应时间
head-on strategy 迎头定位策略
price deal 价格优惠
in anticipation of … 预期某事，为某事做准备
be aligned with … 与……一致

at one's best 在最好的情况下
at one's worst 在最糟糕的情况下
protect … against 保护……
a crowd of 很多……
monosegment positioning 单一细分市场定位
multisegment positioning 多重细分市场定位
standby positioning 备用定位
imitative positioning 模仿定位
anticipatory positioning 预见性定位
adaptive positioning 适应性定位
defensive positioning 防御性定位

1. Positioning is a concept in marketing which was first introduced by Jack Trout and then

Unit 11 Market Positioning

popularized by Al Ries and Jack Trout in their bestseller book *Positioning—The Battle for Your Mind*. 在市场营销中定位这一概念最初是由杰克·特劳特提出来的，后来他和阿尔·里斯合著的畅销书《定位：头脑争夺战》出版了，定位这一概念也因此得到了普及。

杰克·特劳特是定位之父，被摩根士丹利推崇为高于迈克尔·波特的营销战略家，也是美国特劳特咨询公司的总裁。他于 1969 年在《定位：同质化时代的竞争之道》中首次提出了商业中的"定位（positioning）"观念，1972 年在《定位时代》中开创了定位理论，1981 年出版学术专著《定位》，他的定位理论被美国营销协会评为"有史以来对美国营销影响最大的观念"。

2. If a product is well positioned, it will bring about strong sales, and it may become the go-to brand for people who need that particular product. 如果产品定位合理的话，就会提高销售量，那些需要这种产品的顾客就会经常购买。

在本句中，and 连接的是两个并列的分句，第一个分句中 if 引导条件状语从句；第二个分句中使用了 who 引导的定语从句，修饰限定先行词 people。

3. Repositioning a company involves more than a marketing challenge. 对公司进行再定位不仅是营销方面的一个挑战。

再定位（repositioning）是由杰克·特劳特和阿尔·里斯提出来的。所谓再定位，就是对品牌重新定位，旨在摆脱困境、使品牌获得新的增长与活力。它不是对原有定位的一概否定，而是企业经过市场的磨炼之后，对原有品牌战略的一次扬弃。

4. It is particularly appropriate when individual segments are small, as is generally the case in the early stages of the product's life cycle. 单个的细分市场规模不大，在这种情况下采用多重细分市场定位策略是非常得当的，在产品周期的早期阶段也是这样的。

在本句中 as 引导非限制性定语从句，代表整个主句的意思，这在定语从句中是很常见的，例如：

He tended to arrive at the conclusion without consideration of all possible results, as was indicated in the failure of his previous plan. 他作出决定的时候总是不考虑后果，他的上一个计划也是这么失败的。

I Answer the following questions according to the text.

1. Speaking of positioning, what do individuals and businesses have in common?
2. How can you understand "It is not what you do to a product or service, but what you do to the mind of the prospect."?

3. In what way does the market positioning influence businesses?
4. What are the three types of positioning concepts?
5. How can you understand repositioning?
6. What are the seven market positioning strategies?
7. What are the advantages and disadvantages of monosegment positioning?
8. When will firms turn to standby positioning according to the passage?
9. What will happen if firms adopt anticipatory positioning?
10. According to the passage, what is the purpose of Procter & Gamble to develop seven brands of laundry detergents?

II Decide whether the following statements are true or false.

1. Individuals always position themselves, and it's true of businesses.
2. The firm selects its target market, closely following positioning itself in the targeted segment.
3. The sole reason for the failure of a product in the market lies in the wrong positioning.
4. Positioning is what you do to the mind of the potential customers rather than what you do to a product or service.
5. From the definitions about positioning, we can see that it is the most important step of a marketing strategy.
6. Market positioning is bound to bring about sales for the firms.
7. Functional positions can solve problems, provide sensory and cognitive stimulation as well as benefits for customers, and get a favorable perception by potential customers.
8. With the help of sufficient information, firms may reposition to change their perception among the public.
9. Difficult as it is to predict the changes, firms are able to influence the perceptions of customers by means of positioning strategies.
10. The implementation of monosegment positioning strategy will trigger sales from customers from different segments.

III Fill in each blank with the proper form of the word in the bracket.

1. Companies need to see how consumers perceive their product, and how differences in presentation can impact _____ (perceive).
2. Positioning can be_____ (manipulation), but doing so isn't a simple task.
3. Repositioning involves attempting to change the identity of _____ (compete) products, relative to the identity of your own product, in the collective minds of the target market.

Unit 11 Market Positioning

4. Companies which _____ (anticipation) and shape market trends have the best opportunity for long-term prosperity.
5. This will ultimately give you a strong advantage over the competition and gives customers a unique, _____ (desire) product.
6. Today's marketplace is crowded, with companies constantly _____ (introduce) new products to the public.
7. The success of his firm _____ (popular) that marketing strategy.
8. Economic crises recur _____ (periodical).
9. She was promoted to some kind of _____ (manager) job.
10. They hope to _____ (fulfillment) their objectives by 2020.

IV Fill in each blank with a proper preposition.

1. Companies also engage _____ repositioning, in which they attempt to alter the perception of other brands.
2. Also positioning is defined as the way _____ which the marketers create impression in the customers' mind.
3. This is especially true _____ small and medium-sized firms, many of which often lack strong brands for individual product lines.
4. A well-positioned business is closely aligned _____ the needs of its target segments, both current and emerging.
5. Beyond having a strong customer franchise in the marketplace, gaining access _____ a strong customer relationship is a favored tactic.
6. He traveled in Europe _____ the interest of a business firm.
7. _____ its best, his plan can ease the current situation.
8. Greatest success goes to a business which have a highly differentiated position in the market, and which establishes barriers _____ entry for competitors.
9. Product positioning involves developing a product and marketing plan that will appeal _____ the selected market segment.

V Fill in the blanks with the words and phrases given below. Change the form where necessary.

| more often than not | vulnerable | dubious | in hope of | generate |
| protect … against | specify | belongingness | a crowd of | minimize |

1. The first method is obviously about shaping the nature of market demand to _____ a desired market positioning.

2. Those figures alone are a _____ basis for such a conclusion.
3. This procedure has improved, but it is still _____ to criticism.
4. What steps did the firm do to maximize profits and _____ loss?
5. They are conducting research _____ getting a better understanding of the wants of customers.
6. He saw _____ people are getting together talking about the advertisements.
7. _____, customers tend to frequent their favorite stores.
8. You'd better _____ the characteristics and perceptions of the target customers.
9. The warm jacket will _____ you _____ the cold.
10. _____ is the human emotional need to be an accepted member of a group.

VI Cloze.

Perceptual mapping is one of the few marketing research techniques that 1_____ direct input into the strategic marketing planning process. It allows senior marketing planners 2_____ a broad view of the strengths and 3_____ of their product or service offerings relative to 4_____ of their competitors. The marketing planners are 5_____ to survey the customer and the competitor 6_____ in the same realm. It is a graphics technique that attempts to visually display the 7_____ of customers or potential customers. Typically the position of a product, product line, brand, or company is displayed 8_____ to their competition.

Perceptual maps can have any number of dimensions 9_____ the most common is 10_____ dimensions. 11_____ consumers' perceptions of related products is only half the story. Many perceptual maps also display consumers' ideal points which reflect ideal combinations of the two dimensions as seen by a consumer. Areas 12_____ there is a cluster of ideal points indicate a market segment. Areas 13_____ ideal points are sometimes referred to as demand voids. A company considering 14_____ a new product will look for areas with a 15_____ density of ideal points.

1. A. provide	B. provided	C. have provided	D. provides
2. A. taking	B. to be taking	C. to take	D. taken
3. A. weaknesses	B. plans	C. policies	D. strategies
4. A. that	B. those	C. offerings	D. strengths
5. A. engaged	B. devoted	C. enabled	D. determined
6. A. simultaneously	B. spontaneously	C. synthetically	D. substantially
7. A. decisions	B. perceptions	C. attitudes	D. ideals
8. A. related	B. inclined	C. referred	D. relative
9. A. and	B. so	C. but	D. however
10. A. two	B. three	C. many	D. four

11. A. To display	B. Display	C. Having displayed	D. Displaying
12. A. that	B. where	C. which	D. when
13. A. with	B. have	C. without	D. \
14. A. introducing	B. to introduce	C. to introducing	D. having been introduced
15. A. low	B. much	C. little	D. high

VII Translation.

1. The market selected by a company as the target for their marketing efforts is critical since all subsequent marketing decisions will be directed toward satisfying the needs of these customers.
2. In today's globalizing and continuously developing economies, the competition among enterprises grows quickly, the market share gets narrower; and in order to gain new markets, companies are trying to create superiority over their rivals by positioning new products aimed at consumer behaviors and perceptions.
3. Because product or market positioning is dependent on the attitudes of the target market, marketing management, either tries to change product specifications according to their attitudes, or tries to change the attitudes of the market.
4. A positioning strategy consists of three steps: to reveal possible competitive advantages to create a positioning, to select the right competitive advantages and to choose a comprehensive positioning strategy.
5. The goal of product positioning is to keep your product on top of your customers' mind when they're considering a purchase.

Extended Reading

Product Positioning: Stand Out From the Crowd

Positioning shows the place where existing or to be issued products are put in the marketplace by the customers. Whether in the consumer market or in the industrial market, after selection of a specific section, enterprises should also specify which position they want to be. Product positioning, a part of market positioning, has long been recognized as a vital strategic marketing decision tool in the tangible product marketplace, which helps to influence the market's perception of your products. It is what comes to mind when your target market thinks about your products compared with those of your competitor's. As a marketing strategy, it is a crucial ingredient in the buying process and should never be left to chance. Correct and meaningful product positioning enables you to cut through the relentless advertising and helps gain market dominance and increase sales and profits for your company. On the other hand, the absence of appropriate product positioning is unlikely to end well. With or without your effective input, customers will position your product most probably based on information from your competitors, which will not flatter you.

You can position a product using a positioning statement, a written description of the objectives of a positioning strategy. It states how the firm defines its business or how a brand distinguishes itself, how the customers will benefit from its features, and how these benefits or aspects will be communicated to the intended audience. The most common mistakes in crafting a positioning statement include: not precisely defining the target customer; listing multiple differentiators/benefits (the benefit promise should be singular); developing benefits that are not unique or sustainable; not including the reason customers should believe the benefit promise.

The following is the product positioning to-do list: conduct a market segmentation; define your target market; identify the product attributes; data collection from the target market on the identified product attributes; determine the product's share of heart and mind (of the total potential mindshare); place your product in the right space; determine what you need to do to reach that position in the minds of your market.

Marketers manage product positioning by focusing their marketing activities on a positioning strategy. Pricing, promotion, channels of distribution, and advertising all are geared to maximize the chosen positioning strategy. However, product positioning strategies are numerous, and the selection of one over another is crucial to how your company will market its products or services. With appropriate strategies, firms will be in a better position to stand out from crowd.

First-mover strategy

Position your product by being first to market. This first-mover strategy enables you to quickly gain market share. Typically, customers view the first product on the market as the leader. Once you have positioned yourself as the market leader, you enjoy first-mover advantage. In other words, you can gain control of resources that followers may not be able to match. Therefore, you must deliver a quality product that supports your market-leading status. Otherwise, you risk tarnishing your brand image, which can have a long-term negative impact on sales of your products.

Multi-branding strategy

A multi-branding strategy can help you create the market positioning of similar products. For a multi-branding strategy, you create multiple products you market under different brand names. In effect, you are creating your own competition with your own products and leaving little room for competitors to enter the market with ease. You can differentiate the products by price, features or quality differences. This positioning strategy can allow you to dominate the market by offering options for customers at all price points and feature requirements, while obtaining economies of scale for your business.

Demographics strategy

Position your products by targeting your products to different demographic groups. You can differentiate based on age, income, education, gender and other demographic factors. Remember to support your positioning strategy by means of advertising and packaging. Consider using a demographic positioning strategy when you are introducing your product after market leadership has been established, or if a niche market could command a premium price.

Words and Expressions

issue *v.* 发布	first-mover advantage 先占优势
tangible *a.* 有形的	quality product 高品质产品
ingredient *n.* 组成部分	tarnish *v.* 使失去光泽；玷污
be left to chance 疏忽	brand image 品牌形象
cut through 处理，应付	multi-branding strategy 多品牌策略
relentless *a.* 无情的	with ease 容易地，轻而易举地
flatter *v.* 奉承，赞美	demographics strategy 人口策略
singular *a.* 单独的，单一的	market leadership 市场领导地位
benefit promise 利益承诺	niche market 小众市场
economy market 大众产品市场	premium price 溢价
first-mover strategy 先占策略	

Comprehension

I   Answer the following questions according to the passage.

1. What is the importance of product positioning?
2. How can you understand "As a marketing strategy, it is a crucial ingredient in the buying process and should never be left to chance"?
3. How will product positioning influence businesses?
4. What is a positioning statement?
5. What mistakes will marketers make in crafting a positioning statement?
6. How can firms carry out product positioning?
7. What is called first-mover strategy?
8. What is called multi-branding strategy?
9. What is called demographics strategy?
10. What does the writer mainly talk about in this passage?

II. Write "T" for true, and "F" for false.

1. It's totally up to the customers to position products and services.
2. Market positioning, a part of product positioning, has long been proved to play a vital role in the marketplace.
3. Product positioning should never be given any chance.
4. Customers can position products with the help of firm's information or information offered by the competitors.
5. The benefits for the customers should be either unique or sustainable.
6. Marketers are to determine how important their products are viewed in the eyes of potential customers.
7. It's an easy task to choose an appropriate market positioning strategy since there are numerous strategies.
8. With the first-mover advantage, you are bound to dominate the segmented market.
9. Multiple products under different brand names will undoubtedly do great harm to the sales of existing products.
10. With demographics strategy, you can differentiate your products through demographic factors.

Additional Terms

attribute 产品属性	imitative strategy 模仿战略
consumer benefit 消费者利益	market positioning analysis 市场定位分析
consumer perception 消费者感知	new-product development 新产品开发
current customer 现有顾客	perceptual mapping 定位认知图,知觉图
customer preference 顾客偏好	positioning base 定位基础
customer retention 顾客维系	product user 产品使用人
decider 决策者	repositioning 再定位
evolution of market 市场演变	targeting strategy 目标市场选择战略
existing market 现有市场	
follower 追随者	
high-end product 高端产品	

Unit 12

Market Expansion

Businesses around the globe crave for growth and stability, but this cannot be achieved without a very important factor: the market. It is the sole desire of firms to always maximize profits while satisfying human wants through the products and services they provide. To maximize profit the firm would not only study market trends but must expand its market frontiers. Increasingly, more and more companies have come to see expansion into foreign markets as a key strategy in their quest for growth, profits and shareholder value creation.[1] The importance of global expansion as a growth opportunity has been stated most clearly by Dr. Lucius Riccio, professor at Columbia Business School: "It is a time of global transformation and change made possible by logistics innovation. A time when the smallest companies can compete with the largest ones—sometimes with the advantage of being more nimble and quicker to seize opportunities."

In most countries of the world, international trade represents an important share of gross domestic product. In considering alternatives to grow your company, it will be worth investigating this accelerating trend which is the outcome of increasing industrialization, transportation and communication tools. You can follow the footsteps of large corporations that are already looking more beyond their country borders for growth. In many cases such as General Electric, Coca-Cola and Proctor & Gamble, offshore earnings are beginning to outstrip domestic profits.[2]

Market expansion is the process of offering a product or service to a wider section of an existing market or into a new demographic, psychographic or geographic market; it's a growth strategy in which an organization targets existing products to new markets, market development by targeting new geographic markets, new demographic or psychographic segments, or totally new users.

While trying to expand market and sales volumes, companies are supposed to have confidence in the quality of their products and services. Only with the confidence can it then think of expanding its frontiers penetrating into more markets internationally which would give rise to more turnovers.[3] In addition, numerous customers may give it more confidence not only to patronize the firm but also to invest therein whenever the need arises.

As we move into the new millennium, advances in communication, transportation, and other technologies have made the world a much smaller place. Today, almost every firm, large or small, faces international marketing issues. Business owners aspire to grow their business. Expansion is among any business owner's top priorities.[4] Deciding whether to invest in business expansion is a common and important strategic business decision any companies will face sooner or later. Rapid growth often brings its own unintended consequences. The commitment of pushing revenues to new levels can strain a company's resources to the breaking point. Management also faces the challenge of recruiting employees who can handle expanded responsibilities, without sacrificing the cost and quality controls. Expanding business means paying for more space, people and inventory in many instances, but it also means potential for increased revenue and profits. Nothing is perfect and market expansion is no exception.[5] In other words, it has both disadvantages and advantages. The disadvantages are listed as follows.

Increased costs

Business expansion is bound to trigger more costs. There will be increased operating expenses including the establishment of facilities abroad, the hiring of additional staff, traveling of personnel, specialized transport networks, information and communication technology. In addition, training/retraining and hiring become increasingly crucial as companies expand their business, because many employees' skills do not grow with the organization. Expanding business internationally means that the companies may need to conform to new regulations and standards. This may call for changes such as in the production process, inputs and packaging, as well as advertisements, thus bringing about additional costs.[6] Besides, international trade may cause delays in payments, adversely affecting the firm's cash flow.

Compromised quality

Product quality is increasingly becoming an important competitive issue. In a recent study of the business units of major North American companies, managers ranked "producing to high quality standards" as their chief current concern. However, rapid growth may give rise to declining quality. One example is Toyota, whose executives aimed to own 15% of the global auto market in 2012, according to *The New York Times*. However, two major recalls changed Toyota's plan. The company had no alternative but to halt production of eight models accounting for half domestic profits. In other words, Toyota compromised its reputation for quality, which had been central to its corporate identity.

Financial challenges

Another drawback of business expansion is that when a company invests money and other resources to expand, it has less capital available for other business transactions. This makes it especially important that you carefully weigh the market potential of expansion before making the investment. Consider the potential return on investment from each product or new market you could expand into before investing your capital into a path of expansion. Without careful considerations, your investment will turn sour.[7]

Spread too thin

Another risk of business expansion is that you could spread your company's resources and expertise too thin.[8] Often, company leaders think they have to expand if things are going well. However, getting involved in too many markets or products can cause the company to spread its abilities out to the point that it does not perform well in any area. Business expansion only makes sense if your company has adequate people and resources to cover the new area with expertise.

While there are obvious disadvantages to expansion, the advantages and benefits received from expanding a business are easy to recognize. As is known to all, Amway expanded into Australia in 1971. In the 1980s, it expanded into 10 more countries, and quickened its pace since then. By 1994, Amway was firmly established in 60 countries. Today Amway sells its products in 80 countries and international profits account for more than 70% of the company's overall revenues. The advantages are listed as follows.

New personnel

One clear advantage to expanding a business is the opportunity to staff the company with new, qualified employees. Since people are often recognized as the most important asset of a company, acquiring new and talented personnel is a clear-cut advantage to business expansion. These people can help streamline processes, bring fresh ideas to the organization and bring a sense of camaraderie to the organization.

New customers

A primary merit of business expansion is the ability to attract and retain new customers. When you move into new markets, you can bring in previously untapped customer markets. Reaching out to these new customers with expansion is one thing, but maintaining long-term relationship with them is of primary importance. Growing a loyal customer base is the best way to achieve stable and growing profits over time. Business expansion often has the advantage of exposing the business to a wider audience. This increased pool of potential customers can dramatically improve sales, resulting in increased profitability. Customers, like employees, are important in operating a successful company. In other words, expanding your business widens your customer base. Expansion, when done properly, can place the company at the forefront of many customers' minds.[9]

New market opportunities

International business presents companies with new market opportunities. These new markets provide more opportunities for expansion, growth, and income. That is to say, with more markets, the companies are enabled to enjoy more resources and opportunities. A bigger market means more customers, increased revenue, a larger profit margin, and allows the business to realize economies of scale.

Economies of scale

When you expand your business, you often spread the risks of reducing the potential of one product or one poor decision damaging your business. Operating in multiple markets or in many product areas also allows companies to spread the costs of doing business across more markets or customers. This makes the costs of doing business less on a per-customer basis, which improves the potential to profit by adding new customers.

Favorable financing opportunities

Successful business expansion can put the firm in a positive place when it comes to acquiring necessary financing.[10] This financing can be a lifeline to the business during the expansion process and a fallback after the expansion has occurred. A company with increased market share and a solid financial position can typically acquire financing with little or no problem.

It goes without saying that market expansion can pose a series of problems for companies that are not ready for the challenges of growth. While there are some very obvious benefits to business growth, there are some disadvantages as well. It is important that you consider both, as they're closely related to your particular situation, before making any decisions. It is essential that the company, while expanding, view successful expansion on a profitability level, not just from a sales growth level. Since the point of expanding the business is to make it more profitable, business owners should periodically review the return on investment from an expansion. Additionally, there should be a clear reason for the expansion—entering into new, potentially profitable market segments, for example.

As is ever mentioned by Niccolò Machiavelli, the famous medieval author of *The Prince*, there is nothing more difficult to plan, more doubtful of success, nor more dangerous to manage than unwarranted expansion.[11] As we live in a society where bigness is viewed as a symbol of success, be careful that you do not identify success with the speed at which you can expand your business. It's universally acknowledged that overexpansion is a root cause of business failure. Many companies reaped dramatic increases in sales as well as great losses. Growth without profit can only lead to cash shortages and piles of unpaid bills. It's not a pleasant situation at all. Therefore, attention should be paid to slow and steady growth.

Unit 12　Market Expansion

Vocabulary

stability　*n.* 稳定	surpass　*v.* 超过，超出
sole　*a.* 唯一的，单独的	recall　*n.* 召回
quest　*n.* 寻求	compromise　*v.* 妥协
nimble　*a.* 敏捷的，敏锐的，机警的	drawback　*n.* 缺点，不足
accelerating　*a.* 加速的	expertise　*n.* 专门知识
offshore　*a.* 离岸的	thin　*a.* 稀少的
outstrip　*v.* 超过，越过	staff　*v.* 配备人员
demographic　*a.* 人口统计的	clear-cut　*a.* 清晰明了的
psychographic　*a.* 消费心理的	streamline　*v.* 使（企业、组织等）简化并更有效率
geographic　*a.* 地理的	camaraderie　*n.* 友情
penetrate　*v.* 渗透，进入	untapped　*a.* 未开发的，未利用的
patronize　*v.* 赞助	forefront　*n.* 最前线
therein　*ad.* 在那里	lifeline　*n.* 生命线
aspire　*v.* 渴望	fallback　*n.* 可依靠的东西
recruit　*v.* 招募	unwarranted　*a.* 无保证的，不必要的
inventory　*n.* 存货	reap　*v.* 收获
adversely　*ad.* 不利地	

Phrases and Expressions

crave for　渴望	account for　占……
conform to　符合	profit margin　利润率
cash flow　现金流量，现金流通	economies of scale　规模经济
have no alternative but to do sth.　除了做某事之外别无选择	identify … with …　将……与……等同起来
turn sour　变得糟糕	root cause　根本原因
corporate identity　企业形象	cash shortage　现金短缺

1. Increasingly, more and more companies have come to see expansion into foreign markets as a key strategy in their quest for growth, profits and shareholder value creation. 越来越多的公司开始拓展市场，将其视为追求发展、增长利润，以及创造股东价值的重要战略。
本句中"see ... as ..."的意思是"把……当作"，"expansion into foreign markets"的意思是"拓展市场"。例如：
Using the Internet is seen as one of the newest and easiest ways to grow your business. 利用互联网被看作最新的、最便捷的发展业务的方式。

2. In many cases such as General Electric, Coca-Cola and Proctor & Gamble, offshore earnings are beginning to outstrip domestic profits. 美国的通用电气、可口可乐、宝洁等公司，其海外收入额已经超过了国内的利润额。
本句中首先要了解几个专有名词，其次要注意"outstrip"的意思是"超出，超过"。例如：
The demand is outstripping current production. 现在需求逐渐超过了生产能力。
Demand for organic food was outstripping supply. 人们对有机食物的需求超过了供应量。

3. Only with the confidence can it then think of expanding its frontiers penetrating into more markets internationally which would give rise to more turnovers. 只有满怀信心，公司才会想到要拓展市场，进入更多的国际市场，获得更多的收益。
很显然，本句使用了倒装结构。"only+介词短语/副词短语"位于句首时，句子要使用倒装结构，目的在于强调后面的内容。例如：
Only in this way can we succeed in expanding our businesses into new markets. 只有通过这种方式，我们才能成功地开拓新的市场。
此外，短语 give rise to 的意思是"造成，产生，引起"，其中 to 属于介词。例如：
The new regulations are bound to give rise to many complaints. 这些新制定的规章制度必然会怨声载道。

4. Expansion is among any business owner's top priorities. 拓展市场对于任何一位企业家来说都是头等大事。
本句中 priority 的意思是"优先事项，最重要的事，当务之急"，例如：
The government's priority is to build more power plants. 政府的首要任务是建造更多的发电站。
The fight against inflation took priority over measures to combat the deepening recession. 抵制通货膨胀比抑制日益加剧的经济衰退更为重要。
The development of the national economy is a top priority. 发展国民经济是头等大事。

Unit 12　Market Expansion

5. Nothing is perfect and market expansion is no exception.　世上没有十全十美的事情，市场拓展也不例外。

本句中 exception 的意思是"例外"，例如：

This is considered an exception to the rule.　我们把这看作该规则的例外。

The law makes no exceptions.　法律不允许搞特殊。

Yesterday was a day off for everybody, with the exception of Lawrence.　昨天所有人都放一天假，劳伦斯除外。

6. This may call for changes such as in the production process, inputs and packaging, as well as advertisements, thus bringing about additional costs.　这就要作出一些调整，比如，生产过程、资金投入、产品包装、广告宣传等，这样一来就会增加成本。

在本句中，短语 call for 的意思是"需要，要求"，例如：

This project calls for great care and courage.　这个项目需要细心和胆量。

Your plan calls for a lot of money.　你的计划需要大笔资金。

More work does not necessarily call for more men.　更多的工作不一定需要更多的人手。

此外，句子末尾处的"thus bringing about additional costs"用 -ing 形式表示结果，例如：

Another way to expand your business via people power is to hire sales representatives and consultants to add your products to their inventory, thus increasing your sales and profits.　借助于人力来拓展业务的另一种途径就是雇用销售代表和顾问，提高产量，增加库存，从而提高产品销售量和利润额。

7. Without careful considerations, your investment will turn sour.　不经过深思熟虑，你的投资就会出问题。

在本句中，短语 turn sour 的意思是"变得糟糕，出现问题"，turn 是系动词，后面跟形容词，例如：

His original enthusiasm has turned sour.　他最初高涨的热情已经消退了。

Luckily I dropped out before the deal turned sour.　幸运的是，在交易变糟糕之前我已经退出了。

8. Another risk of business expansion is that you could spread your company's resources and expertise too thin.　拓展业务所面临的另外一种风险就是这会消耗公司的大量资源和技术。

在本句中，spread too thin 是常见的美国习惯用语，意思是"过分地扩散"，如果该习惯用语用在人的身上，那就意味着一个人要做的事太多，给自己增加了很多压力，到无法应付的地步。例如：

I'm afraid Karen is spread too thin this year. She's taking three part-time jobs, and works 20 hours a week in the bookstore. She looks tired all the time and keeps falling asleep while sitting in the office.　我担心凯伦今年给自己的压力太大，她要做 3 份兼职，每个星期要在书店工作 20 个小时，她看起来总是很疲惫的样子，在办公室的时候经常打瞌睡。

此外，还有一个与 thin 相关的习惯用语 wear thin，意思是"某一样东西在一段时间里，它的功能和价值在逐步降低"，例如：

Your patience with another person may wear thin if he keeps doing something you don't like. 要是一个人老是做你不喜欢的事，那你对他就会越来越没有耐心。

Parliament has not yet begun to combat the deepening economic crisis, and public patience is wearing thin. 议会还没有着手应对日益严重的经济危机，公众日渐失去了耐心。

9. Expansion, when done properly, can place the company at the forefront of many customers' minds. 市场拓展如果操作无误的话，公司就会成为顾客所关注的焦点了。

在本句中，when done properly 属于插入成分，可以看作省略了其中的"it is"，由于与主句的主语一致，在这种情况下就可以省略从句的主语。例如：

While expanding business, the company is supposed to draw up a solid plan without which it's easy to get lost along the way. 在拓展业务的同时，公司应该制订可行的计划，否则的话，就很容易迷失方向。

10. Successful business expansion can put the firm in a positive place when it comes to acquiring necessary financing. 谈到获得必要的资金，如果成功地拓展业务，公司就会处于有利的地位。

本句中短语 when it comes to 的意思是"谈到，提到"，例如：

When it comes to going international, the real danger for any expanding business is that it does so too quickly or in an uncontrolled way. 谈到打入国际市场，任何一家公司所面临的真正的风险就是业务拓展速度过快，或者是不加以节制。

11. As is ever mentioned by Niccolò Machiavelli, the famous medieval author of *The Prince*, there is nothing more difficult to plan, more doubtful of success, nor more dangerous to manage than unwarranted expansion. 正如《王子》的作者，著名的中世纪作家 Niccolò Machiavelli 所说的那样，毫无道理的市场拓展是最难计划的，其成功是最令人难以置信的，也是管理起来最危险的。

本句中使用了 as 引导的非限制性定语从句，代表整个主句的意思，例如：

As is known to all, Mr Smith is very popular among his employees. 众所周知，史密斯先生非常受员工的爱戴。

As had been expected, the promotion plan bore fruit. 正如我们所预料的那样，促销计划成功了。

本句还使用了比较级的形式来表示最高级的概念，这种表达方法在英语中是非常常见的，目的在于增强表达效果，加强语气。例如：

Nothing is more important than a thorough market research. 展开详细的市场调查是最重要的事情。

It can't be less boring. 这太无聊了。

Unit 12 Market Expansion

I Answer the following questions according to the text.

1. What is the author's purpose to quote Dr. Lucius Riccio?
2. What is market expansion according to the passage?
3. What are the disadvantages of market expansion?
4. What is the author's purpose to mention the example of Toyota?
5. How can you understand that going international will spread your company's resources too thin?
6. What are the merits of business expansion?
7. Why are people considered as the most important asset of a company?
8. What role do the new customers play in the process of business expansion?
9. How are economies of scale achieved?
10. What is Niccolò Machiavelli's view of business expansion?

II Decide whether the following statements are true or false.

1. Market exerts powerful effect on businesses' goal of growth and stability.
2. The only desire of the firm is to maximize profits without consideration of human wants.
3. General Electric, Coca-Cola and Proctor & Gamble are mentioned as successful examples of business expansion.
4. Self-confidence really counts in business expansion.
5. Every firm in the world is supposed to go international.
6. Business expansion is of the foremost importance for firms.
7. Business expansion is bound to cause delays in payments.
8. In 1980, Amway expanded into 10 more countries, and quickened its pace since then.
9. Most of Amway's overall revenues come from its business expansion.
10. It is more important to maintain long-term relationship with new customers than reach out to them.

III Fill in each blank with the proper form of the word in the bracket.

1. Companies selling in global industries have no alternative but _____ (international)

their operations.
2. Expanding globally allows a business to increase its _____ (profit) in ways not available to purely domestic businesses.
3. Some advertisements lead to children's excessive _____ (expose) to violence.
4. Are there any rules to follow when facing a business _____ (expand)?
5. The manager's first task is to bring some _____ (stable) to the team.
6. We want to get _____ (maximize) benefit from the contract.
7. While _____ (try) to go international, firms tend to decide the mode of entry first.
8. This will _____ (able) users to conduct live video conversations.
9. Going global requires _____ (specialize) training and skills.
10. The drug has so far had no _____ (adversely) effects on patients.

IV Fill in each blank with a proper preposition.

1. When it comes _____ global marketing program, companies must decide how much, if not all, to adapt their marketing mix to local conditions.
2. These national differences in customer tastes and preferences call _____ a change in approach to marketing.
3. Make sure that you do not identify success _____ how fast you can expand your business.
4. They crave _____ success of their marketing strategies.
5. The sale exposed the company _____ widespread criticism.
6. This strategy is offered as an alternative _____ intense competition in the domestic market.
7. It was a well-organized centre staffed _____ qualified and professional people.
8. By 1900, Coca-Cola had already penetrated _____ numerous foreign markets, including Cuba, Puerto Rico, and France.
9. The meeting was viewed _____ a great success.
10. There are some workers who are employed _____ a seasonal or temporary basis.

V Fill in the blanks with the words and phrases given below. Change the form where necessary.

| quest | wants | arise | weigh | profitability |
| outstrip | penetrate | aspire | trigger | turn sour |

1. Luckily we soon _____ his disguise and reduced company's loss to the minimum.
2. More recently, the firm's increased focus on emerging markets like India, and Indonesia

has _____ its brand's global success.
3. With the advent of faster communication, transportation and financial flows, many company owners _____ to become successful in international marketing.
4. The products failed to satisfy the needs and _____ of current consumers.
5. In the past two decades, new problems _____ from the changes of global marketing environment.
6. Before going abroad, the companies have to take into considerations many factors besides _____, such as the market size, competitive advantage and risk level.
7. Without careful consideration of the merits and demerits of global marketing, the firm's plan to survive in the international markets will _____.
8. These costs must be _____ against the environmental benefits.
9. Demand for organic food is _____ supply.
10. In the _____ for great increase in sales, companies have to take into account many factors.

VI Cloze.

What could be more American than Coca-Cola? The brand is as 1_____ as baseball and apple pie. In 1893 Coke got its start in an Atlanta pharmacy, 2_____ it sold for five cents a glass. From there, the company's first president, Asa Candler, set out to convince America that Coca-Cola was "the pause that refreshes". The beverage quickly became an all-American phenomenon; by 1895, the company 3_____ plants in Chicago, Dallas, and Los Angeles. By 1900, it had already penetrated beyond America's borders 4_____ numerous countries, including Cuba, Puerto Rico, and France. As the time went by, strong marketing abroad fueled Coke's popularity throughout the world. Its worldwide success resulted 5_____ a skillful balancing of global standardization and brand building with local 6_____. For years, the company has 7_____ the motto "Think globally, act 8_____".

9_____ Coke's taste and positioning are fairly 10_____ worldwide, the company carefully adapts its mix of brands and flavors, promotions, price, and distribution 11_____ local customs and preferences in each market. 12_____, beyond its core Coca-Cola brand, the company makes nearly 300 different beverage brands, created 13_____ for the local consumers. It sells a pear-flavored drink in Turkey, a berry-flavored Fanta for Germany and a honey-flavored green tea in China.

Thus Coca-Cola is truly an all-world brand. 14_____ in the world you are, you'll find it "15_____ an arm's length of desire". Yet, Coca-Cola also has a very personal meaning to consumers in different parts of the globe. Coca-Cola is as American as baseball and apple pie. But it's also as 16_____ as Big Ben and afternoon tea, as German as bratwurst and beer, as Chinese as Ping-Pong and the Great Wall. Consumers in more than 200 countries 17_____ Coca-Cola as 18_____. In Spain, Coke has been used as a mixer 19_____ wine; in Italy, Coke is served with meals 20_____ wine; in China, the beverage is served on special government occasions.

1. A. German   B. Chinese   C. English   D. American
2. A. where   B. when   C. which   D. as
3. A. had set out   B. set out   C. had set up   D. set up
4. A. into   B. towards   C. in   D. away
5. A. in   B. on   C. of   D. from
6. A. changes   B. adaptation   C. innovation   D. reform
7. A. attributed to   B. taken to   C. adhered to   D. led to
8. A. locally   B. reasonably   C. carefully   D. thoroughly
9. A. So   B. Therefore   C. But   D. Although
10. A. popular   B. consistent   C. delicious   D. wonderful
11. A. for   B. with   C. to   D. of
12. A. For example   B. In addition   C. Besides   D. Hence
13. A. specially   B. particularly   C. extremely   D. especially
14. A. No matter what B. No matter when   C. No matter where   D. No matter who
15. A. within   B. beyond   C. in   D. out
16. A. Chinese   B. American   C. German   D. English
17. A. think of   B. regarded   C. witness   D. considered
18. A. theirs brand   B. their beverage   C. its brand   D. their beverages
19. A. in   B. into   C. with   D. on
20. A. instead of   B. in the place of   C. replace   D. in place of

VII Translation.

1. Nothing better illustrates Coca-Cola's skill in balancing standardized global brand building with local adaptation than the explosive global growth of Sprite.
2. Foreign firms are expanding aggressively into new international markets, and home markets are no longer as rich in opportunity.
3. Governments are placing more regulations on foreign firms, such as acquiring joint ownership with domestic partners, mandating the hiring of nationals, and putting limits on the profits that can be taken from the country.
4. A global firm is one that, by operating in more than one country, gains marketing, production, R&D, and financial advantages that are not available to purely domestic competitors.
5. The rapid move towards globalization means that all companies will have to answer some

basic questions: what market position should we try to establish in our country, in our economic region, and globally? Who will our global competitor be, and what are their strategies and resources? Where should we produce or source our products? What strategic alliances should we form with other firms around the world?

 Extended Reading

In today's market, many business owners are making endeavors to find ways to weather the economic storm and keep their businesses profitable. Some try to cut costs internally by trimming headcount, salary or employee hours, or seeking ways to reduce production costs or improve efficiency, while some business owners could benefit a lot from considering business expansion.

Breaking into a foreign market is exciting but not to be taken lightly. In considering making the move, you should bear it in mind that foreign markets operate differently. The investment decisions should not be rushed, and every step should be given thorough research and consideration before being put into action. Remember that due diligence pays, as you should identify and research all areas of the business before entering a market. Businesses of all sizes have the opportunity to do business in a foreign market. Doing your homework to discover the best opportunities will put you on the path to successfully breaking into a foreign market.

Not all companies need to venture into international markets to survive. After all, operating domestically is easier and safer. Business owners need not learn another country's language and laws, face political and legal uncertainties, or redesign their products to suit different customer needs and expectations. However, some factors will draw the company into the international arena. Global competitors might attack the company's domestic market with high-quality goods and low prices. The company might want to counterattack them to tie up their resources, or higher profits opportunities in foreign markets might appeal to companies in the home market. In contrast, the company's domestic market might be stagnant or shrinking, or the company might need to enlarge its customer base to achieve economies of scale. The company might want to reduce its dependence on any one market to minimize its risk, or the company's customers might move to a foreign land and require international services. Finally, the company is troubled by overcapacity and needs to find additional markets for its goods.

Make sure you conduct a thorough research before arriving at a decision. If you rush a decision, then you will pay for it sooner or later. Making a decision without taking adequate time to explore and digging into all aspects of the decision in the end does great harm to productivity. Without this roadmap, it's easy to get lost along the way, making changes to your business that are either too costly or not well thought out. In other words, planned expansion can take a business to a whole new level, while over-expansion is one of the biggest dangers of a growth phase. It's easy to get carried away in the heat of the moment and to expand beyond the needs and the financial capacity of the business. Remember, a business may go through several periods of expansion and it's best to phase these according to demand.

Before going abroad, the company is supposed to define its international marketing objectives and policies. For example, it should decide what volume of foreign sales it longs for. The company also needs to decide how many countries it wants to market in. It must be careful not to spread itself too thin or to expand beyond its capacities by operating in too many countries too soon. Next, the company needs to decide on the types of countries to enter. A country's appeal lies in geographical factors, income and population, political climate, and other factors. Possible global markets should be ranked based on such factors as market size, market growth, competitive advantage and risk level. Once a company had decided to take the initial steps toward expansion, consider exactly how you will make it happen. In other words, it must determine the best mode of entry, including exporting, joint venturing and direct investment.

The simplest way to enter a foreign market is exporting. Export strategy is to ship commodities to other places or countries for sale or exchange. In economics, an export is any good or commodity, transported from one country to another country in a legitimate fashion, typically for use in trade. It will boost sales and hence raise revenues as well as enhance overall profitability.

Selling to numerous markets allows firms to branch out their business and spread their risk. Companies who have excess production can sell their items in an overseas market and not be forced to give huge concession or even dispose of their excess production. On the other hand, some enterprises will face some challenges when venturing in the international marketplace. It's a waste of time and costs. When exporting, companies may need to modify their products to meet foreign country safety and security codes, and other import restrictions.

Joint venture (JV), a good way for companies to partner without having to merge, refers to the cooperation of two or more individuals or businesses in which each agrees to share profit, loss and control in a specific enterprise. In a joint venture, both parties are equally invested in the project in terms of money, time, and effort. Since the cost of starting new projects is generally high, a joint venture allows both parties to share the burden of the project, as well as the resulting profits.

Since money is involved in a joint venture, it is necessary to have a strategic plan. In short, both parties must be committed to focusing on the future of the partnership, rather than just the immediate returns. Thus honesty, integrity, and communication within the joint venture are very necessary.

There are four types of joint ventures, namely, licensing, contract manufacturing, management contracting, and joint ownership. A JV can be brought about in the following major ways: foreign investor buying an interest in a local company; local firm acquiring an interest in an existing foreign firm; both the foreign and local entrepreneurs jointly forming a new enterprise; together with public capital and/or bank debt.

Foreign direct investment (FDI), the biggest involvement in a foreign market, is direct investment into production or business in a country by a company in another country, either by buying a company in the target country or by expanding operations of an existing business in that country. Foreign direct investment is in contrast to portfolio investment which is a passive investment in the securities of another country such as stocks and bonds.

The party making the investment is usually known as the parent enterprise, and the party invested in can be referred to as the foreign affiliate. Together, these enterprises form what is known as a transnational corporation. Many parent enterprises provide FDI because of the tax incentives that they get. Governments of certain countries invite FDI because they get additional expertise and technology. So they provide tax incentives for foreign investors, which ultimately benefits all parties. Different international markets have different tastes, preferences and requirements. By investing in a company in such a country, an enterprise ensures that its business practices and products match the needs of the market in that country specifically. Though this is not such a big factor, some markets prefer locally produced goods due to a strong sense of patriotism and nationalism, making it very hard for international enterprises to penetrate such a market. FDI helps enterprises enter such markets and gain a foothold there.

The main disadvantage of direct investment is that the firm faces such risks as restricted or devalued currencies, falling markets, or political changes. Enterprises go down this path after carefully studying the advantages and disadvantages of foreign direct investment, so they are always well prepared for the worst. When handled properly, FDI can prove to be beneficial to both parties. But if it goes wrong, then things can get very ugly for everyone involved as well. So this is a double-edged sword that needs to be handled with lots of caution.

Words and Expressions

weather v. 平安度过	enlarge v. 扩大，扩充
trim v. 削减	overcapacity n. 生产过剩
headcount n. 人数	roadmap n. 路线图，发展蓝图
move n. 行动，步骤	over-expansion n. 过度拓展
rushed a. 仓促的，莽撞的	exporting n. 出口
venture v. 冒险	legitimate a. 合法的
domestically ad. 国内地	licensing n. 许可，执照
counterattack v. 反击，反攻	specifically ad. 特别地，专门地
stagnant a. 萧条的，停滞的	foothold n. 立足之地
shrink v. 缩水；减少	trim headcount 裁员，减少总人数

take … lightly 对……掉以轻心，对……没有认真对待	mode of entry 进入国际市场的模式
make a move 采取措施	joint venturing 合资经营
bear in mind 记住	direct investment 直接投资
put into action 实施	branch out 扩展范围
due diligence 尽职调查	dispose of 处理
put sb. on the path to … 使某人走上……道路	strategic plan 战略计划
	immediate return 即期回报，即期收益
international arena 国际舞台	contract manufacturing 合约制造，合同制造
high-quality goods 高质量的产品	management contracting 管理承包
tie up 占用，阻碍	joint ownership 共同所有权
get carried away 忘乎所以	portfolio investment 证券投资
financial capacity 财务能力	parent enterprise 母公司
international marketing objective 全球市场目标	foreign affiliate 外国联署企业
long for 渴望	transnational corporation 跨国公司
spread too thin 过分拓展市场	tax incentive 税收优惠
decide on sth. 决定……	falling market 市价跌落
risk level 风险水平	double-edged sword 双刃剑

Comprehension

I Answer the following questions according to the passage.

1. What measures have been taken to survive the present market?
2. How can you understand the sentence "Remember that due diligence pays, as you should identify and research all areas of the business before entering a market."?
3. What does the writer mainly talk about in paragraph 3?
4. What are the advantages and disadvantages of developing domestically?
5. What does the word "roadmap" in paragraph 4 refer to?
6. What decisions should the firms make before going international?
7. What are the decisive factors in terms of a country's appeal?
8. What are the advantages and disadvantages of exporting?
9. What are the four types of joint ventures?
10. What are the merits and demerits of direct investment?

Unit 12　Market Expansion

II　Write "T" for true, and "F" for false.

1. Having failed to keep their business profitable, some firms begin to shift their focus from the home market to some foreign markets.
2. Businesses, large or small, stand a chance of succeeding in the foreign markets.
3. All companies do not need to venture into international markets to survive.
4. Easier and safer as it is to develop domestically, some businesses have to conduct businesses in foreign markets.
5. Over-expansion is the biggest danger in the course of business expansion.
6. Business expansion is supposed to be conducted on the basis of scales of economies.
7. Joint venture means the cooperation of businesses in which each agrees to share profit, loss and control in a specific enterprise.
8. Both parties must focus on not only the immediate returns but also the future of the partnership.
9. Licensing, contract manufacturing, management contracting, and joint ownership can bring about a joint venture.
10. Bonds are an active investment in the safety of another country.

Additional Terms

adapted marketing mix　适应性市场组合
adoption process　适应过程
brand extension　品牌延伸
cash investment　现金投资
channel level　渠道层级
click-only company　点击企业
co-branding　合作品牌
communication adaptation　策略沟通调适
core competence　核心竞争力, 核心能力
cosmocorp　宇宙公司
dumping　倾销
economic community　经济共同体
exchange control　外汇管理
export credit　出口信贷
export earning　出口收益
export financing　出口融资，出口信贷
export-led　由出口带动的
export license　出口许可证
export market　出口市场
export market need　出口市场需求
export market development program　出口市场拓展计划
export-oriented　出口为主，出口导向
export performance　出口业绩
export price　出口价格
export value　出口货值
exporting　出口
external asset　对外资产
external commercial relation　对外贸易关系
external competitiveness　对外竞争力
external equilibrium　对外均衡

external investor　外来投资者
external price competitiveness　对外贸易价格竞争能力
external trade　对外贸易
extra statutory concession　法外宽减
extrinsic value　外在价值，非固有价值
greenfield investment　全新投资项目
industrial economy　工业经济
industrializing economy　工业化经济
internalization advantage　内部化优势
investment advisor　投资顾问
investment bank　投资银行
investment climate　投资环境
investment grade　投资等级
investment risk　投资风险
investment vehicle　投资媒体
joint venture agreement　合资合同
Joint venture strategy　合资经营战略
location specific advantage　区位优势
majority ownership　过半数所有权
market growth rate　市场增长率
market potential　市场潜力
multinational corporation　跨国公司
ownership advantage　所有权优势
partnership agreement　合作协议
partner selection　协作伙伴选择
price escalation　价格升级
price transparency　价格透明
product adaptation　产品调适
product invention　产品创新
rate of return　回报率
standardized marketing mix　标准化营销组合
straight product extension　直接产品延伸
subsistence economy　自给自足经济
venture investment　风险投资
whole channel view　整体渠道观点

PART IV

Strategy Analysis

Unit 13
Marketing Competition Strategy

Competition is one of the business challenges faced by entrepreneurs when building a successful business from scratch. [1]Business is a war; so is marketing. We can gain an insight of marketing firms by classifying firms by the roles they play in the target market: leader, challenger, follower, and nicher. 40 percent of the marketers are in the hands of a market leader; another 30 percent is in the hands of a market challenger; another 20 percent is in the hands of a market follower a firm that is willing to maintain its market share and not rock the boat. The remaining 10 percent is in the hands of market nichers, firms that serve small market segments not being served by larger firms.[2]

In today's world, there is a rise in both the number of products and the number of competitors in the market. Naturally everyone wants to be ahead of the competition. Is everyone successful? Definitely not. It is the dream of an entrepreneur to see his company among the spotlight as an example for others to follow. Capturing substantial market share does not happen overnight but requires determination, commitment and diligence in the long run.[3]

Many industries contain one firm that is the acknowledged market leader. Market leadership is the position of a company with the largest market share in the relevant product market and usually leads the other firms in price changes, new product introductions, distribution coverage, and promotional intensity or highest profitability margin in a given market for goods and services. Market share may be measured by either the volume of goods sold or the value of those goods. Steve Jobs, the co-founder of Apple, suggests the following for anyone who wishes to become a market leader.[4]

- Own and control the relevant technology in whatever market you are in, either through the use of patent or other proprietary protections.
- Adopt and implement better technologies immediately, whenever they become available,

regardless of whether or not any other organizations are currently using them.
- Be the first to use a technology or create a category for a product. Then, make it an industry standard.

Market leadership is a particularly useful and relevant concept in the Internet age, where first-movers in new markets can quickly gain monopolies for services or products. Examples of digital market leadership are as follows.
- Microsoft's position of the operating system (Windows) and web browser (Internet Explorer) markets.
- Apple's share of portable media player sales (iPod).
- Comcast's dominance in broadband Internet access (cable modems) in many areas of North America.
- Friendster, followed by MySpace and now Facebook's position (social networking).

Well-known products generally hold a distinctive position in consumers' minds. Nevertheless, unless a dominant firm enjoys a legal monopoly, its life is not altogether easy. It must maintain constant vigilance. For instance, under constant pressure from fast growing snack makers of all kinds, Hershey's had found that domination of the US chocolate candy business is not developing increasingly, consumers are passing up Hershey's candies for chips.[5] To maintain profit targets, Hershey's has cut costs, dropped weak product lines, cut hundreds of slow-selling package sizes, improved distribution by increasing high-margin convenience store presence, and introduced extension of its strongest brands. To more broadly compete and sustain growth, however, Hershey's is even considering other new snack products.

Remaining number one calls for effective market leader strategies, which in general consist of three main tasks including expanding the total market, protecting its current market share through good defensive and offensive actions, as well as increasing its market share, even if market remains constant.

The dominant firm normally gains the most when the total market expands. For example, if Americans increase their consumptions of ketchup, Heinz stands to gain the most because it sells almost two thirds of the country's ketchup. If Heinz can convince more Americans to use ketchup or to use ketchup with more meals or to use more ketchup on each occasion, Heinz will benefit considerably. In general, the market leader should look for new customers or more usage from existing customers. Of course, the risk analysis is absolutely necessary because expansion failure can be fatal. Many companies reaching the limits of growth in their core business look to new products, mergers, or acquisitions for future expansion. But diversification is inherently risky and the odds of success are poor. Failed growth strategies waste company resources—human and financial.

Protecting the market share is more difficult. The lower barrier there is to entry into business, the more attractive the current customer segment is from competitor point of view. Customer satisfaction is a key parameter that makes protecting market share possible, for it indicates possible weakness in operations and addresses areas where to charge. Measuring customer satisfaction is therefore an important task of marketing department of the company. Other important task is to benchmark competitors, and try to find out how they tempt customers, what will be their following moves and implement lucrative moves first.

Expanding the market share is also possible for market leader. Keyword to expanding market share is innovation. Product, market segment, distribution and promotion are the areas on which innovations may lead to bigger share of market. The bigger market share is however not the only target which should be pursued. The most profitable level of market share should be pursued, and it is not always the highest level. Somewhere goes the borderline of optimal market share after which the profitability starts to fall down. This is because keeping all the current customers with the lower margin will cost sometimes more than giving up part of the customers and keeping the rest with better profit margin.

A market challenger is a company that is working hard to earn a higher share of a particular consumer market, and is posing something of a threat to the businesses which are the front runners in the industry.[6] While the current share of the challenger is less than that of the market leader who accounts for the majority of the sales made in that market, an up and coming business will intentionally compete with and show signs of capturing more clients from the leader over a period of time. Given the right set of circumstances, a market challenger can eventually become a market leader in its own right.[7]

One of the easiest ways to understand the concept of a market challenger is to consider the launch of a new brand of soda. With the market already dominated by a handful of industry leaders, the new brand will pursue an aggressive marketing strategy to reach consumers and entice them to give the product a try. Assuming that the strategy does reach a significant number of consumers and they find the soda to compare favorably with older established brands, the market challenger will, over several years, build market share that is captured from those industry leaders. Given enough time, the sales of the challenger may come to rival those of the traditional leaders, allowing that challenger to be recognized as a leader within the beverage industry.

The strategies used by a market challenger to build rapport with consumers will vary, depending on the nature of the competition within the marketplace and the goals of that company. In some cases, the basis for the competition may be a price war, with the challenger touting a product of similar quality but available for a lower price, a move that may cause leaders to offer some price incentives of their own. At other times, the focus may be on presenting the newer products as being superior to other established products on the basis of taste, ease of use, or some other defined criteria. The market challenger may even compete on the basis of being an operation that is more environmentally friendly than the competition.

Typically, a market challenger will demonstrate some potential for capturing a significant amount of market share. That potential is often made manifest by appealing to certain sectors or groups within the broader consumer market, the use of modern technology to compete with the traditional leaders in the market, and the fact that the marketing efforts of the business are in fact leading to a steady increase in sales volume. While there is no magic formula that defines every aspect of being a market challenger, it is not unusual for any company that is new on the scene and is obviously gaining new customers to be perceived as a viable threat to the old regime.

Many companies don't try to be the best of the best. Instead, they prefer to follow rather than challenge the market leader. Many runner-up companies do not challenge the market leader. This type of business owner has a low-risk, "play it safe" strategy that involves using tactics that work well for competitors—a tactic known as leap-frogging.[8] In this way, they can reduce risks, avoid extra costs, capitalize on the success of the market leader, and reduce the likelihood of a competitive attack. Instead of exhausting efforts and resources on trying to be the "top dog", a market follower uses time-tested techniques to retain current customers and employs borrowed strategies to win new ones.[9] There are four follower strategies.

- **Counterfeiter**. The counterfeiter duplicates the leader's products and packages and sells it on the black market or through disreputable dealers. Music firms have been plagued by the counterfeiter problem.
- **Cloner**. The cloner copies the leader's products as it is as well as name, packaging with slight variations.
- **Imitator**. The imitator introduces brands similar to leaders by copying some of the things but maintaining differentiation of packaging, advertising, pricing or location.
- **Adaptor**. The adaptor introduces improved products than leader's products.

A niche market is the subset of the market on which a specific product is focusing. The market niche defines the specific product features aimed at satisfying specific market needs, as well as the price range, production quality and the demographics that is intended to impact. It is also a small market segment. For example, sports channels target a niche of sports lovers. So to speak, the niche market is a highly specialized market aiming to survive among the competition from numerous super companies. Even established companies create products for different niches, for example, Hewlett-Packard has all-in-one machines for printing, scanning and faxing targeted for the home office niche while at the same time having separate machines with one of these functions for big

businesses.[10] Then how to develop a niche strategy?
- Select a segment of the market that has a special need.
- Carry out market research to identify if the market size makes the idea feasible.
- Ensure that exclusivity through branding, patents or trademarks can be obtained.
- Prepare inventory and delivery channels.
- Prepare a promotion plan to reach the particular market.
- Implement the plan.
- Monitor market continuously to ensure that niche characteristics and market continue to be feasible.

Vocabulary

entrepreneur *n.* 企业家	受的
remaining *adj.* 剩下的，其余的	rival *vt.* 与……竞争
spotlight *n.* 公众注意的中心	tout *vt.* 兜售
overnight *adv.* 一夜之间，突然	manifest *adj.* 明显的
commitment *n.* 承诺；献身	regime *n.* 管理体制
diligence *n.* 勤奋	runner-up *adj.* 第二名的
acknowledge *vt.* 承认，公认	tactic *n.* 策略
relevant *adj.* 相关的	leap-frogging *n.* 蛙跳战略
co-founder *n.* 共同创立者	likelihood *n.* 可能性
domination *n.* 控制	time-tested *adj.* 经受时间考验的
considerably *adv.* 大量地，可观地	counterfeiter *n.* 伪造者
constant *adj.* 不变的	disreputable *adj.* 名誉不好的，不体面的
fatal *adj.* 致命的	plague *vt.* 使痛苦，造成麻烦
inherently *adv.* 固有地	cloner *n.* 复制者
odds *n.* 可能性，胜算	imitator *n.* 模仿者
tempt *vt.* 引诱，吸引	adaptor *n.* 改编者
lucrative *adj.* 获利多的，赚钱的	subset *n.* 分组，子集
optimal *adj.* 最佳的，最优的	all-in-one *adj.* 一体化的，集成的
up and coming *adj.* 有前途的	
established *adj.* 已被认可的，已被接	

Unit 13 Marketing Competition Strategy

Phrases and Expressions

market challenger　市场挑战者
market follower　市场追随者
market nicher　市场补缺者
be in the hand of ...　在……掌握中
rock the boat　破坏现状，捣乱
be ahead of　比……强，占优势
in the long run　从长远来看
distribution coverage　分销领域
promotional intensity　销售集中程度

proprietary protection　产权保护
operating system　操作系统
Internet access　互联网接入，上网
social networking　社交网络
capitalize on　利用
niche market　利基市场
so to speak　可以这么说
promotion plan　促销计划

1. Competition is one of the business challenges faced by entrepreneurs when building a successful business from scratch.　激烈的竞争是企业家白手起家、成功创业所面临的挑战之一。

   在本句中，短语 do sth. from scratch 的意思是"白手起家，从无到有"，例如：
   Hong Kong's manufacturing industry did not start from scratch in the post-war period.　战后，香港制造业的兴起并非从零开始的。
   此外，scratch 还有一些常见的固定搭配，例如：scratch the surface of（触及表面，隔靴搔痒）；not come up to scratch（未达到标准，不令人满意）；scratch one's head（绞尽脑汁）。
   例如：
   Managers say they've only scratched the surface of the problem.　经理们说他们只不过是触及了问题的表面。
   The director always made me feel I wasn't coming up to scratch.　董事长总是让我觉得自己不够优秀。
   The institute spends a lot of time scratching its head about how to boost American productivity.　该协会花费大量时间苦苦思索如何提高美国的生产力。

2. 40 percent of the marketers are in the hands of a market leader; another 30 percent is in the hands of a market challenger; another 20 percent is in the hands of a market follower a firm that is willing to maintain its market share and not rock the boat. The remaining 10 percent is

in the hands of market nichers, firms that serve small market segments not being served by larger firms. 百分之四十的商人由市场领导者控制；另外百分之三十由市场挑战者控制；百分之二十由市场追随者控制，市场追随者愿意保持原有的市场份额，而不愿意改变现状。其余的百分之十由市场补缺者控制，他们为细分市场提供服务，而这些细分市场是无法从大公司获得相应服务的。

企业在特定市场的竞争地位，大致可分为市场领导者、市场挑战者、市场追随者和市场补缺者四类。市场领导者为了保持自己在市场上的领先地位和既得利益，可能采取扩大市场需求、维持市场份额或提高市场占有率等竞争策略。为扩大市场需求，市场领导者采取发现新用户、开辟新用途、增加使用量、提高使用频率等策略。为保护市场份额，市场领导者采取创新发展、筑垒防御、直接反击等策略。市场挑战者是指那些在市场上居于次要地位的企业，它们不甘于目前的地位，通过对市场领导者或其他竞争对手的挑战与攻击，提高自己的市场份额和市场竞争地位，甚至取代市场领导者的地位，其策略有价格竞争、产品竞争、服务竞争、渠道竞争等。市场领导者与市场挑战者的角逐，往往是两败俱伤，从而使其他竞争者通常要三思而行，不敢贸然向市场领导者直接发起攻击，更多的还是选择市场追随者的竞争策略，其策略有仿效跟随、差距跟随、选择跟随等。几乎所有的行业都有大量中小企业，这些中小企业盯住大企业忽略的市场空缺，通过专业化营销，集中自己的资源优势来满足这部分市场的需要，其策略有市场专门化、顾客专门化、产品专门化等。

3. Capturing substantial market share does not happen overnight but requires determination, commitment and diligence in the long run. 占有大量的市场份额并不是一下子就能实现的，而是需要决心、承诺和勤奋，持之以恒。

在本句中，overnight 的意思是"突然，一下子，一夜之间"，例如：

The rules are not going to change overnight. 这些规定不会说变就变。

He's realistic enough to know he's not going to succeed overnight. 他很现实，知道自己不会一下子成功。

4. Steve Jobs, the co-founder of Apple, suggests the following for anyone who wishes to become a market leader. 苹果公司的创始人之一史蒂夫·乔布斯，为那些想成为市场领导者的人提出了以下建议。

史蒂夫·乔布斯，世界著名发明家、企业家、美国苹果公司联合创办人及前行政总裁。1976年4月1日乔布斯和朋友成立苹果公司，先后推出了iMac、iPod、iPhone等风靡全球的电子产品，深刻地改变了现代通信、娱乐乃至生活的方式。2011年10月5日他因病逝世，享年56岁。乔布斯是改变世界的天才，他凭借敏锐的触觉和过人的智慧，勇于变革，不断创新，引领全球资讯科技和电子产品的潮流，把电脑和电子产品变得简约化、平民化，让昂贵的电子产品变为现代人生活的一部分。

5. For instance, under constant pressure from fast growing snack makers of all kinds, Hershey's had found that domination of the US chocolate candy business is not developing increasingly,

consumers are passing up Hershey's candies for chips. 例如，面对各种食品制造商带来的压力，好时公司发现，美国巧克力的统治地位有所下降，好时食品对消费者的吸引力正在逐步减弱，取而代之的是薯条。

好时公司是美国最大的巧克力制造商，也是最早的巧克力制造商，具有100多年的历史，总公司位于宾夕法尼亚州。好时巧克力的创始人米尔顿·好时先生（Milton Hershey）于1903年初创巧克力制造业时，这里还是一片少有人烟的牧场。好时先生以他的智慧和长远的眼光创建了世界一流的巧克力工厂，牧场专送的新鲜牛奶、精心筛选的可可豆、传统的经典工艺使得好时巧克力纯正、幼滑。整座好时小镇变成了一个香味满溢的巧克力王国。

6. A market challenger is a company that is working hard to earn a higher share of a particular consumer market, and is posing something of a threat to the businesses which are the front runners in the industry. 市场挑战者试图努力提高在某一特定消费者市场的市场份额，对于该行业的领军企业来说这会构成某种威胁。

在本句中，that 引导定语从句，用来修饰限定 company，该定语从句中 and 连接两个并列的分句，句尾是 which 引导的定语从句，修饰限定 businesses。此外，短语 something of 的意思是"有点，有几分"，例如：

Women are still something of a rarity in senior positions in business. 在商界位居高职的妇女仍然十分罕见。

短语 pose a threat to 的意思是"威胁……"，例如：

The rapid growth of online shopping had posed a threat to traditional way of shopping. 网上购物的迅猛发展对传统的购物方式造成了威胁。

7. Given the right set of circumstances, a market challenger can eventually become a market leader in its own right. 条件成熟的话，市场挑战者最终会凭借自己的能力成为市场领导者。

在本句中，短语 in one's own right 的意思是"凭借某人自己的能力"，例如：

This small company has developed into a market leader in this industry in its own right. 这家小公司凭借自己的实力，已经发展成为该行业的市场领导者。

8. This type of business owner has a low-risk, "play it safe" strategy that involves using tactics that work well for competitors—a tactic known as leap-frogging. 这种类型的企业所有者采用低风险、"无争议性"策略，采用竞争对手惯用的策略，即蛙跳策略。

在市场营销领域，迂回进攻是一种非直接的攻击战术。公司可以采取蛙跳式策略进入新的技术领域，以替代现有产品。挑战者不是愚蠢地效仿竞争对手的产品，而是耐心地开发新的技术，这样就可以在自己占有优势的新战场向对手发起挑战。

9. Instead of exhausting efforts and resources on trying to be the "top dog", a market follower uses time-tested techniques to retain current customers and employs borrowed strategies to win new ones. 市场追随者不会为了成为"优胜者"而绞尽脑汁，耗尽所有的资源，相反，他会

采用百试不爽的策略，保留公司现有的顾客，采纳他人的策略以获得新的顾客。

在本句中，短语 top dog 的意思是"优胜者，胜利者"，主句中使用的是两个并列的谓语动词"uses"和"employs"，后面各自跟着 to 引导的不定式表示目的，ones 代替上文提到的 customers。

10. Even established companies create products for different niches, for example, Hewlett-Packard has all-in-one machines for printing, scanning and faxing targeted for the home office niche while at the same time having separate machines with one of these functions for big businesses.

即使是那些知名公司也会为不同的利基市场生产产品，例如，惠普公司拥有集打印、扫描、传真为一体的机器，这是专门为家庭办公市场量身定制的，与此同时，惠普还拥有单独为大公司提供服务的机器，这些机器只具备这些功能中的某一种功能。

惠普（Hewlett-Packard, HP）公司建于 1939 年，惠普由斯坦福大学的两位毕业生威廉·休利特及戴维·帕卡德创办，经过几十年的发展及一系列收购活动，现已成为世界上最大的科技企业之一，在打印、成像领域和 IT 服务领域都处于领先地位，总部位于加利福尼亚州帕罗奥多市，2002 年与康柏公司合并，是全球仅次于 IBM 的计算机及办公设备制造商。惠普公司是面向个人用户、大中小型企业和研究机构的全球技术解决方案提供商，其提供的产品涵盖信息技术基础设施、个人计算与接入设备、图像与打印设备，包括台式计算机与工作站、笔记本电脑与平板电脑、打印与多功能一体机、掌上电脑、投影仪、扫描仪、数字影像、存储设备、服务器、网络设备、耗材与附件等。

I Answer the following questions according to the text.

1. How are firms classified on the basis of the roles they play in the target market?
2. What suggestions does Steve Jobs give those who want to become market leaders?
3. What firms are considered as digital market leaders?
4. What is the author's purpose to mention the example of Hershey's?
5. What can be called effective market leader strategies?
6. Will the company definitely become a market leader with expansion of the total market?
7. What are the important tasks of marketing department of the company?
8. What can be learnt from the example of launching a new brand of soda?
9. How does a market challenger employ different strategies to build rapport with consumers?
10. What are the advantages of follower strategies? Please name some of the strategies.

Unit 13 Marketing Competition Strategy

II Decide whether the following statements are true or false.

1. Marketing is also a kind of war according to the passage.
2. It is out of the question for everyone to be ahead of the competition in today's world.
3. Comcast is dominant in broadband Internet access in many areas in America.
4. Facebook has replaced Friendster and MySpace in the terms of social networking.
5. Examples of digital market leadership include Microsoft, Apple, Comcast, Friendster, MySpace, Facebook, Best Buy and so on.
6. Heinz is responsible for two thirds of the world's ketchup.
7. Customer satisfaction is of great importance because it indicates possible weakness in customer preferences and addresses areas where to charge.
8. The most profitable level of market share should be pursued because it symbolizes the highest level.
9. It's not advisable to keep all the current customers with the lower margin.
10. The market challenger stands a slim chance of becoming the market leader.

III Fill in each blank with the proper form of the word in the bracket.

1. It's necessary to _____ (class) different types of potential customers.
2. These products are characterized by the emphasis on the _____ (maintain) of health.
3. The three parties will meet next month to work out _____ (remain) differences.
4. You don't have to _____ (commitment) to anything over the phone.
5. He adapted himself to the new job and came to know some _____ (establish) names of Paris fashion.
6. He warned the public to be _____ (vigilance) and do not believe all the commercials.
7. No single factor appears to _____ (domination).
8. Because of mismanagement, this bar has become the noisiest and most _____ (reputable) place.
9. Some small companies tried in vain to _____ (imitator) this high-quality product.
10. There are some _____ (specialize) agencies for advertising.

IV Fill in each blank with a proper preposition.

1. After graduation he ran a Portuguese restaurant which specializes _____ seafood.
2. They started _____ scratch and needed men, fund and technology.
3. Large concentrations of capital were _____ the hands of merchants.
4. Being ahead _____ the fierce competition calls for effective marketing strategies.
5. _____ the long run, prices are bound to rise.

6. Never pass _____ a golden opportunity to improve yourself.
7. We need to appeal _____ a wider customer base.
8. Advertisers capitalize _____ the grandness and elegance it brings to their products.
9. He likes to be _____ the spotlight.
10. The expansion of his business posed threat _____ other firms in this industry.

V Fill in the blanks with the words and phrases given below. Change the form where necessary.

| considerably | optimal | plague | rock the boat | manifest |
| odds | likelihood | so to speak | build rapport with | lucrative |

1. The _____ are that they will meet their waterloo.
2. They seldom _____ or annoy board with unusual budget requests.
3. He tried every means to _____ potential customers.
4. The new manager is, _____, easy to get along with.
5. The tariff may be nationally _____, but it still means a net loss to the world.
6. The project wasted a _____ amount of time and money.
7. Inflation will remain a recurrent _____ in this country.
8. The fall in sales is a _____ failure of his promotion plan.
9. He decided to turn his hobby into a _____ sideline.
10. Once people have seen that something actually works, they are much more _____ to accept change.

VI Cloze.

Being first in any category is 1_____ to give you the edge—being the leader comes from being first. It's 2_____ to get into the mind of consumers first than try to 3_____ people you have a better product or service than 4_____ they did get there first. Improvements are always 5_____ to product/service inventions and innovations but the first has a head start. Once you are the leader, a position mostly 6_____ by being first, it is pretty hard for competitors to dislodge you, as long as you keep your products up to date and 7_____ comparable quality.

"When you're number four or five in a market, when number one sneezes, you get pneumonia. When you're number one, you control your destiny. The others keep 8_____; they have difficult times. That's not the same if you're number four, and that's your only businesses. Then you have to find strategic ways to get stronger." says Jack Welch, the legendary former CEO of GE.

So it's quite necessary to evolve a game plan, a business strategy 9_____ on what the company does best. Become more concrete, more focused. In business, the strong 10_____, the

Unit 13 Marketing Competition Strategy

weak do not. The big, fast ones get to play, while the small ones are left behind. There is a competitive 11_____ of being the best—or the second best—that can, and should, be exploited. Winners and market leaders will be those who insist 12_____ being the number one or number two fastest, leanest, lower-cost, world-wide producers of quality goods or services and those 13_____ have a clear technological edge or a clear competitive advantage in their chosen 14_____.

The market leader is 15_____ in its industry and has substantial market share. If you want to lead the market, you 16_____ be the industry leader in establishing an innovation-friendly organization, developing new business models and new products or services. You must be on the cutting 17_____ of new technologies and innovative business processes. Your customer value proposition must offer a superior solution 18_____ a customer's problem, and your product must be well differentiated.

Once you are the first and get the consumers to buy your brand, often they won't 19_____ to switch. People tend to stick with 20_____ they've got.

1. A. to go	B. going	C. to going	D. being going
2. A. more easier	B. more difficult	C. much difficult	D. much easier
3. A. believe	B. persuade	C. convince	D. advise
4. A. the one	B. ones	C. the ones	D. the one what
5. A. taken	B. taking	C. making	D. made
6. A. gained	B. is gained	C. has been gained	D. being gained
7. A. with	B. for	C. of	D. at
8. A. merging	B. to merge	C. merge	D. being merged
9. A. depended	B. decided	C. based	D. agreed
10. A. beat	B. succeed	C. win	D. survive
11. A. situation	B. advantage	C. condition	D. merit
12. A. upon	B. with	C. for	D. in
13. A. that	B. who	C. what	D. which
14. A. place	B. market	C. industry	D. niche
15. A. superior	B. dominant	C. important	D. strong
16. A. should	B. can	C. must	D. might
17. A. edge	B. advantage	C. force	D. power
18. A. of	B. for	C. with	D. to
19. A. want	B. bother	C. like	D. likely
20. A. which	B. that	C. what	D. how

| VII | Translation.

1. Once a company becomes a market leader, it is hard for the competitors to get ahead, so other companies should try to gain extensive market share for their products otherwise it is a possibility that in the long run their product will be overlooked.
2. As a market leader the company should figure out the weaker points of its competitors and then work upon those weak aspects to retain its top spot within the market.
3. Working together as a team towards achieving one objective adds up to the chances of becoming a market leader.
4. Size of the entry barrier varies a lot from business to business, depending on the investments required, skills and other charges needed.
5. Before making your marketing plan, identify what makes your business special in comparison to what the competitors are offering.

Extended Reading

Edge Out Competitors

How stiff is the competition in your industry? How do you intend to stay ahead of competition in business? Entrepreneurs face stiff competition every day. Some have survived and their businesses are thriving and growing at an exponential rate. How did they survive competition? They didn't survive by rolling dice and praying for luck; instead, they survived competition by being tough and strategic in their marketing approach.

Being a smart marketer can mean the difference between whether your business succeeds or fails. Developing a strategic marketing plan will not only help you to edge out the competition, but also grow a booming business. Only in this way can you learn more about the strategies early and expansion stage companies can use to put themselves in the best position to bury the competition. It's good to have a competitor. You can also benefit from your competitors' brands in the same way that Foursquare is mentioned every time anyone brings up Facebook check-ins, or Quora is mentioned every time someone brings up Facebook Q&A.

Business is a game and only the team with the best players will win. To beat the competition will require everyone's collective effort. It's not just a task for the marketing department or top management; it's everyone's responsibility. So as the leader of your business, it's very important you enlist the support of the whole organization. If you are ready to outperform your competitor, then below are six marketing tactics you can implement to stay ahead of competition.

Unit 13 Marketing Competition Strategy

1. Define your brand

No two businesses are alike just as no two customers are alike, hence the need for branding. What sets your business apart from the competition? What does your business name or product stand for in the heart of your customers? What's your unique selling proposition? What does your business stand for? What's different about your business in comparison to other businesses in your industry? What do you want to be known for in the marketplace? Is there anything special about your business?

You see when new competitors enter into your line of business, whether you like it or not, be prepared to lose some market share. No one business can appeal to everybody. So your best response is to define your brand and consistently communicate your own unique selling proposition. It is the businesses that don't clearly stand for something that often get eaten up by competitions. If your business doesn't stand for something, it will fall for anything.

Aliko Dangote set his company apart with speedy delivery and uniform price. Wal-Mart became a brand with its unique pricing strategy; Apple became a brand with innovation and Virgin Atlantic grew because it offered first class service to an ignored niche. To remain competitive, you've got to be distinctive. To outsmart your competitors, you need to be unique. You need to find your strength, work on it and broadcast it to the world.

2. Develop a competitive strategy

Your mission to survive or stay ahead of competition begins with strategic planning. You must identify your competitor; spot out the competitor's strengths and weaknesses, and plan your strategy based on the information gathered. Concentrate all your attacking effort on your competitor's weaknesses while avoiding and defending against the strengths.

When developing a competitive strategy, don't do it alone, do it together with your business team. Your competitive strategy must not only include plans to defeat competition; it must also include plans that will strengthen the business from the inside as well as on the outside.

Once you surmised what you are up against, you can begin to develop your marketing plan. Identify one or two extraordinary aspects of your business and use them as the lead for all marketing. This could include your pricing structure, on-time delivery, or expertise in your field.

Jack Welch, the former CEO of General Electric (GE) was right when he said "if you don't have a competitive advantage, don't compete". In other words, don't bother getting into the game if you haven't first figured out a plan on how to win. There are basically three key areas to focus on when choosing a competitive advantage:quality,price and service.

Most of the time it is not so easy to measure up well on all three key areas. However, it's important to include service in any of the combinations you want to focus on. Why? The other two forms of competitive advantage can cost you a lot and often time customers can choose otherwise. There's always an alternative to quality; if you focus on only offering the highest quality at a premium price, customers will scout around for a lower quality at a cheaper price. There's always an alternative to price; if you focus on offering the cheapest price possible it will require that you find a way to drive down your cost to the barest minimum, and this can turn out in form of low quality products or services and customers will start to complain.

Pick either of the two: price or quality as your competitive advantage and complement it with service. Without the element of service in your competitive strategy you can never deliver happiness to your customers. People may not remember how great your product or service is; they may not remember how much you make them pay, but they will never forget how you make them feel.

3. Focus on a niche

Don't try to be all things to all people. Concentrate on selling something unique that you know there is a need for, offer competitive pricing and good customer service. Most businesses try to be everything to everyone; don't join them. Find a niche market and serve that niche to the best of your effort. In every industry, there's an under-served, abandoned niche that the big corporations consider too small to be served. It's up to you to find such niche and focus your entire marketing effort on it. Don't try to be everything to everyone; be something to someone.

Virgin Atlantic was able to breakthrough because it focused on business men and students while British Airways strives to serve everyone. Facebook was able to breakthrough because it focused on youths. So if you are going to stay ahead of competition, then get focused.

4. Create a customer database

Do you know that it cost 20 times more to get a new customer than it cost to keep an old customer? Customers are very expensive to attract and that is why smart businesses focus on a customer's lifetime profitability (CLP) rather than on a one-off purchase. In other words, they place more emphasis on building an enduring relationship with their customers rather than on making a sale. They have realized that it is wiser to have their customers for life rather than having them for a while. Because your greatest success in business will come from the number of repeat purchases you're able to generate from your loyal customers. This was the idea behind our membership strategy. Initially it seemed like a lot of work and a lot of cost on our side, but in the long run, the benefits outweighed the cost and the efforts expended to create our own customer database through the membership strategy. There is nothing more powerful than having a communication link between you and your customers. It is the cheapest but most effective tactic against intense competitions.

5. Connect with customers emotionally

What is good for our customers is also in the long run good for us. All businesses try to communicate with the customers but not all connect with the customers. So stop talking about your products and services. Customers don't care about products and services, they care about themselves. One question on the mind of all your potential customers is "Wii-FM," meaning "what is in for me." The answer to the "WII-FM" question is the key to successfully connecting with your customers emotionally. Connecting with your customers entails knowing your customer's need and touching them at the point of that need. If you can successfully do this, you have nothing to fear about competition.

6. Strive to achieve quality and innovation

You must insist on quality and make quality a standard in your business. Insistence on quality at an affordable rate can set you apart from competition. Never trade quantity and cheapness over quality because it's going to back fire.

How did Apple become one of the most respected companies in the world? They made it through innovation. Steve Jobs ever said that innovation distinguishes between a leader and a follower. Concentrating on innovation was Apple's overall strategy to stay competitive in the market place. Apple's strategy was to stay competitive by providing the customers with constant innovative products that solves basic problems. Being innovative doesn't mean spending millions of dollars in research and inventions; being innovative simply means being willing to try out new products and techniques to improve the value of your offered services. Being innovative is simply searching outside the box for faster solutions to people's problems, so you can choose to compete with innovation or not, but know that a company driven by innovation will always stay ahead of the pack.

Words and Expressions

thriving adj. 兴盛的，兴隆的	mission n. 使命
exponential adj. 快速增长的	surmise vt. 推测，猜测
strategic adj. 战略的，战略性的	extraordinary adj. 非凡的，特别的，不同寻常的
booming adj. 快速发展的	
Foursquare n. 四方（基于地理位置的社会网络服务）	under-served adj. 服务不足的，服务不够的
check-in n. 登记	initially adv. 最初
Quora n. 问答网站	entail vt. 引发，带来
enlist vt. 赢得	insistence n. 坚持
outperform vt. 做得比……更好	edge out 取代，胜过
alike adj. 相同的	in comparison to 与……相比
speedy adj. 快速的	line of business 行业
uniform adj. 统一的，一致的	fall for anything 一事无成
outsmart vt. 用计谋打败	spot out 指出，找出

be up against 面临，面对	的努力
competitive advantage 竞争优势	strive to do sth. 尽力做某事
measure up 测量，估计	customer database 顾客数据库
scout around 侦查，寻找	one-off purchase 一次性购买
drive down 压低	for life 终身
to the barest minimum 最小化	repeat purchase 重复购买率
to the best of one's effort 尽某人最大	back fire 适得其反，事与愿违

Comprehension

I Answer the following questions according to the passage.

1. What is the main idea of the passage?
2. How do entrepreneurs survive the competition?
3. Can you give us some examples to illustrate the benefit of having a competitor?
4. How can you understand the sentence "If your business doesn't stand for something, it will fall for anything."?
5. What examples are mentioned to exemplify the importance of defining the brands?
6. What are the areas to consider when choosing a competitive advantage? What is the importance of service?
7. How can you understand the sentence "Don't try to be everything to everyone; be something to someone."?
8. Why companies are encouraged to create a customer database?
9. What is the philosophy behind membership strategy?
10. What are the advantages of connecting with customers emotionally?

II Write "T" for true, and "F" for false.

1. Faced with fierce competition, entrepreneurs survive by rolling dice and praying for luck.
2. Quora and Foursquare are competitors according to the passage.
3. The success of businesses results from the collective effort of everyone involved.
4. The unique brand is likely to stop customers from coming to patronize you.
5. The absence of service in your competitive strategy will lead to unhappiness of your customers.

6. It's impossible for our competitors to imitate our services as well as the way we treat our customers.
7. It's very expensive to focus on a customer's lifetime profitability.
8. The emphasis on building an enduring relationship with customers means focusing on their life.
9. Finding the niche market is the cheapest but most effective tactic against intense competitions.
10. Businesses are not expected to run after quantity and cheapness at the expense of quality.

Additional Terms

attack strategy 进攻型战略	innovation-friendly organization 创新型企业
bypass attack 绕道进攻	market challenger strategy 市场挑战者战略
contraction defense 收缩防御	
cost control 成本控制	market focus 市场焦点
counter-offensive defense 反击式防御	market follower strategy 市场追随者战略
covert-offensive strategy 秘密进攻战略	market force 市场力量
defense strategy 防御型战略	market-nicher strategy 市场补缺者战略
efficient market hypothesis 有效市场假说	mobile defense 运动防御
encirclement attack 包围进攻	multiple niching 多重利基
exit barrier 退出壁垒	overt-offensive strategy 公开进攻战略
expansion stage company 处于扩展期的公司	position defense 阵地防御
	pre-emptive defense 先发制人防御
flanking defense 侧翼防御	product imitation 产品模仿
frontal attack 正面进攻	product innovation 产品创新
guerrilla attack 游击进攻	return on investment 投资回报率
high-profile customer 高端客户	sustainable competitive advantage 持续竞争优势

Unit 14
Target Marketing Strategy

Market segmentation allows managers to identify one or more market segments that provide opportunities for the organization. Once they have segmented their markets based on different characteristics, the next task is to choose one or more target market segments. Developing different marketing strategies for different customer groups is very important in that we can't be all things to all people, and no one particular strategy would satisfy all customer groups with different characteristics, lifestyles, backgrounds and income levels. The selection of target marketing strategy depends on how the organization understands its potential customers.

When selecting their target markets, companies have to make a choice of whether they are going to be focused on one or few segments or they are going to cater to the mass market. The choice that companies make at this stage will determine their marketing mix. In all there are four generally recognized target marketing strategies, namely, undifferentiated targeting strategy or mass marketing, differentiated targeting strategy, concentrated targeting strategy and micro-marketing (one-to-one marketing).

When everyone might be considered a potential user of its product, a firm uses an undifferentiated targeting strategy, which means that although there are differences within a population, the organization decides to ignore them in its marketing efforts. For this reason, it is sometimes also referred to as mass marketing. Obviously, such a targeting strategy focuses on the similarities in needs of the customers as opposed to the differences. There may be no strong differences in customer characteristics. Alternatively, the cost of developing a separate marketing mix for separate segments may outweigh the potential gains of meeting customer needs more exactly. Under these circumstances a company will decide to develop a single marketing mix for the whole market.

A company using an undifferentiated targeting strategy essentially adopts a mass market philosophy. It views the market as one big market with no individual segments. The company uses one marketing mix for the entire market and assumes that individual customers have similar needs that can be met with a common marketing mix.[1] The first company in an industry normally uses an undifferentiated targeting strategy. There is no competition at this stage and the company does not feel the need to tailor marketing mixes to the needs of market segments. Since there is no alternate offering, customers have to buy the pioneer's product. Ford Model T[2] is a classical example of the undifferentiated targeting strategy.

The primary benefit of this strategy lies in its lower cost. It reduces the cost of marketing research, production of marketing materials (advertising copies, brochures, direct mails, etc.) and media (television and radio air time, newspaper inserts, etc.).

Companies adopting this strategy have either been ignorant of differences among customers or have been arrogant enough to believe that their product will live up to expectations of all customers till some competitors invade the market with more appropriate product. Undifferentiated marketing usually generates lower response rates because it fails to connect sufficiently with the varying leisure needs and interests of different groups within a given population. The strategy is usually used for many basic commodities, such as salt or sugar. However, even those firms that offer salt and sugar now are trying to differentiate their products.

When market segmentation reveals several potential target segments that the company can serve profitably, specific marketing mixes can be developed to appeal to all or some of the segments. A differentiated marketing strategy attaches more importance to the differences between marketing segments by designing a specific marketing mix for each segment.

Conde Nast has more than 20 niche magazines focused on different aspects of life—from *Vogue* for fashionistas to *Bon Appetit* for foodies to *GQ* for fashion-conscious men to *The New Yorker* for literature lovers to *Golf Digest* for those who walk the links. [3]Another example is the car market which is most clearly segmented. There are segments for small cars, luxury cars, sports utility vehicles, etc. Most car makers like General Motors, Ford, Toyota, Honda and others offer cars for all the segments. Though Toyota entered the US market with small cars, it eventually chose to operate in most of the segments.

Firms embrace differentiated targeting because it has the potential to generate higher response levels among target markets, sales volume, higher profits, larger market share and economies of scale in manufacturing and marketing. Providing products or services that appeal to multiple segments helps diversify the business and therefore lowers the company's overall risk. Even if one magazine suffers a circulation decline, the impact on the firm's profitability can be offset by revenue from another publication that continues to do well. But a differentiated strategy is likely to be more costly for the firm in that it involves greater product design, production, promotion, inventory, marketing research and management cost, which are often significantly more expensive as more market segments are targeted. Another potential cost is cannibalization, which occurs when sales of a new product cut into sales of a firm's existing products. Anyway, it is possible to control cost, however, by reducing the number of segments targeted or by consolidating several segments into one. Another means to control cost is to refocus existing marketing materials from one segment to another, especially when minimal content alterations are feasible.

When an organization selects a single, primary target market and focuses all its energies on providing a product to fit that market's needs, it is using a concentrated targeting strategy. Newton Running[4], for instance, has concentrated its targeting strategy on runners—but not all runners, only those that seek to land on the forefoot. This design is thought to be more natural, efficient, and less injury producing than other more traditional running shoes. In comparison, although also known for running shoes, Nike uses a differentiated targeting strategy because it makes shoes for several segments including basketball, football, skateboarders, and provides the fashion-conscious with its subsidiary brand, Cole-Haan.

Companies have discovered that concentrating resources and meeting the needs of a narrowly defined market segment is more profitable than spreading resources over several different segments. Starbucks became successful by focusing exclusively on customers who wanted gourmet coffee products. The strategy is suited for companies with limited resources as these resources may be too stretched if it competes in many segments. Small firms often benefit from this strategy as focusing on one segment enables them to compete effectively against larger firms.

Companies following concentrated targeting strategies are obviously putting all their eggs in one basket. If their chosen segments were to become unprofitable or shrink in size, the companies will be in problem. Such companies also face problems when they want to move to some other segments, especially when they have been serving a segment for a long time. They become so strongly associated with serving a segment with a particular type of product or service, that the customers of other segments find it very difficult to associate with them.[5]

The downside of concentrated marketing is that there is higher risk associated with it. If the organization is unable to sustain a high level of performance serving the one target market it has selected, it has no other segments to fall back on as a safety net. Another risk factor is the possibility that the segment on which an organization has concentrated may change, become too small to support the organization, or even disappear.

When a firm tailors a product or service to suit an individual customer's wants or needs, it is undertaking an extreme form of segmentation called *micromarketing or one-to-one marketing*. Small producers and service providers generally can tailor their offering to individual customers more easily, whereas it is far more difficult for larger companies to achieve this degree of segmentation. Nonetheless, companies like Dell (computers) and Lands' End[6] (shirts) have capitalized on Internet technologies to offer custom products. Dell allows the customers to choose the size, color, parts, and the software included in their computer. Lands' End allows the customers to choose from a variety of options in the fabric, type of collar, sleeve, shape.

Unit 14　Target Marketing Strategy

　　The chief advantages of mass customization are twofold. First, customers who contact an organization provide most of the necessary information about themselves. Not only does this allow the organization to offer highly personalized responses, but it also reduces marketing research costs. Second, production costs are reduced because the organization can operate "on demand", that is, providing a product or service in response to customer demand rather than stockpiling merchandise.

　　In some markets, the requirements of individual customers are unique and their purchasing power is sufficient to make designing a separate marketing mix. Many service providers such as marketing research firms, architects and solicitors vary their offerings on a customer to customer basis.

　　The decision of marketing strategy depends on several factors.

　　● Limited organizational resources suggest a *concentrated strategy* will be the most efficient. The organization will probably not have adequate resources to target several different segments, while an undifferentiated strategy will probably not generate a sufficient response.

　　● A homogeneous market—one in which leisure needs and interests are widely shared—allows an organization to implement an *undifferentiated strategy* with fair prospects for success. There would be little sense in developing a differentiated or concentrated strategy for such a market.[7]

　　● Organizations facing a market in which its competitors are already well established in several segments should probably follow a *differentiated strategy* by targeting those remaining segments in which its competitors are not so strongly present.

　　● Any organization wishing to follow a *concentrated strategy* should carefully consider the following before becoming overly committed: whether that segment can sustain the organization's current level of activity and future growth, what is required to be successful in delivering products and services to that segment, and whether the organization has the capacity to perform at the required level.

 Vocabulary

segment　*v.* 细分，划分	forefoot　*n.* 前足，前脚
alternatively　*adv.* 轮流地，交替地	fashion-conscious　*adj.* 赶时髦的，追逐时尚的
fashionista　*n.* 赶时髦的人	
foodie　*n.* 美食家	downside　*n.* 缺点
embrace　*v.* 欣然接受，支持	twofold　*adj.* 双重的
offset　*v.* 抵消，补偿	overly　*adv.* 过度地，过分地

Phrases and Expressions

undifferentiated targeting strategy 无差异性营销	期望
differentiated targeting strategy 差异性营销	response rate 反应率
concentrated targeting strategy 集中性营销	leisure need 休闲需求
micro-marketing 微观营销	cut into 削减
one-to-one marketing 一对一营销	subsidiary brand 副品牌
tailor ... to ... 调整使适应	spread over 分散
advertising copy 广告稿，广告文案	gourmet coffee 极品咖啡
air time 广播时间	put all one's eggs in one basket 孤注一掷
newspaper insert 报纸插页	fall back on 依赖，依靠
be ignorant of 不知道	safety net 安全网
live up to expectation of 不辜负……的	in response to 响应，回应
	stockpiling merchandise 储备商品
	homogeneous market 同质市场

Notes

1. The company uses one marketing mix for the entire market and assumes that individual customers have similar needs that can be met with a common marketing mix. 公司针对整个市场都采用一种营销组合，认为顾客们的需求是相似的，同样的营销组合就能满足他们的这些需求。
   在本句中，谓语动词 assume 后面跟的是 that 引导的宾语从句，在从句中 needs 后面使用了 that 引导的定语从句，that 在定语从句中作主语。

2. Ford Model T：福特 T 型车诞生于 1908 年 9 月 27 日，它的面世使 1908 年成为工业史上具有重要意义的一年：T 型车以其低廉的价格使汽车作为一种实用工具走入了寻常百姓之家，美国亦自此成为了"车轮上的国度"。福特汽车公司生产的大多数 T 型车都是黑色的，创始人亨利·福特相信 T 型车是每个人都需要的，并拒绝他人的改进建议，而此时他的竞争对手正在以更低的价格生产更加舒适、外观新颖的汽车，T 型车不断丢失市场份额，最终其销量在 1927 年被雪佛兰公司超越。福特汽车公司不得不在 1927 年 5 月 26 日将 T 型车停产，全面投向 A 型车的生产。

3. Conde Nast has more than 20 niche magazines focused on different aspects of life—from *Vogue* for fashionistas to *Bon Appetit* for foodies to *GQ* for fashion-conscious men to *The New Yorker* for literature lovers to *Golf Digest* for those who walk the links. 康泰纳仕集团旗下有 20 多种杂志，着眼于生活的方方面面——从时髦人士的《时尚》、美食家的《美食》、时尚男士的《智族》、文学爱好者的《纽约客》，到高尔夫球爱好者的《高尔夫球辑要》。

   Conde Nast：康泰纳仕集团素以出版最精美和最具影响力的杂志而闻名于世，对内容原创性及卓越品质的一贯追求，使该集团在杂志界居领先地位长达百年之久。时至今日，康泰纳仕集团继续秉承着自身的高标准，致力于革新。旗下最著名的杂志有：《时尚》是时尚杂志，收录时尚、生活与设计的相关内容，创办于 1892 年，现发行于 18 个国家，每月一刊；《美食》是美国主流的美食、烹饪、生活杂志，其名字来自法语，Bon Appetit 意为"祝您好胃口"；《智族》是一本男性月刊，内容着重于男性的时尚、风格、文化，也包括美食、电影、健身、音乐、旅游、运动、科技的文章，作为当前世界排名第一、最具影响力的男性时尚杂志，以精美的制作、深入的报道，超越国内其他男刊，在广告商及读者群中获得了极高的信任度及美誉度，对中国精英男性的生活产生了广泛而深刻的影响。然而"GQ"这个词，今天已经成为日常生活中的语汇了，代表穿着打扮考究、有品位的一类男人；《纽约客》也译作《纽约人》，是一份美国知识、文艺类的综合杂志，内容覆盖新闻报道、文艺评论、散文、漫画、诗歌、小说，以及纽约文化生活活动向等；《高尔夫球辑要》主要介绍高尔夫球及其训练要点，报道国际赛事、运动员和教练员的情况。

4. Newton Running：牛顿跑鞋是美国著名的专业跑鞋品牌，其设计师成立了独立的实验室，潜心研究多年，完美地运用牛顿力学原理，使牛顿跑鞋成为备受美国专业运动员追捧的专业跑鞋。

5. They become so strongly associated with serving a segment with a particular type of product or service, that the customers of other segments find it very difficult to associate with them. 他们为某一细分市场提供特定的产品或者服务，与之联系密切，这样一来其他细分市场的顾客就会觉得与这些公司之间没有什么联系。

   本句主要使用了 so ... that ... 的句型，so 后面的第一个 with 是短语 become associated with 的一部分，第二个 with 则是 serve ... with 的一部分。that 后面的句子中使用了 it 作形式宾语，真正的宾语是句尾的不定式 to associate with them。

6. Lands' End：兰兹角是一家服装、箱包和日用百货领域内的老牌零售商，公司早在 1995 年就展开了互联网战略，当时有大约 100 种商品，其后，该公司的网站逐渐提供了下列服务：实时的、个性化的交互式导购员，以及"大家一起购物"系统（能够使不同地点的顾客在网上交谈）和购物广告。这些技术和服务，进一步扩展了消费者的购物体验，网站上在线的导购专家可以通过网上聊天的方式帮助你找到自己想要的商品。

7. There would be little sense in developing a differentiated or concentrated strategy for such a market. 在这样的市场上采用差异性营销或者集中性营销是没有什么意义的。

   在本句中，sense 的意思是"意义，好处"，例如：

There's little sense in trying to outspend a competitor with a much larger service factory. 试图比竞争对手花更多的钱建一个大得多的维修厂没有什么意义。

I Answer the following questions according to the text.

1. What do managers have to consider while selecting their target markets?
2. What are the generally recognized target marketing strategies?
3. When will companies adopt undifferentiated targeting strategy?
4. What are the merits and demerits of undifferentiated targeting strategy?
5. When will companies adopt differentiated targeting strategy?
6. What are the main disadvantages of differentiated targeting strategy? What measures can be taken to tackle the problem?
7. When will companies adopt concentrated targeting strategy?
8. What are the risks connected with concentrated targeting strategy?
9. When will micromarketing become popular with companies?

II Decide whether the following statements are true or false.

1. Of all the four target marketing strategies, differentiated targeting strategy is the most popular one.
2. The undifferentiated targeting strategy attaches more importance to similarities instead of differences of customers in target markets.
3. Undifferentiated marketing usually generates lower response rates in that there are fewer customers at the early stage of the target market.
4. It's highly advisable for companies with such basic commodities as salt and sugar to adopt undifferentiated targeting strategy.
5. Nike adopts concentrated targeting strategy while Newton Running favors differentiated targeting strategy.
6. Conde Nast became successful by focusing exclusively on customers who favor its products.
7. If companies are so strongly associated with a particular type of product or service, that it's hard for them to expand scope of business.
8. Despite the higher marketing research costs, micromarketing reduces lower products costs.

Unit 14 Target Marketing Strategy

9. The decision of marketing strategy mostly depends on the number of competitors in the market.

III Fill in each blank with the proper form of the word in the bracket.

1. This is an _____ (exclusively) agency for the sale of Ford cars in the town.
2. The two methods can be used _____ (alternate).
3. They're used to _____ (stretch) their budgets.
4. It's far better than vegetarian _____ (offer) in other restaurants.
5. The negotiation drafted by your team is _____ (feasible) in operation and will end up in failure.
6. The future of the company will depend crucially on how consumers _____ (response).
7. We must _____ (concentrated) our efforts on finding ways to reduce costs.
8. Their wage increases would be _____ (offset) by higher prices.
9. The increase of media choices, especially the Internet, threatens to _____ (cannibalization) the readership of newspapers.
10. _____ (segment) of the market allows the bank to tailor its approach to the customers' requirement.

IV Fill in each blank with a proper preposition.

1. He interviewed the young man in response _____ Mary's request.
2. This marketing strategy has cut _____ sales of some existing products.
3. This course is spread _____ fifteen weeks.
4. You can always fall back _____ him when you are in difficulties.
5. They tried to tailor their products _____ the needs of their potential customers.
6. This company seeks _____ the needs of individual customers.
7. There's no sense _____ pretending that nothing has happened.
8. _____ this reason, it is unlikely that many such engines were built.
9. It's hard to say _____ this stage how the market will develop.
10. His request is unreasonable _____ that he knows we can't afford it.

V Fill in the blanks with the words and phrases given below. Change the form where necessary.

ignorant of	live up to expectations of	fall back on
tailor ... to ...	have the capacity to do sth.	associate with
downside	put all one's eggs in one basket	consolidate
embrace		

1. Only by so doing could they _____ the company.
2. We are still _____ the causes of the disease.
3. The new policy has been _____ by all the departments of the company.
4. IBM, which _____ some operations last summer, has made clear that it needs to continue to streamline them.
5. With proper marketing strategy, the firm _____ meet needs of potential customers.
6. To buy stock in a single company is _____.
7. They were trying to _____ their strategy _____ the varying market.
8. I haven't _____ the project over the last year.
9. The _____ of this approach is a lack of clear leadership.
10. You can always _____ him when you are in difficulties.

VI Cloze.

Undifferentiated targeting occurs 1_____ the marketer ignores the apparent segment differences that exist 2_____ the market. The marketing strategy is intended to 3_____ to as many people as possible. In essence, the market is viewed 4_____ a homogeneous aggregate. Traditionally, undifferentiated marketing (also known as "mass marketing") has focused on radio, television, and newspapers as the medium used to 5_____ this broad audience. By reaching the largest audience possible, 6_____ to the product is maximized. In theory, this is closely related to a 7_____ number of sales. It is the technique of trying to spread our marketing message to anyone that is 8_____ to listen. A truckload of general advertising is done to the mass market in the hope that some of them will hit a 9_____. It 10_____ us to reach a wide range of services to take any job that comes on our way.

For certain types of widely 11_____ items, the undifferentiated market approach makes the most 12_____. For example, toothpaste isn't made 13_____ for one consumer, and it is sold in huge quantities. A company or individual who manufactures toothpaste wishes to get more people to buy their particular brand over 14_____. The goal is that when a consumer has the 15_____ to select a tube of toothpaste, he would remember the product that was marketed. 16_____ through any supermarket, and you will observe hundreds of food products that are perceived as nearly 17_____ by the consumer and are treated 18_____ by the producer, especially generic items. Many mass marketed items are considered staple items. These are items people 19_____ new when their old ones wear 20_____.

1. A. where   B. when   C. which   D. /
2. A. outside   B. on   C. in   D. within
3. A. contribute   B. attribute   C. appeal   D. lead
4. A. like   B. seem   C. alike   D. as

Unit 14 Target Marketing Strategy

5. A. reach   B. arrive   C. get to   D. touch
6. A. inclination   B. exposure   C. guidance   D. approach
7. A. more   B. fewer   C. smaller   D. larger
8. A. willing   B. devoted   C. reluctant   D. eager
9. A. record   B. target   C. goal   D. success
10. A. encourages   B. sets   C. enables   D. urges
11. A. popular   B. produced   C. consumed   D. purchased
12. A. profits   B. progress   C. contribution   D. sense
13. A. extremely   B. particularly   C. specially   D. especially
14. A. another   B. the other   C. other   D. others
15. A. opportunity   B. option   C. ability   D. mood
16. A. Walking   B. Walk   C. Walked   D. Being walking
17. A. same   B. different   C. expensive   D. identical
18. A. such as   B. such that   C. as such   D. as to
19. A. used to buy   B. are used to buy C. are used to buying D. used to buying
20. A. out   B. away   C. down   D. off

VII Translation.

1. Understanding people's needs is an even more complex task today because technological and cultural advances in modern society have created a condition of market fragmentation.
2. Marketers select a target marketing strategy in which they divide the total market into different segments based on customer characteristics, select one or more segments, and develop products to meet the needs of those specific segments.
3. When marketers want to segment regional markets even more precisely, they sometimes combine geography with demographics by using a technique called geodemography.
4. Psychographic data are useful to understand differences among consumers who may be statistically similar to one another but whose needs and wants vary.
5. Ideally, marketers should be able to define segments so precisely that they can offer products and services that exactly meet the unique needs of each individual or firm.

 Extended Reading

Create Successful Marketing Strategy

Marketing strategy is defined by David Aaker as a process that can allow an organization to concentrate its resources on the optimal opportunities with the goals of increasing sales and achieving a sustainable competitive advantage. It allows you to use pathways and footholds that apply your limited marketing budget more effectively. Marketing strategy facilitates your ability to apply marketing money to the correct half of the Wanamaker equation—the half you are not wasting on audiences who do not value your message.

Creating a marketing strategy is vital for any business, without which your efforts to attract customers are likely to end up in failure. The focus of your strategy should be making sure that your products and services meet customers' needs and developing long-term and profitable relationships with those customers. To achieve this, you will need to create a flexible strategy that can respond to changes in customer perceptions and demands. It may also help you identify new markets that you can successfully target.

Effective marketing starts with a considered, well-informed marketing strategy. A good marketing strategy helps you define your vision, target your products and services to the people most likely to buy them, realize your mission and business goals, build a strong reputation for your products and outlines the steps you need to take to achieve these goals. Your marketing strategy affects the way you run your entire business, so it should be planned and developed in consultation with your team.

A marketing strategy sets the overall directions and goals for your marketing, and is therefore different from a marketing plan, which outlines the specific actions you will take to implement your marketing strategy. Your marketing strategy could be developed for the next few years, while your marketing plan usually describes tactics to be achieved in the current year.

One of the key elements of a successful marketing strategy is the acknowledgement that your existing and potential customers will fall into particular groups or segments, characterized by their needs. The focus of your strategy should be identifying these groups and their needs through market research, and then addressing them more successfully than your competitors.

You can then create a marketing strategy that makes the most of your strengths and matches them to the needs of the potential customers. For example, if a particular group of customers is looking for quality first and foremost, then any marketing activity aimed at them should draw attention to the high quality service you can provide.

Once this has been completed, decide on the best marketing activity that will ensure your target market know about the products or services you offer, and why they meet their needs. This could be achieved through various forms of advertising, exhibitions, Internet activity and by creating an effective "point of sale" strategy if you rely on others to actually sell your products. Limit your activities to those methods you think will work best, avoiding spreading your budget too thinly.

Once you have created and implemented your strategy, monitor its effectiveness and make any

Unit 14　Target Marketing Strategy

adjustments required to maintain its success, which is often overlooked. This control element not only helps you see how the strategy is performing in practice, but also helps inform your future marketing strategy. A simple device is to ask each new customer how they heard about your business.

There was a time back in the fifties when microwave ovens were first seriously marketed. They were marketed to women, but, women were afraid of them. Kitchens at the time were small and there was no room. More importantly, housewives thought that they were shirking their duties by using this new fangled gadget. At that time, women were expected to cook. Not to cook fast, but to slave over a hot oven. So some marketing gurus at the time came up with a creative idea. They sold microwaves to men. Men loved the technology so much, that they talked their wives into buying one. They were first used for defrosting, or reheating leftovers. They soon became a staple of modern culture, and forced their way into the lives of people.

With an understanding of your business' internal strengths and weaknesses and the external opportunities and threats, you can develop a strategy that plays to your own strengths and matches them to the emerging opportunities. You can also identify your weaknesses and try to minimize them.

The next step is to draw up a marketing plan to set out the specific actions to put that strategy into practice. The plan should be constantly reviewed so it can respond quickly to changes in customer needs and attitudes in your industry, and in the broader economic climate.

If you can choose the right combination of marketing across product, price, promotion, place and people, your marketing strategy is more likely to be a success.

Words and Expressions

pathway　*n.* 途径	in consultation with　与……磋商
considered　*adj.* 经过仔细考虑的	make the most of　最大限度地利用，充分利用
shirk　*v.* 逃避	
fangled　*adj.* 新款式的，流行的	first and foremost　首先
gadget　*n.* 小器具，小装置	make adjustment　调整
defrost　*v.* 除霜	slave over　辛苦地工作
leftover　*n.* 残羹剩饭	marketing guru　营销天才，营销大师
staple　*n.* 主要部分，重要内容	talk sb. into doing sth.　说服某人做某事
Wanamaker equation　沃纳梅克方程式	
end up in failure　以失败告终	force one's way into ...　挤进，强行通过

Comprehension

I Answer the following questions according to the passage.

1. What can be called marketing strategy?
2. What does "the correct half of the Wanamaker equation" refer to?
3. What is supposed to be the focus of the marketing strategy?
4. What are the characteristics of a good marketing strategy?
5. What is the difference between a marketing strategy and a marketing plan?
6. What are the key elements of a successful marketing strategy according to the passage?
7. Please illustrate the way managers make the most of their strengths and match them to the needs of the potential customers.
8. How can you make your potential customers know about the products or services you offer?
9. What is the purpose of the writer to mention the example of microwave ovens and microwaves?
10. Why should the marketing plan be constantly reviewed?

II Write "T" for true, and "F" for false.

1. With successful marketing strategy, companies can apply their limited marketing budget more effectively.
2. If customer perceptions and demands change, the marketing strategy should change accordingly.
3. The top executives are totally responsible for its planning and developing.
4. A marketing plan sets the overall directions and goals for your marketing, and is therefore different from a marketing strategy.
5. Companies are supposed to make full use of their strengths and make them in line with needs of customers.
6. A marketing strategy may be short-term or long-term, which depends on the needs of customers.
7. Women were thought to shirk their duties by using microwave ovens.
8. Finally some marketing gurus succeeded in forcing housewives to buy microwaves.
9. It's easy for companies to identify weaknesses and try to minimize them.
10. It's advisable to change your marketing plan to adapt to the changes in customer needs and attitudes in your industry.

Additional Terms

accessibility 可接近性
actionability 可行性
behavioral segmentation variable 行为细分变量
benefit segmentation 利益细分
competitive intensity/rivalry 竞争强度
competitor positioning 竞争性定位
deep segmentation variable 深度细分变量
demand variability 需求变动性
differentiability 差别性
geodemographic segmentation 地理人口细分
geographic segmentation variable 地理细分变量
image differentiation 形象差异化
fragmented market 分散型市场
loyalty segmentation 忠诚度细分
market attractiveness 市场吸引力
market failure 市场失灵
market profitability 市场收益率
measurability 可衡量性
perceptual mapping 知觉图
product line differentiation 产品线差异化
psychographic segmentation 消费心态细分
repositioning strategy 再定位策略
segment attractiveness 细分市场吸引力
segment profile 市场状况
segment size 细分市场规模
segment structural attractiveness 细分市场结构吸引力
segmentation variable 细分变量
service differentiation 服务差异化
user category 用户类别

Unit 15
Product Strategy

Small businesses can fail for various reasons, including the lack of necessary funding to sustain a company's stability, poor leadership of a management team, and an inadequate business plan. Another major reason behind a company's lack of success can be accounted for by commercial failure, the state at which a company's product experiences poor sales. In addition, entrepreneurs may have the tendency to assume that customers will want their products, and instead of investing their money in testing their business ideas, they end up spending a lot of money in advertising campaigns. [1]This common mistake is extremely risky and can eventually lead to bankruptcy.

Then what is a product? In marketing terms, marketers broadly define a product as a good, idea, method, information, object or service created as a result of a process and serves a need or satisfies a want. In short, a product is anything that can be offered to a market to satisfy a want or need. It has a combination of tangible and intangible attributes (benefits, features, functions, uses) that a seller offers a buyer for purchase. For example, a seller of a toothbrush not only offers the physical product but also the idea that the consumer will be improving the health of their teeth. From this definition, we can see that it includes both physical products and services. Therefore, we have to consider the product from the target customer's perspective. Like the cosmetic companies are combining chemicals to make lipsticks, vitamin manufacturers produce little pills, watch makers produce mechanical devices that keep time. They are basically enhancing their products for their target markets—as lipstick has become beauty and hope, vitamins become hope for a healthier life and watches become status symbols. A product is a bundle of physical, chemical and/or intangible attributes that have the potential to satisfy present and potential customer wants.[2]

Consumers often think that a product is simply the physical item that he or she buys. In order to actively explore the nature of a product further, let's consider it as three different products—the core product, the actual product, and finally the augmented product. This concept is known as the three levels of a product. The core product is not the tangible physical product. You can't touch it.

That's because the core product is the benefit of the product that makes it valuable to you. A benefit is what the product does for the customer. Customers buy benefits. So with the car example, the benefit is convenience, i.e., the ease at which you can go wherever you like, whenever you want to.[3] Another core benefit is speed since you can travel around very quickly. The actual product is the tangible, physical product. You can get some use out of it. Again with the car, it is the vehicle that you test drive, buy and then collect. You can touch it. The augmented product is the non-physical part of the product. It usually consists of lots of added value, for which you may or may not pay a premium. So when you buy a car, part of the augmented product would be the warranty, the customer service support offered by the car's manufacturer and any after-sales service. The augmented product is an important way to tailor the core or actual product to the needs of an individual customer. Often the augmented benefits of a product are the key determinant of whether a customer decides to buy. Many successful businesses really understand this. A great example was cosmetics leader Elizabeth Arden. She certainly knew what she was selling. It wasn't pots of cream and cosmetics, it was much more than that, she understood what her customers need. She ever said, "I don't sell cosmetics. Instead, I sell hope."

Therefore, product strategy involves more than producing a physical good or service.[4] It is a total product concept that includes decisions about package design, brand name, trademarks, warranties, guarantees, product image, and new-product development. Most business marketing directors will develop a clear and realistic product strategy before the launch of a new product into its intended market. Technology-based firms must choose from multiple strategies for developing the new and improved products that generate corporate growth.[5]

What is a successful product strategy? A successful product strategy is the use of a firm's product-related resources in such a way as to maximize growth and profitability opportunities. In reality, developing the product strategy is one of the toughest challenges that companies face. Product Strategy is perhaps the most important function of a company. It is developed and written by the organization's marketing team, and requires final approval by the chief executive officer . It begins with a strategic vision that states where a company wants to go, how it will get there, and why it will be successful.[6] It's said that it is like a roadmap, and like a roadmap it's useful only when you know where you are and where you want to go. Similar to making effective use of a map, you first need a destination, and then you can plan your route. Just as a business has a strategic vision of what it wants to be when it grows up, the product has its own strategy and destination. The product strategy enables the company to focus on a specific target market and feature set, instead of trying to be everything to everyone.

Therefore, the product strategy is of great importance to businesses. On the part of some product managers, however, they have mistaken ideas about the product strategy. Some consider a mission statement as the product strategy. A mission statement is a "big" thing—it's designed to show a company what they should be trying to accomplish right now. Your product is a much more focused item—it needs to have a smaller scope that fits your product. Some product managers who when asked what their product strategy was would talk about a list of goals for the year. Once again, this is a good thing to have, but it is most definitely not a product strategy. A list of goals for your product is too vague. Goals can be all over the map and although they may be a good thing to do, they don't clearly show the direction that you want to move your product in. Still other product managers attempt to use a resource plan as a product strategy. This never works out because a resource plan is simply too unfocused. It's a great way to make sure that you'll have everything that you need when you need it, but it doesn't tell you why you need them or even what they need to do once you have the resources. Hence, every product manager has the responsibility to create a strategy for their product. The key is to realize the fact that a product strategy is not a mission statement (too big), not a list of goals (too vague), nor is it a resource plan (too unfocused).

Instead, a product strategy is something that you create in three steps. The first is to determine the nature of the business challenge that your product is currently facing, the next is to create a policy that you can use to guide your product so that it will be at an advantage, and finally it's a set of actions that you can execute.

Products and consumer perceptions are variable, so changes in strategy may be required to better meet customer needs, technological developments, new laws and regulations, and the overall product life-cycle. By monitoring external conditions and shifting product development accordingly, a company can better target its consumers and learn to react to their needs. The major factors that can make a change in the product strategy are as follows.

- **Customer preferences**. Fluctuations in the cost of materials, and changing brand awareness are just a few of things that can lead to changes of consumer needs. Keeping close track of customer response to a product and taking their demands into consideration are important for maintaining market share.[7]

- **Technological advances**. A new technological development can result in a change in a product line in order to remain competitive. For example, fiber optic cables have replaced older cables in certain applications and many businesses have switched from main frame computers to personal computers. Being aware of these advances can help a business take the lead in a certain field.

- **Laws and regulations**. The implementation of new governmental regulations can cause certain products or manufacturing methods to be restricted, limiting their consumer appeal. Product development strategies must shift with the legal landscape.

- **Product life-cycles**. To preserve the rate of growth in profit and sales, many industrial companies decide to alter, discontinue, or replace older products with newer models or more recent upgrades. These changes are usually made periodically, allowing existing products that reach maturity or decline to be phased out or modified, thus retaining their appeal.[8]

Vocabulary

fund　*vt.* 资助，提供资金	multiple　*adj.* 多样的，多重的
inadequate　*adj.* 不足的，不充分的	mistaken　*adj.* 错误的
risky　*adj.* 危险的	unfocused　*adj.* 未聚焦的，没有重点的
bankruptcy　*n.* 破产	fluctuation　*n.* 浮动，变动
tangible　*adj.* 有形的	preserve　*vt.* 保留，保持
intangible　*adj.* 无形的	discontinue　*vt.* 停止
convenience　*n.* 便利	upgrade　*n.* 升级
guarantee　*n.* 担保，保证书	

Phrases and Expressions

physical product　物质产品	mission statement　公司宗旨
core product　核心产品	resource plan　资源计划
actual product　实体产品，实际产品	be at an advantage　处于优势
augmented product　扩大产品，附加产品	product life-cycle　产品生命周期
test drive　试驾	customer preference　消费者喜好
package design　包装设计	product line　产品线
new-product development　新产品开发	main frame computer　大型计算机
marketing team　营销团队	phase out　逐步淘汰
feature set　特色设置	

1. In addition, entrepreneurs may have the tendency to assume that customers will want their products, and instead of investing their money in testing their business ideas, they end up spending a lot of money in advertising campaigns.　此外，企业家们也许会认为，顾客会喜欢他们的产品，于是，他们不但没有为检验自己的商业想法进行投资，反而将巨资投入到广告宣传活动中。

在本句中，短语 have the tendency to do sth. 的意思是"往往会做某事"，例如：
He has a tendency to give up easily. 他经常很轻易地放弃。
当然，这一短语在实际运用过程中，也会有些变化形式，例如：
Prices continue to show an upward tendency. 物价继续呈上升的趋势。
此外，短语 invest in 的意思是"投资于……"，例如：
After market research, they decided to invest in children's toys. 在我们市场调查后，他们决定投资儿童玩具。

2. A product is a bundle of physical, chemical and/or intangible attributes that have the potential to satisfy present and potential customer wants. 因此，我们可以说产品是物理、化学和无形特性的组合，或者说是有形特性与无形特性的组合，该组合能够满足现有和潜在顾客的各种需求。
在本句中，that 引导了宾语从句，作动词 say 的宾语。第二个 that 引导了定语从句，修饰限定先行词 attributes，that 在从句中充当主语。短语 have the potential to do sth. 意思是"有做某事的潜力"，例如：
She has the potential to become a good entrepreneur. 她具备成为一名优秀企业家的潜力。
The boy has great potential. 这个男孩非常有潜力。

3. So with the car example, the benefit is convenience, i.e., the ease at which you can go wherever you like, whenever you want to. 以汽车为例，其优点就是便利，也就是说，有了汽车，你可以想去哪儿就去哪儿，想什么时候去就什么时候去。
在本句中，使用了介词前置的定语从句，关系代词 which 作引导词。短语 at ease 的意思是"安逸地，自由自在地"，例如：
He was more at ease in the office than on a platform. 他在讲台上不像在办公室里那样自在、无拘无束的。
此外，ease 还可以与 with 搭配，with ease 的意思是"轻易地，轻而易举地"，例如：
They gained the advertising campaign with ease. 他们轻而易举地就在广告宣传活动中获胜。

4. Therefore, product strategy involves more than producing a physical good or service. 因此，产品策略不仅是生产物质产品或者提供服务。
在本句中，involve 的意思是"涉及，牵涉"，后面一般跟名词或者 -ing 形式，例如：
Nicky's job as a public relations director involves spending quite a lot of time with other people. 作为公共关系主管，尼基需要花很多时间与别人打交道。
此外，短语 more than 的意思是"不仅是"，例如：
More than an opportunity, it's a great challenge for China to enter WTO. 中国加入世贸组织不仅是一种机遇，也是一种挑战。

5. Technology-based firms must choose from multiple strategies for developing the new and improved products that generate corporate growth. 技术型公司必须从众多策略中选择一种适合自己的策略，开发新的、改进的产品，以便促进公司的发展。

在本句中，that 引导的定语从句，修饰限定先行词 products，that 在从句中充当主语。technology-based 的意思是"技术型，科技型"，-based 的意思是"以……为基地的"，例如：a London-based company 一家驻伦敦的公司。

动词 generate 的意思是"产生，带来，引起"，例如：
In the 19th century waterpower was widely utilized to generate electricity. 19世纪人们大规模使用水力来发电。
New business we'll generate should far exceed what's lost. 我们新招揽的生意会远远超过丢失的那部分。
We need someone to generate new ideas. 我们需要有人出新主意。

6. It begins with a strategic vision that states where a company wants to go, how it will get there, and why it will be successful. 制订产品策略首先要有战略眼光，能够看出公司发展的趋势、发展的方式及成功的原因。

在本句中，that 引导的是定语从句，that 在从句中充当主语。其中 strategic vision 的意思是"战略眼光"，例如：
All business leaders tonight are outstanding achievers in your respective fields. You have a wealth of successful experiences and strategic vision. 今晚与会的各位企业家，都是你们所在行业的佼佼者，具有丰富的成功经验和战略眼光。

7. Keeping close track of customer response to a product and taking their demands into consideration are important for maintaining market share. 密切关注顾客对产品的反应，充分考虑他们的各种需求，这对于保持原有的市场份额是至关重要的。

在本句中，两个并列的-ing 短语作主语，看作复数。短语 keep track of 的意思是"记录，追踪，了解"，例如：
As a product manager, Brooks has to keep track of the latest developments in packaging design. 作为产品经理，布鲁克斯必须了解产品包装的最新发展动态。
此外，短语 take ... into consideration 的意思是"把……考虑在内"，例如：
Companies are supposed to take customers preferences into consideration. 公司应该把顾客的喜好考虑在内。

8. These changes are usually made periodically, allowing existing products that reach maturity or decline to be phased out or modified, thus retaining their appeal. 通常情况下，这些变化是周期性的，现有的产品如果已经处于成熟期或者衰退期，那么就会逐步被淘汰或者进行产品修正，这样就可以继续吸引顾客的眼球。

在本句中，主句使用了被动语态，后面使用了-ing 短语，该短语中包含一个 that 引导的定语从句，修饰限定先行词 products，其中使用了短语 allow ... to do，thus retaining their appeal 表示一种结果。

本句提到的 maturity 和 decline 是产品寿命周期的两个重要阶段，一般来讲，产品的寿命周期分为 4 个阶段，即引入期、成长期、成熟期、衰退期。

引入期：产品投入市场，处于试销阶段，销售额的年增长率一般低于10%。这时产品设计尚未定型，工艺不够稳定，生产批量小，成本高，用户对产品不太了解，竞争者少，一般没有利润，甚至发生亏损。本阶段的主要对策有：尽量缩短其时间长度，以减少经济损失；进一步加强产品设计和工艺流程；加强市场调查与预测、宣传与促销，努力增加销售额。

成长期：销售量迅速上升，销售额的年增长率一般在10%以上，产品设计、工艺基本定型，生产批量增大，成本降低，利润上升，市场出现竞争者。本阶段的主要对策有：加强综合计划，改进生产管理；适时进行技术改造，提高产品质量和生产能力；加强广告促销与售后服务，努力开拓市场。

成熟期：市场趋近饱和，销售量的年增长率一般为–10%～+10%，利润达到高峰，较多竞争者进入市场，竞争非常激烈。本阶段的主要对策在于努力提高产品竞争能力，扩大销售。采取措施改进产品质量，改进生产管理，加强广告、促销与技术服务，合理调整产品价格。

衰退期：新产品开始进入市场，逐渐取代老产品，销售量出现负增长，销售额的年增长率小于–10%，利润日益下降。本阶段的主要对策有：采取优惠价格、分期付款等方式促进销售；在保证经济性的前提下，设法延长产品寿命周期，如扩大产品用途、改善产品质量、降低产品价格、改进产品包装、改善技术服务；在适当时机果断地淘汰老产品，发展新产品，实现产品的更新换代。

I Answer the following questions according to the text.

1. Why do some small businesses fail?
2. What is a product? Give an example to illustrate the definition.
3. How can you understand that "A product is a bundle of physical, chemical and/or intangible attributes that have the potential to satisfy present and potential customer wants."?
4. What are the three levels of a product? Please illustrate them with examples.
5. What is the purpose of the writer to mention the example of Elizabeth Arden?
6. What does a product strategy include?
7. What can be called a successful product strategy?
8. What is the similarity between a product strategy and a roadmap?
9. What are the mistaken ideas about product strategies?
10. What are the major factors that can make a change in the product strategy?

Unit 15 Product Strategy

II Decide whether the following statements are true or false.

1. Commercial failure is the most important reason why small businesses fail.
2. A product can be anything that can satisfy customers' wants or needs.
3. Benefits, features, functions, uses are the tangible attributes of a product.
4. A product can be sold at the price of three different products.
5. The core benefits of a product are the key determinant of whether a customer decides to buy.
6. The product produced by the cosmetics leader Elizabeth Arden is not cosmetics but hope.
7. Product Strategy is definitely the most important function of a company.
8. The product strategy is like a roadmap to show your destination and route.
9. A mission statement is not focused than a product strategy.
10. Fluctuations in the cost of materials, and changing brand awareness are just a few of things that can lead to changes of consumer needs.

III Fill in each blank with the proper form of the word in the bracket.

1. Hopefully, present _____ (sustain) economic growth can be achieved without inflation.
2. People have been used to a _____ (stability) economic situation.
3. The company needs to maintain an _____ (inadequate) supply of trained workers.
4. The decision is a politically _____ (risk) one.
5. Years of mismanagement has left the company virtually _____ (bankruptcy).
6. The scheme will bring _____ (tangible) benefits to these firms.
7. Many people enjoy the pleasures and _____ (convenient) of living in a city center.
8. The annual sales are considered as one of the most important _____ (determine) for the bonus of each employee.
9. He was under the _____ (mistake) impression that his plan would succeed.
10. I'm afraid that the products have been _____ (continue).

IV Fill in each blank with a proper preposition.

1. A number of factors account _____ the failure of his product strategy.
2. They held a meeting to decide whether they could invest _____ glassware.
3. People gain valuable work experience and, _____ addition, employers can afford to employ them.
4. We entered into European market _____ relative ease.
5. The marketing team consists _____ 12 employees.
6. We failed to take all the factors _____ consideration.

7. Market research is _____ great help for marketers to make some decisions.
8. The fall in sales was due to a lack of judgment _____ his part.
9. His inefficiency resulted _____ his bankruptcy.
10. Things worked _____ pretty well in the end.

V Fill in the blanks with the words and phrases given below. Change the form where necessary.

| tailor | keep track of | phase out | have the tendency to | guarantee |
| fund | at an advantage | end up | potential | enable |

1. She _____ spending the night at a small hotel due to the fault of her business partner.
2. Products of high quality and low price _____ them to enjoy popularity both at home and abroad.
3. Over the following three years, the old system will be _____.
4. All our products are _____ to the needs of customers.
5. Even financial businesses in this small city _____ join in the globalization.
6. They put forward a system to _____ their expenses.
7. Our common goal is to maximize our _____ for economic growth.
8. She was _____ in the election of the new product manager because employees trust her.
9. That company is _____ research into new product design and packaging.
10. The government provides help for some small businesses, but it can't _____ their success.

VI Cloze.

Product strategy is a 1_____ component of the overall marketing strategy. The product itself guides decisions that a business 2_____ to achieve marketplace success. Research is used to 3_____ needs and desires of target customers to develop the product strategy. This is not limited 4_____ consumer products; it includes products for 5 _____ as well. In the trade, this is 6_____ as a B2B product strategy. 7_____ used B2B product strategies to identify special needs of business travelers, and 8_____ introduced business-class seating and loyalty rewards programs. Food manufacturers identify the existence of busy working parents to introduce a wide array of 9_____ complete meals and "heat and serve" food items.

Consumer-products manufacturers heavily 10_____ on strong product strategies. Because billions of dollars and market share are at stake, manufacturers of 11_____ recognized food and household-goods products will 12_____ millions in product development to introduce new brand variations. For example, the product strategy for a laundry detergent can be based on the 13_____ of a fragrance, a fabric-softener additive or use in cold water.

Unit 15 Product Strategy

Companies market products to 14 _____ the needs of targeted customers. They develop a "positioning" for the product to compete 15_____ other products and brands in the marketplace. 16_____ plays an important part in product strategy. In some 17_____, the distribution strategy may even determine the positioning. This is often used for direct-to-consumer products that are 18_____ as "not available in stores" or "as seen on TV", and 19_____ require mail or telephone ordering. In some instances, product strategies are based on price alone. Shoppers purchase items like toilet paper or canned foods 20_____ a lower cost, but also complete the rest of their shopping at the store. Membership-based or "club" stores are totally driven by a product-pricing strategy.

1. A. core   B. important   C. basic   D. elementary
2. A. has   B. made   C. makes   D. having
3. A. recognize   B. realize   C. assure   D. identify
4. A. within   B. towards   C. to   D. upon
5. A. individuals   B. businesses   C. groups   D. organizations
6. A. referred to   B. referred   C. think of   D. thought
7. A. Companies   B. Businesses   C. Managers   D. Airlines
8. A. therefore   B. accordingly   C. subsequently   D. adequately
9. A. frozen   B. delicious   C. cold   D. inexpensive
10. A. base   B. rest   C. carry   D. depend
11. A. internationally B. nationally C. locally   D. globally
12. A. cost   B. spend   C. pay   D. take
13. A. collection   B. increase   C. addition   D. demonstration
14. A. recognize   B. investigate   C. understand   D. meet
15. A. against   B. with   C. for   D. on
16. A. Promotion   B. Distribution   C. Production   D. Design
17. A. conditions   B. situations   C. firms   D. cases
18. A. regarded   B. considered   C. advertised   D. taken
19. A. /   B. which   C. what   D. that
20. A. at   B. for   C. with   D. on

VII Translation.

1. Product modification involves altering a product's characteristic, such as its quality, performance, or appearance, to try to increase the product sales.
2. This section describes the role of the product manager who is usually responsible for this, and analyzes three ways to manage a product through its life cycle: modifying the product, modifying the market, and repositioning the product.

3. Trading down often exists when companies engage in downsizing—reducing the content of packages without changing package size and maintaining or increasing the package price.
4. Brand equity resides in the minds of consumers and results from what they have learned, felt, seen, and heard about a brand over time.
5. A company may use private branding, often called private labeling or reseller branding, when it manufactures products but sells them under the brand name of a wholesaler or retailer.

Extended Reading

Product and Business Strategies

There's a sore spot at many companies, and it's painfully evident in some of these businesses. What is this problem? Actually that has to do with the fact that many companies can't accurately articulate the differences between business strategy and product strategy. When asked where the business strategy is, the senior executives always show a blank look. The team wants to make more money so these are the features they want to add, or so their reasoning goes. Sadly, being able to do so is of utmost significance to them. Many—maybe even most—companies confuse the two. In other cases, they just combine the two until you can't discern either. What is the result of this misunderstanding? Poorly understood strategies.

A business strategy typically is a document that articulates the direction a business will pursue and the steps it will take to achieve its goals. In a standard business plan, the business strategy results from goals established to support the stated mission of the business. Business strategy is to identify your business objectives and decide where to invest to best achieve those objectives. For example, moving from a direct sales model (your own sales force selling directly to customers) to an online sales model (your customers buy from your site) is a business strategy. Deciding whether to charge for your services with subscriptions or transactions fees or whether you have an advertising-based revenue model is a business strategy. Deciding to move into an adjacent market is a business strategy.

Now, obviously there are some big product implications to each of these business strategies. But they are not one in the same. There are lots of ways to sell online, lots of ways to develop or acquire and integrate an adjacent offering. The product strategy speaks to how you hope to deliver on the business strategy.

Moreover, while the business may believe something is a great business opportunity, you don't yet know if your company can successfully take advantage of this opportunity. Maybe it will cost too much to build. Maybe customers won't value it enough to pay for it. Maybe it'll be too complicated for users to deal with. This is where product strategy comes into play.

Take Amazon as an example. They've got investments including their core e-commerce offerings by category, they've got third-party selling, they've got an infrastructure technology (cloud computing) business, and they've even got their own growing consumer electronics business. Amazon sets a good example because it illustrates so many points of good business strategies and good product strategies.

Amazon may have made their business in selling hardcopy books and they've been a great innovator there, but instead of spending all their time trying to protect that business, they've also got an investment that could one day change that entire business. To Amazon's credit, they realize that if they don't pursue this someone else probably will. Similarly, they have worked hard to create new technologies to allow them to provide a different e-commerce customer experience, yet they also have been leaders in making that technology available to others, because it's possible that cloud computing business will one day be even larger than what they can ever do themselves as an online retailer.

That's a business strategy and you can see their portfolio planning. Now each of these businesses has one or more product strategies. As an Amazon user you can see the evolution of the e-commerce retailing business. You can also see the evolution of the Amazon web services product line; every few months another piece of the puzzle is launched. You can see the evolution of electronic reader and supporting technologies.

So business owners and senior executives are responsible for the business strategy and the business portfolio planning, and the product organization, especially the directors of product management are responsible for the product strategy and the product portfolio planning. Keep these two concepts straight and you will have more understanding in terms of objectives and responsibilities, as well as better managed business and product portfolios. By setting your product and business strategies separately, you'll be better positioned to achieve both.

Words and Expressions

painfully *adv.* 痛苦地	launch *v.* 发起，发动
articulate *v.* 清晰地说出	business strategy 商业策略，经营策略
reasoning *n.* 推理	sore spot 痛处
sadly *adv.* 伤心地	be of utmost significance to 对……至关重要
discern *n.* 分辨，辨别	take ... as an example 以……为例
adjacent *adj.* 邻近的，毗邻的	third-party selling 第三方销售
innovator *n.* 创新者	infrastructure technology 基本设施技术
pursue *v.* 追求	hardcopy book 纸质版图书
portfolio *n.* 投资组合	

cloud computing 云计算	business portfolio planning 业务组合规划
to one's credit 值得赞扬的是	
online retailer 在线零售商	product portfolio planning 产品组合规划

Comprehension

I Answer the following questions according to the passage.

1. What is the problem that troubles many companies?
2. What effect does it have on companies?
3. What is a business strategy?
4. What is the relationship between business strategy and product strategy?
5. What is the purpose of the writer to mention the example of Amazon?
6. What did Amazon do to change the entire business?
7. What is the importance of keeping the two concepts straight?

II Write "T" for true, and "F" for false.

1. In many companies, there is a place that makes everyone sad.
2. All the companies can not tell the differences between business strategy and product strategy.
3. Asked where the business strategy is, the senior executives always demonstrate their indifference.
4. Companies confuse the two concepts because they are not important.
5. Deciding to move into an adjacent market is a product strategy.
6. Business strategy has nothing to do with product strategy.
7. Amazon is such a great innovator that it shifted its business strategy to change even that entire business.
8. Business owners and senior executives are responsible for both the business strategy and product strategy.
9. Setting your product and business strategies separately, you'll find a better position in the market.
10. Amazon is the most successful company with its business strategy.

Unit 15　Product Strategy

Additional Terms

assembly product　组合产品	product characteristic　产品特性
brand equity　品牌资产	product form　产品形态
brand licensing　品牌许可	product concept testing　产品概念测试
brand personality　品牌个性	product development strategy　产品开发策略
branding　品牌化	
business analysis　商业分析	product extension strategy　产品延伸策略
capital item　资本品	
commercialization　商业化	product item　产品项目
consumer product　消费品	product level　产品层次
convenience product　便利品	product line extension　产品线扩展
core benefit　核心利益	product management　产品管理
corporate branding　公司品牌	product mixing　产品组合
customer mentality　消费者心理	product mix depth　产品组合深度
durable goods　耐用品	product mix length　产品组合长度
expected product　期望产品	product modification strategy　产品调整策略
family branding　家族品牌	
generic product　一般产品	product portfolio　组合产品
industrial product　工业品	product portfolio matrix　产品组合矩阵
line extension　产品线拓展	product specification　产品规格
mixed branding　混合品牌	product upgrade　产品升级
multibranding　多品牌	shopping product　选购品
multiproduct branding　多产品统一品牌	specialty product　特殊品
organization marketing　组织营销	test marketing　试销，试售
place marketing　地点营销	trading down　价值降级
potential product　潜在产品	trading up　价值升级
private branding　自有品牌	unsought product　非渴求品
product-based organization　产品型组织	venture team　风险团队

Unit 16
Pricing Strategy

A price is the amount of money, goods, or services that must be given to acquire ownership or use of a product. It is only one of four elements of the marketing mix (along with the other three: product, promotion and place), however, it is the only element of the mix that provides revenue, the other elements are costs (there is cost in building your product or service, promoting it, and placing or distributing it). Pricing is an important strategic issue because it is related to product positioning. It affects other marketing mix elements such as product features, channel decisions and promotion. In addition, it influences how much of a product consumers or organizations purchase. In general, potential customers look for a price that reflects the benefits they think they will receive from the product. They also consider the price of the product relative to that of competitive offerings.[1] Price also influences whether selling the product will be profitable for the organization. What's more, intense price competition for materials and services, more sophisticated customers and less predictability all require a feasible and effective pricing strategy to sustain profitability.

Unfortunately, pricing strategy is often neglected by managers. There are three reasons behind this practice. Firstly, it is hard to do; secondly, managers often believe prices are set by competition and the marketplace, and are not in their hands; finally there is a lot of pressure to justify pricing decisions.[2]

Saturn[3], a division of GM founded in the 1980s, was a brand new concept in car marketing in the United States. It was also an effort by the largest car company in the United States: General Motors. The real innovation came in labor and management relations and "no-haggle" value pricing which contributed to superior quality and high rate of customer satisfaction.[4] It gave employees more say in how they did their jobs.[5] Saturn's success indicates that a high-quality product and a good pricing strategy are important to success in marketing a product.

To select the most profitable price, the marketers must know how much potential customers will buy at various prices. Generally speaking, the lower the price of a product, the greater the demand for it. Each product has its own demand curve, and must follow the general pattern of sloping downward. In other words, when the seller changes the price of a product, the amount demanded also changes. In reality, the marketers don't know what the demand will be at each possible price for certainty; rather, they make estimates. Their estimates are based on demographic and psychological factors of their target markets and on estimates of how sensitive sales of the product are to its price.[6] These demand factors influence the shape of the demand curve for a particular product. Take the auto industry as an example. Demographic data show that car prices have been rising much faster than consumers' incomes. Psychological data suggest that consumers are more likely to look for a low price and unwilling to assume the risks that accompany haggling with a car dealer. Car makers are responding with "value" prices—single, no-hassle prices on models equipped with a generous package of options. List prices for those packages are lower than before, but basic models are no longer available, leading to a slight boost in the overall prices paid. The third basis for estimating demand is the product's price elasticity, a measure of the sensitivity of demand to changes in price. In general, for a product with elastic demand, total revenue increases when the product's prices declines. If a product has inelastic demand, total revenue increases when the product's price increases.

Marketers in practice approach the pricing decision in various ways. These approaches are based on cost, profit, competition, and customer perception. Moreover, these approaches are not mutually exclusive. Actually, the marketers can benefit from considering all of them: the minimum charge to cover costs and earn a profit, an amount that matches or beats competitors' prices, and an amount that equals customers' perceptions of what the product is worth. The Vermont grocery store is a good case in point. Its owner once told one of his suppliers' salespeople, "What you charge tells me how low I can go. What my competitor sets prices at is how high I can go. I just pick a place in between, and that's my price."

- **Pricing based on cost**

As a general rule, the price of a product must be high enough to cover the total cost of product. The total cost includes fixed and variable costs. Fixed costs are the expenses that remain the same over a wide range of quantities. Variable costs are the costs that change along with changes in quantity. For instance, materials and labor costs are greater when the organization produces or sells more goods or services.

The markup pricing or cost-plus pricing is the way marketers add a percentage to the product's cost in order to arrive at the selling price. For example, your widgets cost $20 in raw materials and production costs, and at current sales volume (or anticipated initial sales volume), your fixed costs come to $30 per unit. Your total cost is $50 per unit. You decide that you want to operate at a 20% markup, so you add $10 (20%×$50) to the cost and come up with a price of $60 per unit. So long as you have your costs calculated correctly and have accurately predicted your sales volume, you will always be operating at a profit. An advantage of this approach is that the business will know that its costs are being covered. The main disadvantage is that cost-plus pricing may lead to products that are priced un-competitively.

A variation of cost-based pricing commonly used by marketers is rate-of-return pricing. It involves determining total costs, then adding a desired rate of return on the investment to produce the product. The marketers may add a percentage return or a particular dollar amount.

Cost-based pricing is relatively easy to use, which makes it popular among sellers who handle many different products. Anyway, the marketers must be aware of the limitations. This technique does not consider the effect of price on demand. Suppose the price and the profit are so high enough to cover costs that buyers turn to competing products. If sales are lower than expected, profits may suffer as well. In addition, this method also fails to take into consideration what competitors are charging.

- **Pricing based on profit**

Of course, for a business to prosper, it has to think beyond its costs to its profits. A logical way of pricing based on profit is to identify the point at which profits will be the greatest. One technique is breakeven analysis, which is to identify the sales volume at the price needed to cover cost. The level of sales at which total revenues equal total costs is called the breakeven point. Of course, the marketer doesn't want merely to cover costs; the price should also be set at a level that will generate a profit. Therefore, the marketer adds the desired level of profits to the total fixed costs.

- **Pricing based on competition**

Marketers also must take the competition into account when setting prices. They must be able to meet competitors' prices or show why their own product is worth more. There are four basic approaches to setting prices relative to the competition.

1. **Follow-the-leader pricing.** It means following any price changes made by the industry leaders. For example, when one marketer raises or lowers prices, the others follow suit.

2. **Adaptive pricing.** It refers to a relatively small competitor responding to any price changes made by competitors with large market share. It doesn't necessarily mean that the marketer may precisely match competitors' price changes, but he does alter its prices to adapt to them to some extent.[7]

3. **Opportunistic pricing.** Marketers use this approach to attract customers by pricing their products lower than competing goods or services. To do this, they may make price cuts, or they may avoid raising prices when competitors do so.

4. **Predatory pricing.** It means setting process at very low levels to hurt competitors. However, when the intent of predatory pricing is to drive competitors out of business, it is illegal.

Of course, as conditions change, marketers may move from one pricing approach to another.

- **Pricing based on customer perception**

No matter what the costs, no matter what competitors are charging, potential buyers may not buy the product if they don't think they are getting their money's worth. Therefore, pricing decisions should take into consideration customer perception of the product. Marketers of consumer goods do so when they use demand-backward pricing, which involves setting a price by starting with the estimated price consumers will pay and working backward with retail and wholesale margins.[8] Compaq [9]always uses this approach for its computer. The marketer starts with the list price consumers will be likely to pay. Then the marketer subtracts the markups that the resellers of these products take. The result is the manufacturers' selling price.

Most potential customers are looking for value, the ratio of perceived benefits to price. Therefore, marketers may adopt value pricing. It means setting the price so that the product's value is higher than the value of competing products. With this strategy, the marketer may promote high perceived benefits of the product, or the strategy may emphasize both high benefits and low price. Anyway, sometimes high-priced products are perceived as having greater quality. In other words, setting the price too low may lead customers to conclude that the product offers relatively few benefits, so that its value is also low. Therefore, marketers must conduct market research.

Pricing is a tricky business. You're certainly entitled to make a fair profit on your product, and even a substantial one if you create value for your customers. But remember, something is ultimately worth only what someone is willing to pay for it.

Vocabulary

predictability	n. 可预测性	un-competitively	adv. 没有竞争力地
haggle	n. 讨价还价	prosper	v. 繁荣，发展
accompany	v. 陪伴，伴随	subtract	v. 减去
markup	n.（在成本的基础上）加价	tricky	adj.（形势、工作等）复杂的；微妙的
widget	n. 小器具		

Phrases and Expressions

product feature	产品特点	fixed cost	固定成本
channel decision	渠道决策	variable cost	可变成本
make estimate	预测，推测	selling price	卖价
assume risk	承担风险	total revenue	收入总额
list price	定价，价目表中所列的价格	cost-based pricing	成本导向定价法
price elasticity	价格弹性	markup pricing	加成定价
total cost	总成本	sales volume	销售量

wholesale margin 批发价格限度	follow-the-leader pricing 追随领袖定价法
retail margin 零售价格限度	adaptive pricing 动态定价法
rate-of-return pricing 收益报酬率定价法	opportunistic pricing 机会主义定价法
return on investment 投资回报率	predatory pricing 掠夺性定价法
breakeven analysis 盈亏平衡分析	follow suit 效仿
breakeven point 盈亏平衡点	customer perception 顾客感知
make price cut 降低价格	value pricing 价值定价法
competitive environment 竞争环境	be entitled to do sth. 授权某人做某事

1. They also consider the price of the product relative to that of competitive offerings. 他们还会将产品价格与竞争对手的价格进行比较。
   在本句中，指示代词 that 用来指代上文提到的可数名词 the price，这样可以避免重复。同样 that 还可以指代上文提到的不可数名词；而 those 可以用来指代上文提到的名词复数。例如：
   The quality of our product is much higher than that of your product. 我们的产品质量远远优于你们的产品质量。
   The managers active in pricing strategy are more likely to succeed than those unwilling to engage themselves in this issue. 积极参与制订定价策略的经理比那些不愿意参与此事的经理成功率要大。

2. Firstly, it is hard to do; secondly, managers often believe prices are set by competition and the marketplace, and are not in their hands; finally there is a lot of pressure to justify pricing decisions. 首先，定价策略是很难制定的；其次，经理们总是认为价格是由竞争和市场来决定的，他们是无法加以控制的；最后，压力重重，很难做出正确的决策。
   在本句中，justify 的意思是"认为合理，辩解"，例如：
   It was becoming increasingly difficult to justify such expenditure. 越来越难以为这样一大笔开销做出解释了。

3. 20 世纪 70 年代日本轿车大举进军美国，再加上石油危机等其他因素，美国汽车，特别是大排量的汽车，在本土的销售受到了极大冲击。为了夺回市场，通用汽车公司决定另辟新的生产和销售汽车的途径，与日本车决一高低。1985 年，通用汽车公司决定新建土星（Saturn）分部，试图开发先进的土星牌轿车以抵御外国轿车大规模进入美国市场。在远离汽车城的田纳西州，通用汽车公司在 20 世纪 80 年代中期决定投资 35 亿美元启动"土星计划"，成立一个全新的、享有高度自治的子公司——土星公司。土星是通用汽车公司最年轻的品牌，打造土星的初衷就是抵御外国车进入美国市场，它必然要在外观上和性能上有所创新，在价格上有优势。至 1993 年，土星车挤进了美国汽车市场十大畅销车型，美国人喜欢这个牌子的汽车。土星车成为汽车历史上最为辉煌的成就之一。

4. The real innovation came in labor and management relations and "no-haggle" value pricing which contributed to superior quality and high rate of customer satisfaction. 该公司真正的创新之处在于，侧重工人与管理层之间的关系，采用"不议价"的价值定位策略，这样保证了汽车的质量，顾客的满意度也很高。

在本句中，which 引导的定语从句用来修饰限定先行词 relations 和 value pricing，which 在从句中充当主语。短语 contribute to 的意思是"有助于"，例如：

His carelessness contributed to the failure of the pricing method. 他一时疏忽，定价策略失败了。

5. It gave employees more say in how they did their jobs. 工人在工作时享有很大的发言权。

在本句中，how 引导的是宾语从句，作介词 in 的宾语。短语 give sb. a say in sth. 的意思是"某人在做某事时有发言权"，say 的意思是"发言权"，例如：

The board made the decision. We have no say in this matter. 这是董事会做出的决定，我们没有发言权。

6. Their estimates are based on demographic and psychological factors of their target markets and on estimates of how sensitive sales of the product are to its price. 他们根据目标市场的人口和心理因素，以及产品销售量对于价格变化的敏感性来进行推测。

本句中 and 连接了两个并列句，句子的谓语动词使用的是 be based on（以……为根据），how 引导的是宾语从句，作介词 of 的宾语。后面的短语 be sensitive to 的意思是"对……敏感"，例如：

He takes his work seriously and is sensitive to criticism. 他对待工作很认真，对别人的批评也很敏感。

7. It doesn't necessarily mean that the marketer may precisely match competitors' price changes, but he does alter its prices to adapt to them to some extent. 商家的产品价格不一定就要与竞争对手的价格完全一致，但是他肯定会在一定程度上调整价格。

在本句中 It doesn't necessarily mean that 的意思是"不一定"，例如：

Companies can select one appropriate strategy, but it doesn't necessarily mean that the strategies are mutually exclusive. 各公司可以选择恰当的策略，但是这并不是说各种策略之间是相互排斥的。

8. Marketers of consumer goods do so when they use demand-backward pricing, which involves setting a price by starting with the estimated price consumers will pay and working backward with retail and wholesale margins. 商家使用需求回溯定价法时会考虑顾客的感知，这种定价法指的是先确定顾客能接受的估价，计算零售和批发价格限度，从而确定产品的价格。

在本句中，when 引导的是时间状语从句，which 引导的是非限制性定语从句，在该从句中谓语动词 involve 后面跟了两个并列的宾语，由 and 连接。此外，从句中还包含一个定语从句 consumers will pay，引导词在从句中充当宾语，因此省略掉了。

9. Compaq：康柏电脑曾是全球领先的电脑品牌，是戴尔（Dell）的强劲竞争对手，惠普于美国当地时间 2001 年 9 月 4 日宣布以价值 250 亿美元的股票收购康柏。2002 年 5 月，两公司合并完成。目前，康柏电脑是惠普的子品牌之一，主要产品涉及个人电脑及电子消费类产品。

I Answer the following questions according to the text.

1. Why is price the only element of the mix that provides revenue?
2. Why is the pricing strategy important?
3. What is the main idea of the second paragraph?
4. What is the purpose of the author to mention the example of Saturn?
5. What are the marketers' estimates of demand based on?
6. What are the commonly used pricing methods?
7. What are the advantage and disadvantage of markup pricing or cost-plus pricing?
8. What is rate-of-return pricing?
9. What is breakeven analysis?
10. What are the four basic approaches to setting prices relative to the competition?

II Decide whether the following statements are true or false.

1. Price is the most important element among the marketing mix.
2. An effective pricing strategy enables the company stay profitable.
3. All managers do not attach great importance to pricing strategy.
4. The writer mentions Saturn in order to highlight the importance of its labor and management relations.
5. The marketers know the demand of the consumers for sure.
6. Their estimates of demand are based on demographic and psychological factors.
7. For a product with elastic demand, total revenue increases when the product's prices increases.
8. The pricing approaches are independent of each other and marketers have to select one of

them for their products.
9. Cost-based pricing is high recommended because it is relatively easy to calculate.
10. The lower the prices are, the more purchase the customers will make.

III Fill in each blank with the proper form of the word in the bracket.

1. The meeting is about the _____ (sustain) economic growth of the city.
2. Our fears proved to be _____ (justify).
3. They have the _____ (exclusive) rights to market this kind of product in Africa.
4. The employees who are _____ (entitle) to vote should be aware of the fact.
5. Selecting a pricing strategy proves to be a little _____ (trick).
6. The figures mentioned in the paper are only rough _____ (estimate).
7. That company rewards creativity and _____ (innovate).
8. They conducted a market research on the _____ (feasible) of this product for young men.
9. Some of their new electronic products are highly _____ (profitability).
10. Consumers are getting more _____ (sophistication) and more demanding.

IV Fill in each blank with a proper preposition.

1. Questions have been raised relative _____ the pricing strategy.
2. We should take _____ account his performance in the office.
3. They didn't know the outcome of the experiment _____ certainty.
4. She repeated her demand _____ an urgent review of this system.
5. They had to sell their products _____ lower prices.
6. The CEO had the final say _____ this matter.
7. The competition _____ the larger market share will be fierce.
8. They are aware _____ the difficulties.
9. He bases his design of the product _____ his own imagination.
10. Inexperience contributed _____ the failure of his promotion plan.

V Fill in the blanks with the words and phrases given below. Change the form where necessary.

| assume risks | a good case in point | be entitled to | substantial | option |
| follow suit | demand curve | make price cuts | boost | justify |

1. They began to offer takeout food, and other restaurants _____.
2. How can people _____ spending so much money on cosmetics?

3. The festival has become a major _____ for the local economy.
4. We've discussed all the marketing _____ and decided to go for television advertising.
5. They refused to _____ for fear that their business would suffer great economic loss.
6. The study reveals very _____ differences between population groups.
7. After a careful examination of the _____, they decided to alter the prices of their products.
8. He had to _____ to adapt to the competitors' prices.
9. The old man _____ attend the meeting as a senior consultant.
10. Shoppers tend to think that prices mean high quality. Electrical goods are _____.

VI Cloze.

There are three reasons 1_____ "better pricing" should be your company's top 2_____. First, if your company is not setting the right prices, there are hidden profits 3_____ to be tapped. Second, small changes 4_____ price can lead to 5_____ profits. McKinsey & Company. studied the Global 1,200 and found that if they raised prices 6_____ just 1%—and demand remains 7_____—profits would go up 8_____ average by 11%, for instance. How much will a 1% price increase 9_____ your profits? Finally, in many industries prices can literally be changed on Sunday night and start generating more profits on Monday morning.

So 10_____ the 4 Cs—Confidence, Compensation, Choice, and C-Level—to improve pricing in your company.

11_____ confidence in your front line. Most sales forces don't sell 12_____ a manner that yields the most profit. They need to confidently articulate why the product offers the highest value compared with rivals. To be clear, "value" doesn't mean lowest price. 13_____, it is the offering that provides the best "deal" for clients. It's surprising, but most companies 14 _____ at this most basic task—they cannot articulate the value of their products and services.

You have to do more than say "ours is better". Go the extra step to quantify how being better 15_____ into more profit. Don't worry if your product isn't as good as the competitor's. After all, if customers only purchased the best, we'd all be driving Rolls-Royce cars. It's okay to acknowledge that your product has 16_____ bells and whistles compared with its rivals. The bottom line: if your product is better than the competitor's, demonstrate it and charge more than rivals based on value. Conversely, if your product has fewer features, acknowledge it and 17_____ a lower price.

Increase profits by offering choices. One of the most effective pricing strategies involves 18_____ good, better, and best product versions. I've found that customers appreciate being offered pricing 19_____ instead of just one "take it or leave it" price.

Reap results by involving the C-Level. It is crucial for the C-Level to create a culture focused on pricing for profit and growth. Just as important, setting aggressive profit targets for managers with

P&L responsibilities—who 20_____ might not be interested in pricing—provides an extra incentive for them to focus on pricing as a means to reach their goals.

1. A. why	B. which	C. what	D. /
2. A. choice	B. task	C. strategy	D. priority
3. A. wait	B. waiting	C. to wait	D. waited
4. A. at	B. on	C. in	D. with
5. A. many	B. much	C. lots	D. big
6. A. to	B. by	C. with	D. at
7. A. constant	B. same	C. changeable	D. consistent
8. A. in	B. with	C. on	D. for
9. A. increase	B. arise	C. rise	D. boost
10. A. follow	B. accept	C. take	D. learn
11. A. Put	B. Instill	C. Place	D. Emphasize
12. A. with	B. on	C. at	D. in
13. A. Instead	B. However	C. Therefore	D. Hence
14. A. succeed	B. fail	C. make	D. work
15. A. turns	B. changes	C. falls	D. translates
16. A. less	B. fewer	C. more	D. many
17. A. set	B. shift	C. cut	D. justify
18. A. offering	B. to offer	C. offered	D. being offered
19. A. choices	B. opportunities	C. options	D. chances
20. A. or	B. /	C. probably	D. otherwise

VII Translation.

1. What's more, intense price competition for materials and services, more sophisticated customers and less predictability all require a feasible and effective pricing strategy to sustain profitability.
2. In reality, the marketers don't know what the demand will be at each possible price for certainty; rather, they make estimates.
3. No matter what the costs, no matter what competitors are charging, potential buyers may not buy the product if they don't think they are getting their money's worth.
4. Actually, the marketers can benefit from considering all of them: the minimum charge to cover costs and earn a profit, an amount that matches or beats competitors' prices, and an amount that equals customers' perceptions of what the product is worth.
5. Of course, the marketer doesn't want merely to cover costs; the price should also be set at a level that will generate a profit.

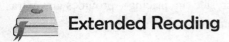

Extended Reading

Effective Pricing Strategies

One of the most difficult, yet important, issues that entrepreneurs, executives and managers are faced with is how much to charge for the products or services. Simple as it may seem on the surface, the company's pricing strategy really counts because it makes great difference between thriving and going bankrupt. The price they set will affect the amount of businesses and profits. What's more, price is often considered as the single most important factor in the customers' decision-making process. The right price can generate more sales, while the wrong price can make the potential customers look elsewhere and in that case the competitors will benefit a lot. If the price is too high, customers fail to afford the products or services, and then the sales will be hurt. But this can also be true if the price is too low. Customers will become suspicious of the quality of the products or services since the price is far below their expectations. Therefore, they will be reluctant to make a purchase decision. The best price is always the one that provides businesses with the long-term profits. It enables the businesses to stand out from the competition.

Many factors are involved in the effective pricing. First of all, businesses are supposed to know something about the product positioning. In other words, they have to decide whether they want to set the price as low as possible (or at least lower than the competitors) or they want to become the exclusive agency with higher prices. Secondly, it's a common practice for companies to set prices once and for all without the consideration of an important factor, namely, the customer demand on the market. Although they can get the exclusive marketing rights, it's only half the battle—dynamic pricing really works. Advertising and careful pricing are needed to increase the demand. Thirdly, companies are expected to bear their potential customers in mind. To be familiar with their shopping habits—whether they are sensitive to the price increase or decrease. Next, companies are advised to make sure they have considered all the costs in making and marketing the products including the fixed and variable costs. The former refers to such costs as electricity, water, and rent; the latter means those like wages, materials, and shipping costs. Lastly, take into account the prices of your competitors.

Since there are a number of different pricing strategies and there is no one single right way to set prices, careful consideration is called for to decide which one makes the most sense for the business. Some commonly used effective strategies are listed as follows.

Product line pricing is used to sell different products in the same product range at different price points based on features or benefits. By using it, some individual products may not make profits, but the goal is for the product line as a whole to turn a profit.

Penetration pricing is the pricing technique to set relatively low price in order to gain market share. Once this is achieved, the price is increased. The strategy works in the hope that customers will switch to the new brand because of the lower price. It is associated with a marketing objective of increasing market share or sales volume instead of making profits in the short term.

Loss leader pricing is the method to set the price at cost or below cost to bring customers to the storefront either physically or digitally. The pricing strategy assumes that while the customer is in the store to buy the low-priced products, they will look around and will be likely to buy other products at regular or higher prices.

Price skimming is a pricing strategy in which the business sets a relatively high price at first to cover costs quickly and earn a quick profit, then lowers the price over a period of time when the product becomes more widely distributed, and more competition enters the market. The purpose is to capture the consumer surplus. This strategy is used when there are enough buyers in the marketplace and the product is in high demand.

Promotional pricing is the strategy to set the price lower than normal levels in order to attract new customers. This technique can be effectively used across numerous industries including food services, cosmetics, and household cleaning supplies.

Psychological pricing is used when the business wants the consumer to respond on an emotional, rather than rational basis. It assumes that certain prices have a psychological impact.

Premium pricing is the practice of keeping the price of a product or service higher than similar products to encourage favorable perceptions among buyers. It is intended to exploit the assumption of the customer that expensive products are of high quality.

Product bundle pricing refers to the practice of combining several products in the same package. Usually slow-moving inventory can be sold with a group of popular items, which will be of great interest to the bargain seekers. This can increase the total profit gained from each customer even if the profit margin on each item sold in the bundle is lower than if they had been sold separately.

No matter which strategy the businesses choose, they have to demonstrate the product is worth the price.

Words and Expressions

be faced with ...　面临，面对	product positioning　产品定位
on the surface　表面上	exclusive agency　独家代理
make great difference　有很多差别	once and for all　永远地，彻底地，一次性地
go bankrupt　破产	
be suspicious of ...　怀疑……	be sensitive to ...　对……敏感
reluctant　*adj*. 不愿意的	product line pricing　产品线定价法

product range　产品系列
penetration pricing　渗透定价法
in the hope that ...　希望……
marketing objective　营销目标
loss leader pricing　特价商品定价法
price skimming　撇脂定价法
cover cost　回收成本
consumer surplus　消费者剩余
in high demand　需求量大
promotional pricing　促销定价法
food service　食品行业

household cleaning supply　家用清洁用品业
psychological pricing　心理定价法
premium pricing　高价位定价法
favorable perception　好感
be of high quality　质量好，质量上乘
product bundle pricing　产品捆绑定价法
slow-moving inventory　呆滞存货
total profit　总利润额

Comprehension

I Answer the following questions according to the passage.

1. What is the main idea of the first paragraph?
2. What influence will the right price and wrong price exert on businesses and customers?
3. What kind of price can be considered as best according to the passage?
4. What are the factors involved in pricing?
5. What pricing strategies are mentioned in the passage?
6. When is product line pricing adopted by the marketers? What is the goal?
7. If the marketer wants to capture the consumer surplus, what strategy should he use?
8. What is premium pricing?
9. For whom is product bundling pricing designed?
10. What does the writer mainly talk about in the passage?

II Write "T" for true, and "F" for false.

1. If the price is far below their expectations, the buyers will make their purchase.
2. The best price is the highest price to maximize the profits.
3. Dynamic pricing is much better than pricing once and for all.
4. All together there are eight pricing strategies.
5. With product line pricing, some individual products will not make money.

6. The ultimate goal of product line pricing is to make profits in the short term instead of increasing market share or sales volume.
7. The loss leader pricing tries to attract customers into the real shop.
8. When there are enough buyers in the marketplace and the product is in high demand, the marketer can use psychological pricing.
9. It's assumed that some prices will affect buyers' emotions.
10. No matter what strategies the marketers use, they have to indicate the worth of the products.

Additional Terms

allowance pricing 折让定价
antidumping 反倾销
assumed latitude 假定纬度
average price 平均价格
average revenue 平均收入
bait and switch 上钩销售法
base price 底价
bedrock price 最低价
captive-product pricing 附属产品定价
cash discount 现金折扣
ceiling price 最高价，顶价
channel member 渠道成员
competitive bidding 竞标，竞争出价
competitive parity method 竞争对抗法
cost inflation 成本上升
cost of distribution 分销成本
customary pricing 习惯性定价法
customer contact 顾客接触
deceptive pricing 欺骗性定价
derived demand 衍生需求
discount 折扣
desired percentage return 预期回报率
discriminatory pricing adjustment 歧视定价调整
dumping 倾销

economy pricing 经济定价
excess capacity 生产力过剩
freight absorption pricing 运费补贴定价法
functional discount 功能折扣
geographical pricing 地理定价
going rate 随行就市
horizontal price fixing 横向价格固定
initiate piece change 主动改变价格
international pricing 国际定价
location pricing 地点定价
marginal analysis 边际分析方法
marginal cost 边际成本
marginal revenue 边际收益
market share leadership 市场份额领先
market price 市场价格
market structure 市场结构
monopolistic competition 垄断竞争
multidimensional scaling analysis 多纬度分层定价
odd even pricing 奇偶定价
oligopoly 寡头垄断
optional product 可选产品定价
organizational buyer 组织购买者
overhead 固定成本

perfect competition 完全竞争	profit maximization 利润最大化
perfect competition structure 完全竞争产业	pure monopoly 独占
	quantity discount 数量折扣
price discrimination 价格歧视	reference price 参考价格
price elasticity of demand 需求价格弹性	reseller 分销商，代理销售商
	seasonal discount 季节性折扣
price escalation clause 价格调整条款	sunk cost 旁置成本，滞留成本，沉没成本
price fixing 价格管制	
price floor pricing 价格底线定价法	target profit pricing 目标利润定价法
price lining 价格底线	time pricing 时间定价
price sensitivity 价格敏感度，价格敏感性	trade in allowance 以旧换新折让
	uniform delivered pricing 统一发货定价法
price sensitivity meter 价格敏感度测试	unit sales 单位产品销售额
pricing discretion 价格自主权	value-based pricing 价值导向定价法
product quality leadership 产品质量领先	vertical price fixing 纵向价格固定
promotional allowance 促销折让	zone pricing 分区定价法

Unit 17
Promotion Strategy

For many artisans and small business owners, creating products is the easy part. Many think the most difficult part is selling those same products, but you'd be wrong. Selling is actually pretty easy when you get the marketing right. In other words, marketing is typically the most difficult piece of the puzzle to solve. One of the best ways to market your products is through promotions. The key to every promotion is to get the word out so make sure you share your promotion with your friends, family, followers, fans and just about everyone else that you can think of to help your promotion reach the most people.[1]

Product promotion is one of the necessities for getting your brand in front of the public and attracting new customers. There are numerous ways to promote a product or service. Some companies use more than one method, while others may use different methods for different marketing purposes. Regardless of your company's product or service, a strong set of promotional strategies can help position your company in a favorable light with not only current customers but new ones as well.[2]

Promotion is one of the key elements of the marketing mix. It deals with any one or two-way communication that takes place with the consumer. These promotional strategies are ways companies communicate information about their products and services with the end goal of increasing sales. Examples of promotional strategies in marketing include advertising, public relations, personal selling and sponsorship.

- **Advertising**

Advertising is a promotional marketing strategy used to create awareness about their products and services, the goal of which is to generate a response from the target customers.[3] You can use a variety of different types of advertising: television and radio advertisements; print advertisements in newspapers, magazines and journals; direct mail advertisements in which you send marketing materials directly to a select list of customers; and outdoor advertising such as posters, banners, signs and bus advertisements.

Advertising is any paid, non-personal presentation of information about a product, brand, company, or store. It usually has an identified sponsor. Advertising is intended to influence consumers' affect and cognitions—their evaluations, feelings, knowledge, meanings, beliefs, attitudes, and images concerning products and brands. In fact, advertising has been characterized as image management: creating and maintaining images and meanings in consumers' minds. Even though advertisements first influence affect and cognition, the ultimate goal is to influence consumers' purchase behavior.

Advertisements may be conveyed via a variety of media—the Internet, TV, radio, prints (magazines, newspapers), billboards, signs, and miscellaneous media such as hot-air balloons or T-shirt imprints. Although the typical consumer is exposed to hundreds of advertisements daily, the vast majority of these messages receive low levels of attention and comprehension. Thus, a major challenge for marketers is to develop messages and select media that expose consumers, capture their attention, and generate appropriate comprehension.

For many years, Nike Corporation used print advertisements and billboards featuring strong visual images of athletes—Carl Lewis long jumping, Michael Jordan leaping for the basket, or unknown ordinary people jogging—and little else. Some outdoor advertisement contained only the Nike "swoosh" logo in the corner and the athletes wearing Nike shoes and clothes. At first, consumers probably had to look twice to comprehend what product was being advertised. But once the association was made, related meanings were easily activated when consumers encountered other advertisements in the series. In markets where the advertisements were run, Nike sales increased an average of 30 percent.

- **Public relations**

Public relations (PR) is the practice of managing the spread of information between an individual or an organization and the public. It is a promotional strategy that seeks to establish and maintain communication and understanding between the company and the public. It provides an organization or individual exposure to their audiences using topics of public interest and news items that do not require direct payment.[4] In addition, it helps communicate positive updates about your company, product or service, and helps you control damage when a problem arises that puts your business in the public spotlight. PR can give consumers and the media a better understanding of how a company works. Within a company, a PR department might also be called a public information department or a customer relation department. These departments assist customers if they have any problems with the company. They usually try to show the company at its best. [5]PR departments also might conduct research to learn how satisfied customers are with the company and its products. Examples of public relations strategies you can use include press releases, media interviews, corporate web videos, company blogs and interactions in social media.

- **Personal selling**

Personal selling, another promotional strategy you can use to market your business, involves hiring one or more sales people to manage personal customer relationships and sell your products and services. Whether you have a large sales force or you do all the selling yourself, personal selling is an important strategy for the majority of businesses. When you determine your personal selling strategy, track and measure the business you bring in through your sales efforts to help establish best practices for effective selling.

Personal selling involves direct personal interactions between a potential buyer and a salesperson. It can be a powerful promotion method for at least two reasons. For one thing, the personal communication with the salesperson may increase consumers' involvement with the product and/or the decision process. Thus, consumers may be more motivated to attend to and comprehend the information the salesperson presents about the product. For another, the interactive communication situation allows salespeople to adapt their sales presentations to the informational needs of each potential buyer.

Certain consumer products, such as life insurance, automobiles, and houses, are traditionally promoted through personal selling. In retailing, personal selling has decreased over the past 20 years as self-service has become more popular. However, some retailers, like Nordstrom, have established a differential advantage by emphasizing personal selling and customer service.[6] Besides lots of personal attention from a courteous sales staff, customers are surrounded by pianos softly playing in the store and champagne at fashion shows.

For other businesses, personal selling by telephone, or telemarketing, has become popular as the total costs of a direct sales call keep increasing. Telemarketing selling differs considerably from face to face selling. The telemarketer usually follows a prepared script, makes 20 to 50 calls per day that last from 1 to 2 minutes, works about 4 to 6 hours per day, and is closely supervised. In contrast, a conventional salesperson often travels, usually must improvise the sales presentation to fit the buyers' needs, makes only 2 to 10 sales calls per day that last about 1 hour each, works about 8 to 12 hours per day, and is loosely supervised.

Both Avon and Mary Kay Cosmetics, among the U.S. marketers of skin care products, were built on personal selling.[7] In their earlier days, neither company spent much on advertising or customer sales promotions. In 2002, Mary Kay did $1.6 billion in wholesale business with little advertising. Most of the Mary Kay promotion budget is spent on sales incentives intended to motivate sales consultants. In addition to symbolic prizes such as medals, ribbons, and commemorative certificates, Mary Kay gives jewelry, calculators, briefcases, and furs as rewards to salespeople. Top sellers receive the use of pink Cadillacs or Buicks. It also spends heavily on motivational and training programs for its 1 million female sales consultants worldwide.

● **Sponsorship**

Sponsorship is a promotional strategy in marketing in which your company pays to be associated with a certain event, cause or other organization. For example, large companies pay to sponsor professional sports teams, television events and international competitions such as the Olympics. In exchange for sponsoring these events, companies get brand exposure and publicity. At the local level, you can sponsor a little league team, local festival or concert to help spread the word about your business.

Sponsorship is the financial or in-kind support of an activity, used primarily to reach specified business goals. It should not be confused with advertising. The latter is considered a quantitative medium, whereas the former is considered a qualitative medium which promotes a company in association with the sponsor. A large number of events these days use sponsorship support to offer more exciting programs and to help pay for rising costs. A company can benefit from sponsorship in many ways, such as enhancing image, driving sales, heightening visibility, differentiating from competitors.

Vocabulary

affect *n.* 感情，情感，心情	supervise *v.* 监督，监管
billboard *n.* 广告牌，告示牌	improvise *v.* 即兴创作
miscellaneous *adj.* 各种各样的，多方面的	loosely *adv.* 粗略地，随意地
feature *v.* 使有特色，描写……的特征	briefcase *n.* 公文包
courteous *adj.* 有礼貌的，客气的	motivational *adj.* 激励的
telemarketing *n.* 电话销售	event *n.* 事件，活动
	cause *n.* 事业

Phrases and Expressions

get sth. right 彻底搞清楚	be exposed to 暴露于
end goal 最终目标	in the public spotlight 成为焦点，备受公众的瞩目
public relation 公共关系	public information department 公共信息部
sponsorship 赞助	customer relation department 客户关系部，客服部
image management 形象管理	
purchase behavior 购买行为	
hot-air balloon 热气球	

English
Unit 17 Promotion Strategy

press release　新闻稿
media interview　媒体采访
corporate web video　公司网络视频
company blog　公司博客
bring in　产生，引进
attend to　注意
adapt ... to　适应
life insurance　人寿保险
differential advantage　差别利益
conventional salesperson　传统的销售人员
skin care product　护肤产品
sales incentive　销售奖励，销售激励
commemorative certificate　纪念证书
brand exposure　品牌曝光率
spread the word　传播消息
in-kind support　友情伙伴
quantitative medium　定量媒介
qualitative medium　定性媒介

Notes

1. The key to every promotion is to get the word out so make sure you share your promotion with your friends, family, followers, fans and just about everyone else that you can think of to help your promotion reach the most people.　促销的关键在于传播信息，确保你的朋友、家人、追随者、粉丝，乃至你所能想起来的每个人都能给你提供帮助，让更多的人了解促销信息。
在本句中，短语 get the word out 的意思是"把消息传开"，that 引导的定语从句"that you can think of"用来修饰限定 everyone else，后面的"to help your promotion reach the most people"是不定式表示目的。

2. Regardless of your company's product or service, a strong set of promotional strategies can help position your company in a favorable light with not only current customers but new ones as well.　不管你的公司生产什么样的产品，提供什么样的服务，一系列有效的促销策略能够帮助公司定位，不仅能得到现有顾客的青睐，而且还能获得新顾客的好感。
在本句中，短语 regardless of 的意思是"不管，不顾"，例如：
The club welcomes all new members regardless of age.　俱乐部对所有新成员不分年龄一律欢迎。
此外，短语"in a favorable light with sb."意思是"获得某人的好感，给某人留下良好的印象"，例如：
Your new products are in favorable light with the teenagers.　你们的新产品获得了青少年的青睐。

3. Advertising is a promotional marketing strategy used to create awareness about their products

and services, the goal of which is to generate a response from the target customers. 广告是一种营销策略，用来提高人们对其产品和服务的认识，让目标顾客对此作出反应。

在本句中，"used to create awareness about their products and services"是过去分词短语作定语修饰限定前面的"strategy"，后面的非限制定语从句用来补充说明主句的情况，阐述广告的目的。

4. It provides an organization or individual exposure to their audiences using topics of public interest and news items that do not require direct payment. 公共关系利用公众感兴趣的话题，以及一些不需要直接付款的新闻，让观众对公司或者个人有一定的了解。

在本句中，现在分词短语"using topics of public interest and news items"与句子主语 it（public relations）形成主动关系，后面的 that 引导的定语从句修饰限定前面的名词"news items"。

5. They usually try to show the company at its best. 这些部门尽量展示公司最好的一面。

在本句中，短语"at one's best"的意思是"处于最佳状态"，例如：

After the success of the promotional plan, the company was at it best. 促销计划成功了，公司处于最佳状态。

6. However, some retailers, like Nordstrom, have established a differential advantage by emphasizing personal selling and customer service. 但是，一些零售商，比如诺德斯特龙，注重人员推销和客户服务，具备了差别利益。

诺德斯特龙（Nordstrom）创立于 1901 年，它的第一家店铺位于美国西雅图，当时的店名叫华林·诺德斯特龙鞋店，是以创始人卡尔·华林和约翰·诺德斯特龙的名字命名的，以销售鞋子为主要业务，并为顾客提供修鞋服务。至 1923 年，在西雅图东北部它有了第二家分店。1928 年，由于两个创始人的合作关系越来越糟，经过协商，他们分别将各自的股份卖给了诺德斯特龙的 3 个儿子。1930 年 8 月，华林·诺德斯特龙鞋店正式更名为诺德斯特龙鞋店。1971 年诺德斯特龙公司正式挂牌上市，1973 年成为美国西海岸最大的服装专卖店，同年将公司正式更名为诺德斯特龙股份有限公司。

7. Both Avon and Mary Kay Cosmetics, among the U.S. marketers of skin care products, were built on personal selling. 雅芳和玫凯琳化妆品公司是美国的护肤品商，就非常注重人员推销。

雅芳（Avon）：全美 500 强企业之一，1886 年"雅芳之父"大卫·麦可尼创立"加州香芬公司"（California Perfume Company）。1939 年，麦可尼先生以莎翁故乡一条名为"AVON"的河流重新为公司命名。一百多年来雅芳人一直恪守着"信任、尊重、信念、谦逊和高标准"的雅芳价值观。如今，雅芳已发展成为世界上最大的美容化妆品公司之一，拥有 4.3 万名员工，通过 440 余万名营业代表向 145 个国家和地区的女性提供两万多种产品。

玫凯琳化妆品公司（Mary Kay Cosmetics）：护肤品和彩妆品直销企业之一，是玫琳凯·艾施女士于 1963 年创办的，总部设在美国得克萨斯州达拉斯市，是一家业务遍布五大洲 30 多个国家和地区、在全球拥有 5 000 名员工和 180 余万名美容顾问的大型化妆品跨国企业。

Unit 17 Promotion Strategy

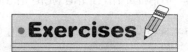

I Answer the following questions according to the text.

1. What is the most difficult part in business?
2. What is promotion according to the passage?
3. What promotional strategies are referred to in the passage?
4. What is the purpose of advertising?
5. What is the problem with advertising?
6. What is the purpose of the author to mention the example of Nike?
7. Why is public relations so important in business?
8. Why is personal selling considered as a powerful promotion method?
9. What is the advantage of telemarketing selling over face to face selling?
10. What is the difference between advertising and sponsorship?

II Decide whether the following statements are true or false.

1. It's commonly acknowledged that marketing is the most difficult part for businesses.
2. Promotion is the best way to market products.
3. Regardless of different marketing purposes, companies may use the same method to promote their products or services.
4. Promotion is the most important element of the marketing mix.
5. Advertising is aimed to influence consumers' evaluations, feelings, knowledge, meanings, beliefs, attitudes, and even images about themselves.
6. Frequently as consumers are exposed to advertisements every day, the vast majority of these messages fail to receive high levels of attention and comprehension.
7. Because of the advertisements, Nike's sales increased by 30%.
8. Within a company there are a public information department and a customer relation department besides a PR department.
9. Personal selling enables consumers to involve in the products or decision process.
10. Nordstrom made great success by means of personal selling.

III Fill in each blank with the proper form of the word in the bracket.

1. The Employment Minister said the reforms _____ (generate) many new jobs since last May.
2. All this _____ (public) has had a snowball effect on the sales of their latest products.
3. The _____ (insure) company paid out for the stolen silver.
4. The company has decided to withdraw from some of its sports _____ (sponsor).
5. He _____ (supervise) and trained more than 400 employees.
6. Her _____ (promotional) to Sales Manager took everyone by surprise.
7. This is a spectacular event _____ (feature) a stunning catwalk show.
8. The managers of departments will be _____ (involve) in this reform.
9. Now that the problem has been _____ (identify), appropriate action can be taken.
10. The ultimate goal of this reform is _____ (motivate) the employees to work even harder.

IV Fill in each blank with a proper preposition.

1. The trade unions bargained away their rights in exchange _____ a small pay rise.
2. We must constantly adapt _____ the growing market.
3. The firm decided to bring _____ a new management team.
4. The lecture exposed them _____ many new ideas.
5. The new promotion plan was _____ the spotlight again.
6. He had been exposed _____ public criticism since his failure two years ago.
7. Regardless _____ the terrible weather, they managed to finish the task on time.
8. The newly appointed general manager was _____ his best when he came to this company.
9. The freighter carries a few passengers in addition _____ its cargo.
10. Great changes have taken place in our company. It differs _____ what it was ten years ago.

V Fill in the blanks with the words and phrases given below. Change the form where necessary.

generate	for one thing	public relations	sales incentives	concerning
sponsorship	brand exposure	bring in	publicity	supervise

1. We must _____ and speed up the fulfilment of assigned tasks.
2. They tried hard to launch advertising campaigns to increase _____.

Unit 17 Promotion Strategy

3. There are an ever-growing number of events that call for _____.
4. The program of _____ is an effective way to make employees more hard working.
5. There are certain skills that are helpful for people in _____ including a high level of communication skills, both written and verbal.
6. The reforms will continue to _____ excitement for a long time.
7. Much _____ was given to the opening ceremony.
8. He asked several questions _____ the future of the company.
9. The firm decided to _____ a new management team.
10. The manager didn't agree to this plan. _____, it was not based on market research; for another, it failed to take the current economic situation into account.

VI Cloze.

Coupons and rebates are both examples of limited offers. These promotions 1_____ the price for one time only, pushing the customer to take 2_____ action. If the marketer has skimmed the market, his main preoccupation is 3_____ the product 4_____ diminishing the perceived value of the premium brand. However, 5_____ the marketer is penetrating the market, he has to be careful 6_____ set a promotional price so low that it will cut 7_____ profits. The time frame when marketers will see a 8_____ on investment is not so easily calculated, since the customer chooses when to 9_____ in the coupon or rebate.

Promotional 10_____ are set by retailers, and the cost of the promotion is usually shared between the retailer and the brand. By designing a sale program that 11_____ with a specific holiday or seasonal time of year, retailers and marketers can predict a spike in consumer spending and recoup losses in sales and inventory. 12_____ the discounted price in conjunction with the length of time is a key factor, because marketers do not want the customer to get so 13_____ to the lower price that they are less willing to pay 14_____ price for the product when the promotional period has expired.

A bulk-buying promotion strategy lowers prices for buying more than one of a specific item. This ensures that marketers will sell more units, and take 15_____ of lower production costs because of economies of scale. Customers who buy low-priced goods 16_____ bulk reap the benefits of this strategy. A bulk-buying promotion doesn't work as well with a price-skimming strategy 17_____ the higher-priced items are not normally manufactured in 18_____ large enough to be considered a bulk purchase.

Customer enrollment in a valued membership club—19_____ she receives exclusive promotional discounts—is something that is used at all price points and can actually fortify perception of the brand. Because membership equates to exclusivity, it doesn't diminish brand equity in a luxury product, and it can spur multiple sales in lower-priced goods. 20_____, by controlling the sales periods for valued customers, marketers can predict when a specific segment of their customers will be more likely to buy. Thus, businesses profit comes from two income streams: a discounted but more predictable income stream, and full-price but less-predictable stream.

1. A. fall	B. drop	C. deduce	D. reduce
2. A. buying	B. selling	C. effective	D. immediate
3. A. discount	B. to discount	C. discounting	D. to discounting
4. A. and	B. but	C. without	D. while
5. A. when	B. as if	C. although	D. if
6. A. to not	B. not to	C. to	D. not
7. A. down	B. in	C. off	D. into
8. A. repay	B. increase	C. decrease	D. return
9. A. cash	B. break	C. hand	D. cut
10. A. profits	B. means	C. periods	D. manners
11. A. coincides	B. meets	C. deals	D. comes up
12. A. Choose	B. To choose	C. Choosing	D. Choice
13. A. accustomed	B. eager	C. happy	D. content
14. A. more	B. less	C. full	D. much
15. A. advantage	B. place	C. away	D. disadvantage
16. A. on	B. in	C. with	D. for
17. A. for	B. because	C. since	D. as
18. A. amounts	B. numbers	C. qualities	D. quantities
19. A. that	B. where	C. which	D. there
20. A. Furthermore	B. However	C. Hence	D. Therefore

VII Translation.

1. Different salespeople can change the message so that no consistent communication is given to all customers.
2. Another promotional alternative, direct marketing, uses direct communication with consumers to generate a response in the form of an order, a request for further information, or a visit to a retail outlet.
3. Three of these elements—advertising, sales promotion, and public relations—are often said to use mass selling because they are used with groups of prospective buyers.
4. Offering value to the consumer in terms of a cents-off coupon or rebate may increase store traffic from consumers who are not store-loyal.
5. By pushing the product through the channel, the goal is to get channel members to push it to their customers.

Extended Reading

The concept of coupons is not new. It has existed as long as business has existed as a marketing tool for business owners to attract new customers and sometimes to retain existing customers. In 1887, the Coca-Cola Company was incorporated in Atlanta with Asa Candler as one of the partners. He transformed Coca-Cola into a profitable business by using innovative advertising techniques. The key to this growth was Candler's marketing strategies including having the company's employees and sales representatives distribute complimentary coupons for Coca-Cola. Coupons were mailed to potential customers and placed in magazines. The company gave soda fountains free syrup to cover the costs of the free drinks. It is estimated that between 1894 and 1913 one in nine Americans had received a free Coca-Cola, for a total of 8,500,000 free drinks. By 1895 Candler announced to shareholders that Coca-Cola was served in every state in the United States. Coupons first saw widespread use in the United States in 1909 when C. W. Post conceived the idea to help sell breakfast cereals and other products. Today, more than 2,800 consumer packaged goods companies offer coupons for discounts on products. In 2011, U.S. consumers used coupons to save 4.6 billion dollars on their purchases of consumer packaged goods.

There are many different types of coupons such as discounts, free shipping, buy-one get-one, first-time customer coupons, and free giveaways. Coupons can be used to research the price sensitivity of different groups of buyers (by sending out coupons with different dollar values to different groups). In addition, it is generally assumed that buyers who take the effort to collect and use coupons are more price sensitive than those who do not. Therefore, the posted price paid by price-insensitive buyers can be increased, while using coupon discounts to maintain the price for price-sensitive buyers (who would not buy at a higher price). Coupons have proven themselves to be highly effective sales tools for every conceivable size and type of business. A recent article states that coupon use rises as the economy in any given area slides. 54% of shoppers surveyed said they had already stepped up use of coupons, and even more are expected to do so.

Savvy marketers cite these reasons for heavy reliance on couponing.

• Coupons have the effect of expanding or increasing your market area. We know that consumers will travel far to redeem a valuable coupon.

• Coupons will entice new customers that have been shopping at your competitor. It's a proven fact that consumers will break routine shopping patterns to take advantage of a good coupon offer.

• Coupons attract new residents when they are actively in the market for products and services.

• Coupons will reactivate old customers. Those customers that have been lured away by your competitor will start buying from you again when you give them a good reason to do so.

● Coupon advertising provides the opportunity for additional profits through sales of related items. When you offer a special "deal" on a coupon to invite a customer to do business with you, you have to remember that the same customer will probably end up buying additional items that carry a full profit margin. In addition, you have the opportunity to "sell-up" to a more profitable product or service.

● Coupons build store traffic which results in additional impulse purchases.

● Coupons are measurable and accountable. Don't overlook that couponing is the most measurable and accountable form of promotion.

Like other sales promotion tools, coupons have their strengths as well as their weaknesses. On the plus side, they have the advantage of passing along savings directly to consumers, as opposed to trade allowances given to retailers by producers. Consumers perceive coupons as a temporary special offer rather than a price reduction, so the withdrawal of coupons usually does not have an adverse effect on sales. In addition, coupons often create added traffic for retailers, who have the option of doubling or even tripling the value of manufacturers-coupons at their own expense to create even more store traffic. Moreover, retailers often receive additional compensation from manufacturers for handling the coupons.

Critics of coupon-oriented sales promotions, however, argue that coupon clutter has dramatically lessened their effectiveness. They question whether coupons actually generate more business from new users, pointing out that the increased quantity of distributed coupons has been paralleled by falling redemption rates. In addition, excessive coupon distribution also increases the likelihood of fraud and misredemption. Coupons that are issued for established brands tend to be redeemed primarily by loyal users who would have purchased the product without a coupon.

There are several ways in which small businesses can distribute coupons, including direct mail, in-store or central location, print media, in-pack and on-pack, and through retailer advertising. Because of its targeted distribution, coupons sent by direct mail historically offer higher redemption rates than coupons distributed by print media. Freestanding inserts in newspapers, which accounted for the vast majority of all coupon distribution throughout the 1990s, are generally regarded as more effective than other coupon distribution methods. Perhaps the most popular coupon distribution method for small businesses, however, is the coupon mailer. This is a strategy wherein a group of retail businesses in a community send out a mailing of individual coupons together; consumers within the community thus receive a variety of coupons for area businesses in one envelope. Sometimes the mailing consists of an actual booklet of coupons for participating businesses, but most are sent out in loose-leaf fashion. Many business communities house businesses that specialize in putting such coupon mailers together. These companies charge a fee for their production and distribution services.

Unit 17 Promotion Strategy

Words and Expressions

transform   *v.* 变化，转换
syrup   *n.* 糖浆，糖汁
cover   *v.* 包括，覆盖
conceive   *v.* 想象
giveaway   *n.* 赠品
savvy   *adj.* 有见识的，有经验的
redeem   *v.* 赎回，偿还，兑现
reactivate   *v.* 使恢复活力，重起作用
measurable   *adj.* 可以衡量的
accountable   *adj.* 可以解释的，可以说明的，负有责任的
withdrawal   *n.* 撤回，收回
double   *v.* 加倍
triple   *v.* 增至三倍
coupon-oriented   *adj.* 使用优惠券的
house   *v.* 给……提供住房
fee   *n.* 费用

existing customer   现有客户
complimentary coupon   免费赠送的优惠券
consumer packaged goods   包装消费品
posted price   标价
in-pack and on-pack   入包装分送
step up   加快
store traffic   客流量
impulse purchase   即兴购买
on the plus side   在有利的方面，从好的方面来看
trade allowance   商业折扣
redemption rate   偿还价格，赎回价格
coupon distribution   分发优惠券
print media   印刷媒体
retailer advertising   零售商广告
freestanding insert   夹页广告

Comprehension

I Answer the following questions according to the passage.

1. What is the main idea of the passage?
2. How did Coca-Cola become profitable?
3. When did coupons become widespread?
4. How many types of coupons are listed in the passage?
5. How can businessmen know about consumers' price sensitivity? What measures can they take accordingly?
6. Why are coupons so popular?
7. What are the advantages and disadvantages of coupons?
8. How do small businesses distribute coupons?
9. Which is considered as the most effective distribution method?

10. What is the most popular coupon distribution method for small businesses?

II Write "T" for true, and "F" for false.

1. The concept of coupon is as old as business.
2. Business is a marketing tool for business owners to attract new customers and sometimes to retain existing customers.
3. It was by adopting the technique of coupons that Asa Candler made Coca-Cola become profitable.
4. Between 1894 and 1913 one in nine Americans in every state had received a free Coca-Cola.
5. Because of Coca-Cola's success, coupons became widely used in 1909.
6. Marketers can increase the posted price paid by price-insensitive buyers, while using coupon discounts to maintain the price for price-sensitive buyers.
7. It's said that people tend to use more coupons when the economy is on decline.
8. However far it may be, customers tend to redeem a valuable coupon.
9. A good coupon offer can make consumers change their shopping habits.
10. The withdrawal of coupons usually does not have an adverse effect on sales because customers have been loyal to the companies.

Additional Terms

advertising budget 广告预算	discount 折扣
after-sale customer survey 售后用户调查	freeby 免费赠品
	holiday promotion 节假日促销
all-you-can-afford budgeting 量力而行预算法	hybrid strategy 混合战略
	institutional advertisement 机构广告
brand alliance 品牌联合	loyalty program 忠诚度计划
brand attitude 品牌态度	mail order marketing 邮购营销
brand awareness 品牌知名度	mass selling 大规模销售
brand purchase intention 品牌购买意向	media audience 媒体受众
comparative advertising 比较广告	media strategy 媒介战略
contest 竞赛	message content 信息内容
cooperative advertising 联合广告	missionary salespeople 倡导销售员
customer appreciation event 答谢顾客活动	objective and task budgeting 目标任务预算法
cutting-edge product 尖端产品	order taker 订单接收员

Unit 17 Promotion Strategy

partnership selling　合伙推销
presentation　产品展示
product advertisement　产品广告
product giveaway　促销赠品
promotion behavior　促销行为
promotion communication　促销沟通
promotion environment　促销环境
promotion objective　促销目标
publicity tool　公共宣传工具
push strategy　推动策略
pull strategy　拉引策略
rebate　回扣
relationship selling　关系推销
sales engineer　销售工程师
sales management　销售管理
sales pitch　推销说辞，销售说辞
self-regulation　自我调节
sweepstake　抽奖
wasted coverage　无效覆盖

Unit 18
Marketing Channel Strategy

You can see the results of distribution every day. You may have bought Lay's Potato Chips at a 7-Eleven store, a book through Amazon.com, and Levi's jeans at Sears.[1] Each of these items was brought to you by a marketing channel of distribution. A marketing channel is a set of practices or activities necessary to transfer the ownership of goods, and to move goods, from the point of production to the point of consumption and, as such, which consists of all the institutions and all the marketing activities in the marketing process.[2] It is commonly acknowledged as a useful tool for management. An alternative term is distribution channel or "route to market". It is a "path" or "pipeline" through which goods and services flow in one direction (from vendor to the consumer), and the payments generated by them flow in the opposite direction (from consumer to the vendor). A marketing channel can be as short as being direct from the vendor to the consumer or may include several inter-connected (usually independent but mutually dependent) intermediaries such as wholesalers, distributors, agents, retailers. Each intermediary receives the item at one pricing point and moves it to the next higher pricing point until it reaches the final buyer.

Reaching prospective buyers, either directly or indirectly, is a prerequisite for successful marketing. Some intermediaries actually purchase item from the seller, store them, and resell them to buyers. For example, Sunshine Biscuits produces cookies and sells them to food wholesalers. The wholesalers then sell the cookies to supermarkets and grocery stores, which, in turn, sell them to consumers.[3] Other intermediaries such as brokers and agents represent sellers but do not actually take title to products—their role is to bring a seller and buyer together. The significance of intermediaries is made even clearer when we consider the functions they perform and the value they create for consumers. Producers come to realize that intermediaries make selling goods and services more efficient because they minimize the number of sales contacts necessary to reach a target market. Intermediaries make possible the flow of products from producers to buyers by performing three basic functions. Firstly, intermediaries perform a transactional function that involves buying, selling, and risk taking because they stock merchandise in anticipation of sales. Secondly, intermediaries perform a logistical function in the gathering, storing, and dispersing of products. Thirdly, intermediaries perform a facilitating function, which assists producers in making goods and services attractive to buyers.

A product can take different routes on its journey from a producer to buyers, and marketers search for the most effective route from the many alternatives available.[4] As the number of intermediaries between producer and buyer increases, the channel is regarded as increasing in length. A direct channel means that a producer and ultimate consumers deal directly with each other. While an indirect channel means intermediaries are inserted between the producer and consumers and perform numerous channel functions.

Besides, advances in electronic commerce have opened new avenues for reaching buyers and creating customer value. Interactive electronic technology has made possible electronic marketing channels, which employ the Internet to make goods and services available for consumption. A unique feature of these channels is that they combine electronic and traditional intermediaries to create time, place, form, and possession utility for buyers.[5] Many services can be distributed through electronic marketing channels, such as car rentals marketed by Almo.com, financial securities by Schwab.com, and insurance by MetLife.com. However, many other services such as health care and auto repair still call for traditional intermediaries.

Many companies also use direct marketing channels to reach buyers. Direct marketing channels allow consumers to buy products by interacting with various advertising media . Direct marketing channels include mail-order selling, direct-mail sales, catalog sales, telemarketing, interactive media, and televised home shopping.[6]

In some cases producers use dual distribution, which means a company reaches different buyers by employing two or more different types of channels for the same basic product. For instance, GE sells its large appliances directly to home and apartment builders but uses retail stores to sell to consumers. A recent innovation in marketing channels is the use of strategic channel alliances, whereby one firm's marketing channel is used to sell another firm's products. For instance, Kraft ever distributed Starbucks coffee in U.S. supermarkets and internationally.

Marketing channels not only link a producer to its buyers but also provide the means through which a firm implements various elements of its marketing strategy. Hence, choosing a marketing channel is of great importance. The final choice of a marketing channel depends on a number of factors that often interact with each other.

- **Environmental factors**

Environmental factors have an important influence on the choice and management of a marketing channel. Advances in the technology of growing, transporting, and storing perishable cut flowers has allowed Kroger to eliminate flower wholesalers and but directly from flower growers around the world. [7]The Internet has created new marketing channel opportunities for a variety of products, including consumer electronics, music, books, videos, and clothing and accessory items.

- **Consumer factors**

Consumer characteristics have a direct bearing on the choice and management of a marketing channel. [8]For example, Ricoh Company, Ltd., studied the serious camera users and concluded that a change in marketing channels was necessary. It terminated its contact with a wholesaler that sold to mass merchandise stores and began using manufacturer's agents who sold to photo specialty stores. These stores agreed to stock and display Ricoh's full line and promote it prominently. Sales volume tripled within 18 months.

- **Product factors**

Generally speaking, highly sophisticated products such as large, scientific computers, unstandardized products such as custom-tailor machinery, and products of high unit value are distributed directly to buyers. Unsophisticated, standardized products with low unit value, such as table salt, are typically distributed through indirect channels.

- **Company factors**

A company's financial, human, or technological capabilities affect channel choice. For instance, firms that are unable to employ their sales force might use manufacturer's agents or selling agents to reach wholesalers or buyers. If a firm has multiple products for a particular target market, it might use a direct channel. Firms with limited product line might use intermediaries to reach buyers.

Vocabulary

vendor	n. 卖主		avenue	n. 途径，手段
geographically	adv. 地理地		accessory	n. 配饰
prerequisite	n. 前提条件		terminate	v. 终止
wholesaler	n. 批发商		unstandardized	adj. 未标准化的
disperse	v. 分散，散开；传播			

Phrases and Expressions

point of production	生产点		take title to	拥有……的所有权
point of consumption	消费点		flow of product	产品流程
distribution channel	分销渠道		transactional function	交易功能
route to market	营销渠道		in anticipation of	预料，预期

Unit 18 Marketing Channel Strategy

logistical function 物流功能	possession utility 占用效用
facilitating function 便利功能	televised home shopping 电视家庭购物
direct channel 直接渠道	dual distribution 双重分销
indirect channel 间接渠道	environmental factor 环境因素
customer value 顾客价值	consumer factor 消费者因素
electronic marketing channel 电子营销渠道	product factor 产品因素
	company factor 公司因素
interactive electronic technology 交互式电子技术	consumer electronic 消费性电子产品
	mass merchandise store 大卖场
interactive media 互动媒体，交互媒体	full line 全产品线
time utility 时间效用	unit value 单位价值
place utility 地点效用	table salt 精盐
form utility 形态效用	

1. You may have bought Lay's Potato Chips at a 7-Eleven store, a book through Amazon.com, and Levi's jeans at Sears.　也许你可以在 7-Eleven 便利店买到乐事的薯条，在亚马逊网站买到书，在西尔斯买到李维斯的牛仔裤。
   西尔斯是西尔斯·罗巴克公司的简称，其创始人理查德·西尔斯在 1884 年就开始尝试邮购商品，专门从事邮购业务，出售手表、表链、表针、珠宝及钻石等小件商品。为顺应市场形势的变化，西尔斯公司不断调整自己的营销策略，从而以惊人的速度发展起来。1900 年成为美国零售业销售额排行榜的第一名。1925 年开始百货商店的经营，陆续开设了 300 多家百货商店，1931 年其零售业务营业额首次超过邮购的营业额。西尔斯公司于 2005 年 3 月 24 日与凯马特公司合并，组成美国第三大零售业集团。
2. A marketing channel is a set of practices or activities necessary to transfer the ownership of goods, and to move goods, from the point of production to the point of consumption and, as such, which consists of all the institutions and all the marketing activities in the marketing process. 营销渠道指的是一系列的实践或者活动，这是转换产品所有权所必需的。产品从生产地到消费地，营销渠道包括营销过程中所有的机构和营销活动。
   本句貌似比较复杂，主句为 A marketing channel is a set of practices or activities，后面是 and 连接的三个并列的结构，前两个都是形容词短语，省略掉了 necessary，第三个是 which 引导的定语从句，which 在从句中充当主语。

3. **The wholesalers then sell the cookies to supermarkets and grocery stores, which, in turn, sell them to consumers.** 之后批发商将曲奇饼干卖给各大超市和杂货店，这些超市和杂货店转而将曲奇饼干卖给消费者。

在本句中，which 引导的是非限制性定语从句，从句中的插入成分 in turn 意思是"转而，反过来"，例如：

Theory is based on practice and in turn serves practice. 理论的基础是实践，反过来理论又为实践服务。

4. **A product can take different routes on its journey from a producer to buyers, and marketers search for the most effective route from the many alternatives available.** 产品可以采取不同的路线，从生产商那里转移到买主手里，营销商试图在众多可供选择的路线中寻找最有效的。

在本句中短语 take different routes 意思是"采取不同的路线，走不同的路线"。形容词 available 意思是"可以得到的，可以使用的"，经常放在所修饰的名词后面，作后置定语，例如：

We are doing our best with the limited resources available. 我们正在利用可获得的有限资源尽最大努力。

5. **A unique feature of these channels is that they combine electronic and traditional intermediaries to create time, place, form, and possession utility for buyers.** 这些渠道所具备的一个独特的特点就是，将电子中间商与传统的中间商结合在一起，为买方创造了时间效用、地点效用、形态效用及占用效用。

本句使用了 that 引导的表语从句，注意从句中的几个术语的理解。企业重视物流的目的就是希望能以最低的成本将产品送达用户手中。事实上，企业物流的作用不仅如此，企业物流更为核心的作用还表现在通过几种经济效用来增加产品或服务的价值。这几种经济效用分别为时间效用、地点效用、形态效用及占用效用。"物"从供给者到需求者之间有一段时间差，由改变这一时间差所创造的效用，称作"时间效用"。也就是说，时间效用是缩短时间差，使人的可用时间增加，使物的获得时间减少，在消费者需要的时间内将产品送达。地点效用又称场所效用、空间效用，指的是有关的社会市场营销机构把产品由产地运到销售地，在适当的时间提供给市场，满足特定地区消费者或用户的需要。其效用的产生是由于供给者和需求者之间往往处于不同的场所，也就是说，供给者和需求者所处的空间位置不同，"物"从供给者到需求者之间有一段空间差。形态效用指的是通过生产、制造或组装过程对商品的增值。物流也可以创造形态价值。占用效用又称拥有效用，主要是通过市场营销活动来创造的，即市场营销使商品从所有者手中过渡到消费者手中。拥有效用与市场营销中的产品推销紧密相关。所谓产品推销，就是直接或间接地与顾客接触，使顾客产生拥有产品的愿望。

6. **Direct marketing channels include mail-order selling, direct-mail sales, catalog sales, telemarketing, interactive media, and televised home shopping.** 直接营销渠道包括邮购销售、直接邮寄销售、目录销售、电话销售、互动媒体销售及电视家庭购物。

在这里，邮购销售指的是通过邮局以邮寄商品目录、发行广告宣传品，向消费者进行商品推介展示的渠道，引起或激起消费者的购买热情，实现商品的销售活动，并通过邮寄的方式将商品送达给消费者的零售业态。顾客根据商店的订货单或广告，将所需购买商品的数量和款项用信函汇寄至商店，商店接到订货单和汇款后，即将货物连同发票邮寄给顾客。这种方式可以节省顾客的往返时间和由此产生的费用，便于远距离顾客的购买。直接邮寄销售指的是通过直接邮件作为企业产品或服务的发盘载体，目标市场成员根据该发盘信息，通过指定的渠道（电话、信函）进行问询或订购。这种方法针对性、选择性强，注意率、传读率、反复阅读率高，灵活性强，但是传播面小，容易造成滥寄的现象。目录销售指的是消费者通过查阅"目录购物商场"定期发行的购物目录，拨打"商场"话务中心的电话订购，再由专业快递公司提供快捷、优质的送货上门服务的购物方式。目录销售是一种销售成本低、覆盖面广、信息传递速度快的销售方式，在国外已经取得了普遍的成功。目录销售实际上是将传统的商业销售向现代化的国际互联网销售转变的过渡阶段。它将以其独特的促销方式和新颖的销售手段，对传统的零售业发起强有力的挑战。电话销售被认为出现于 20 世纪 80 年代的美国。随着消费者为主导的市场的形成，以及电话、传真等通信手段的普及，很多企业开始尝试这种新型的市场手法。电话销售决不等于随机地打出大量电话，靠碰运气推销出几样产品，而是通过使用电话，实现有计划、有组织并且高效率地扩大顾客群、提高顾客满意度、维护老顾客等市场行为的手法。互动媒体销售将平面、视频和音效等多种媒体结合在一起，为人类创造出一种全新的交流沟通方式。电视家庭购物是从美国开始崛起的，早期在美国约有 12 个购物频道，一直到 20 世纪 80 年代末期，才实现商业化。1982 年全世界第一家电视购物公司 HSN 在美国佛罗里达州诞生，随即席卷全美。

7. Advances in the technology of growing, transporting, and storing perishable cut flowers has allowed Kroger to eliminate flower wholesalers and but directly from flower growers around the world.　在鲜花的种植、运输及储存方面的技术不断更新，美国的克罗格公司取消了与鲜花批发商的合作，转而直接从世界各地鲜花种植商那里购买鲜花。

克罗格公司的历史可追溯至 1883 年，伯纳德·克罗格开设了全美第一家连锁店——大西方茶叶公司。经过不懈的努力，克罗格把自己的公司从以经营小型杂货店为主发展到经营超级市场。他在美国商业发展史上扮演了重要的角色，许多美国商业法规都是根据克罗格公司的发展而制定出来的。在世界零售百强中，美国的克罗格公司是具有百年历史的名店之一。围绕着市场消费需求的变化，它不断进行创新，创造了世界零售百年史上的若干个第一。2003 年以 518 亿美元的销售额，成为继沃尔玛、家得宝之后的美国第三大零售集团。

8. Consumer characteristics have a direct bearing on the choice and management of a marketing channel.　消费者的特征对于营销渠道的选择与管理来说具有直接的影响。

在本句中，短语 have a direct bearing on 意思是"与……有直接关系，对……有直接影响"，例如：

Attention should be centered on the links that have a bearing on the situation as a whole.　应该注意那些涉及全局的重要环节。

I. Answer the following questions according to the text.

1. What is the writer's purpose to begin the passage with the examples of 7-Eleven store, Amazon.com and Sears?
2. What is marketing channel?
3. What is the main idea of the second paragraph?
4. What is the difference between direct channel and indirect channel?
5. What has contributed to the development of electronic marketing channels?
6. What is the special feature of electronic marketing channels?
7. Please exemplify direct marketing channels.
8. What is dual distribution? Please give some examples.
9. What are regarded as factors influencing the final choice of marketing channel?

II. Decide whether the following statements are true or false.

1. The results of distribution can be seen every day.
2. Distribution channels enable goods, services, and payments flow in the same direction.
3. The more intermediaries there are, the higher the prices will be.
4. Marketing channel is of great importance to marketing.
5. All intermediaries actually do not purchase item from the seller, store them, and resell them to buyers.
6. Because they stock merchandise in anticipation of sales, intermediaries perform a transactional function that involves buying, selling, and risk taking.
7. Intermediaries also help a lot in making goods and services attractive to buyers.
8. As a product can take different routes on its journey from a producer to buyers, marketers try to find as many effective routes as possible.
9. Mansar Products, Ltd. is an example of a direct channel.
10. Such services as health care and auto repair still need the involvement of traditional intermediaries.

III. Fill in each blank with the proper form of the word in the bracket.

1. We are going to render them economic _____ (assist).

Unit 18 Marketing Channel Strategy

2. The retail dealer buys at _____ (wholesaler) and sells at retail.
3. The _____ (standard) parts can be employed universally.
4. Its _____ (geographically) location stimulated overseas enterprises.
5. This is a very _____ (sophistication) machine.
6. His contract _____ (termination) at the end of this season.
7. They were approached indirectly through two _____ (intermediary).
8. The employees _____ (disperse) after the agreement about pay raise were reached.
9. The _____ (vendor) finally took that machine at $20.
10. With _____ (technology) changes many traditional skills have become obsolete.

IV Fill in each blank with a proper preposition.

1. Originally their team consisted _____ only three persons.
2. Does he take any title _____ this company?
3. He bought extra food in anticipation _____ more clients than he'd imagined.
4. This project calls _____ great experience besides care and patience.
5. The heavy rain has a direct bearing _____ the timely delivery of the ordered goods.
6. Effective marketing channel is _____ great significance to firms.
7. He asked us to assist him _____ carrying through their plan.
8. The secretary filled the guests' glasses _____ turn.
9. She searched her desk _____ the necessary information.
10. He is in direct contacts _____ directors and executives within the firm.

V Fill in the blanks with the words and phrases given below. Change the form where necessary.

| take different routes | consist of | customer value | product line | call for |
| open new avenues | custom-tailor | intermediary | prerequisite | durable |

1. His research has _____ for the further development of the company.
2. Bone China is strong and _____, so it becomes very popular in foreign markets.
3. Stability and unity are the _____ to success of any business.
4. Companies can _____ in terms of marketing channels.
5. His report mainly _____ five parts about the achievements in recent years.
6. A _____ refers to a number of products that are related and developed by the same manufacturer.
7. Typically the _____ offers some added value to the transaction that may not be possible by direct trading.

8. _____ is the benefit that a customer will get from a product or service in comparison with its cost.
9. Business success _____ the joint efforts of different departments throughout the whole firm.
10. A _____ PC is a personal computer system that is assembled from components selected by the end-user.

VI Cloze.

Selecting the best marketing channel is 1_____ great significance because it can mean the success or failure of your product. One of the reasons the Internet has been so successful as a marketing channel is 2_____ customers get to make some of the channel decisions themselves. They can shop virtually for any product in the world when and where they want to, 3_____ they can connect to the web. They can also choose how the product is shipped.

The Internet isn't necessarily the best channel for every product, 4_____. For example, do you want to closely 5_____ the fruits and vegetables you buy to make sure they are 6_____ enough or not overripe? Then online grocery shopping 7_____ not be for you. Clearly, how your customers want to buy products will have an important bearing 8_____ the channel you select. In fact, it should be your 9_____ consideration.

10_____, are you selling to a consumer or a business customer? Generally speaking, these two groups want 11_____ differently. Most consumers are willing to go to a grocery or convenience store to purchase toilet paper. The manager of a hospital 12_____ to replenish its supplies would not. The hospital manager would also be buying a lot more toilet paper than an individual consumer and would expect to be called upon by a 13_____, but perhaps only semi-regularly. Thereafter, the manager might want the toilet paper delivered on a regular 14_____ and billed to the hospital 15_____ automatic systems. Likewise, when businesses buy expensive products such as computers or products that have to be 16_____, they generally expect to be sold to personally via salespeople.

The type of product you're selling will also affect your marketing channel choice. Perishable products often have to be sold through shorter marketing channels than products with 17_____ shelf lives. For example, a yellowfin tuna bound for the sushi market will likely be flown overnight to its destination and handled by few intermediaries. 18_____, canned tuna can be shipped by "slow boat" and handled by more intermediaries. Automakers generally sell their cars straight to car dealers (retailers) 19_____ through wholesalers. The makers of corporate jets often sell them straight to corporations, which demand they 20_____ to certain specifications.

1. A. in   B. of   C. for   D. with
2. A. because   B. why   C. that   D. since

Unit 18 Marketing Channel Strategy

3. A. before   B. on condition that   C. after   D. as long as
4. A. though   B. however   C. too   D. although
5. A. look   B. examine   C. inspect   D. check
6. A. good   B. mature   C. ripe   D. grown
7. A. must   B. can   C. should   D. might
8. A. to   B. on   C. for   D. at
9. A. prime   B. good   C. best   D. suitable
10. A. Therefore   B. However   C. In addition   D. First of all
11. A. to sell   B. to be sold to   C. to be sold   D. to sell to
12. A. tried   B. tries   C. trying   D. who trying
13. A. distributor   B. customer   C. client   D. wholesaler
14. A. time   B. place   C. price   D. basis
15. A. via   B. by   C. with   D. through
16. A. perfect   B. valuable   C. customized   D. useful
17. A. long   B. longer   C. short   D. shorter
18. A. Hence   B. Besides   C. Accordingly   D. By contrast
19. A. as well as   B. rather than   C. or   D. instead
20. A. be customized B. customize   C. would be customized D. might customize

VII Translation.

1. You've managed to sell your products via two channels—say, on TV and on the Web.
2. Distribution strategies help identify sales channels that can maximize sales and profits.
3. Indirect channels include retailers, such as Wal-Mart or Home Depot, that sell products without major modifications; value-added resellers, that add features and services before selling; distributors and wholesalers that typically resell to other channel partners; and telemarketers, who prospect for potential customers.
4. However, if you sell insurance, the best distribution strategy may be a combination of wholesalers and retail brokers and direct telemarketers.
5. Some firms even choose to bypass the retailer and sell directly to the end consumer, which is called direct marketing.

 Extended Reading

   The nature of rural emerging markets makes building a successful marketing channel more challenging. For example, the population is widely dispersed, transportation infrastructure is poor or non-existent, household incomes are low, and traditional methods of creating brand trust and awareness will not work. Any company will face many challenges when building a marketing channel in rural emerging markets.

One of the key issues that may prevent rural consumers in emerging markets from making a purchase is lack of substantial and consistent household income. By better understanding the size and pattern of earnings in rural emerging markets, companies can design both products and purchasing schemes that help unlock the enormous purchasing potential of populations in rural emerging markets. Although consumers in rural emerging markets clearly have low and sporadic incomes, it would be a mistake to assume that these consumers necessarily desire to purchase "cheap" products. Instead, the consumers are very brand-conscious and are motivated to buy quality goods. However, at the same time, they are by necessity very value-conscious. The challenge for companies entering this market is to offer consumers high-quality products and brands while also offering prices and payment schemes that fit with the income levels and patterns of the population.

There are some price and payment schemes that have been used successfully by companies in rural emerging markets. Company should choose the affordability scheme that meets the financial needs of both the target consumers and the company itself.

Offering quality branded products in smaller package sizes allows consumers to make a purchase even when they have very minimal funds available. In Kenya, when Coca-Cola saw its sales slumping because of inflation, the company came out with a smaller and cheaper version of its product to address affordability concerns.

A payment scheme that has worked well for some companies selling consumer durables is small-payment financing. Casas Bahia in Brazil, seller of electronics and other consumer durables, has built a successful business with the help of this model. The company allows customers to make small installment payments over a period of months, and over 90 percent of sales are financed in this way.

Any company selling products and services to consumers must first establish trust with the consumer. For a company like Coca-Cola in the United States, this is easy because the Coca-Cola brand is well known and trusted by the entire consumer population. In addition to the Coca-Cola brand, consumers in the United States will trust a new product offering from Coca-Cola because the country's government enforces laws that guarantee product safety and prevent fakes from being sold. The situation is very different for a company entering into a rural emerging market with a new product or service and an unknown brand. Not only will consumers be less aware of many brands, they will also have less innate trust in new brands because of the lack of access to information and because of the plethora of fake and poor-quality brands being offered in the marketplace. This is not to say that rural consumers are not brand-conscious. As C. K. Prahalad points out, the poor are actually "very brand-conscious" and seek out the brands they know well and trust. The challenge for a company entering a rural emerging market with a new product or service is to establish trust in its brand so that consumers will buy it.

It's proposed that for companies entering into rural emerging markets with unknown brands, the best solution to this problem should be to piggyback on an existing known and trusted brand or local entity. Piggybacking on a trusted brand can boost a company's chance and rate of success. Whirlpool brand is a good case in point. It was introduced to Japanese consumers in Sony stores. Sony also has a strong service operation and reputation in Japan. Whirlpool was able to benefit from this association too. Another famous example of this in an emerging market is Coca-Cola's entry into India in 1993. Although Coca-Cola's brand is strong worldwide, the company wanted to quickly gain brand equity in the Indian market. To accomplish this, Coca-Cola purchased local beverage brands that were popular in India like Thums Up, Limca, and Citra. Thums Up, in particular, is known as the most trusted brand in India. Coca-Cola and its subsidiary brands, are now thriving in India.

Rural consumers' lack of education in topics like hygiene, health, and modern agriculture practices also poses challenges for a company's marketing channels in an emerging market. Often times, before a company can begin sales of its product or service, the company needs to educate consumers about the benefit the product or service will have on their lives. Companies should consider this activity as an exercise in unlocking latent need for their product or service, and it should be considered just as important as branding and distribution.

An important component of marketing channel design that many companies in rural emerging markets overlook is providing quality after-sales service to customers. Companies should consider after-sales service as an important component of building a consumer's trust in the company's brand. If a company's after-sales service is poor, customers will likely not purchase the company's products again and will tell other potential customers about their bad experience.

Given the importance of after-sales service for building and maintaining a consumer's brand trust, it's recommended that a company choose the after-sales service option that will best meet the needs and expectations of its customers. In addition, it is critical that companies take the cost of providing good after-sales service into account when designing their marketing channels and when deciding on the size of the market they want to serve.

By building a marketing channel that can perform these activities effectively and in a cost-efficient manner, a company entering a rural emerging market with a new product or service will greatly increase its chances of succeeding in the marketplace.

Words and Expressions

non-existent   *adj.* 不存在的
substantial   *adj.* 可观的，大量的
consistent   *adj.* 连贯的，一致的
sporadic   *adj.* 零星的，分散的
brand-conscious   *adj.* 有品牌意识的
value-conscious   *adj.* 有价值意识的

minimal *adj.* 最小的，极小的	设施
slump *vt.* 大幅度下跌，暴跌	household income 家庭收入
enforce *vt.* 实施，执行	brand trust 品牌信任
fake *n.* 冒牌货，赝品	quality goods 高品质产品
innate *adj.* 天生的，特有的，内在的	affordability scheme 可承受力计划
plethora *n.* 过多，过剩	per capita consumption 人均消费量
piggyback *v.* 背负式装运	installment payment 分期付款支付
hygiene *n.* 卫生	consumer population 消费者数量
component *n.* 组成部分	local entity 局部实体
cost-efficient *adj.* 合算的，划算的，节约成本的	brand equity 品牌资产
	subsidiary brand 副品牌
by necessity 必然地，不可避免地	decide on 决定
transportation infrastructure 运输基础	

Comprehension

I Answer the following questions according to the passage.

1. What is the nature of the rural emerging markets?
2. How does the lack of household incomes influence the development of rural emerging markets? What should be done to solve the problem?
3. What attitudes do the consumers in rural emerging markets hold towards brands and value of the products?
4. What is the purpose of the author to mention the example of Casas Bahia?
5. Is it easy for a company like Coca-Cola in the United States to establish trust with consumers? Why?
6. Why is the situation quite different in India?
7. How did Coca-Cola gain its brand equity in the Indian market?
8. What is the importance of after-sales services to consumers?
9. What does the author suggest in terms of after-sales services and brand trust?

II Write "T" for true, and "F" for false.

1. It's the nature of rural emerging markets that makes it more difficult to build a marketing channel in rural emerging markets.

Unit 18　Marketing Channel Strategy

2. Lack of substantial and consistent household income is the most serious issue that keeps local consumers from making a purchase.
3. Consumers in rural emerging markets tend to favor cheap products for short of money.
4. In Kenya, Coca-Cola ever saw its sales slumping because of mismanagement.
5. Small-payment financing has been proved to be effective for companies in Brazil.
6. Piggybacking on a trusted brand is bound to boost a company's chance and rate of success.
7. Educating consumers about the benefit the product or service isn't considered as important as distribution.
8. More importance should be attached to the after-sales services.
9. Companies are advised to meet the needs and expectations of customers without the slightest consideration of their cost.

Additional Terms

administered system　管理型体系	full-service wholesaler　全面服务批发商
attendance service　辅助服务	industrial distributor　工业分销商
backward integration　后向一体化	intensive distribution　密集分销
broker　经纪人	limited-service wholesaler　有限服务批发商
channel captain　渠道首领	
channel conflict　渠道冲突	manufacturer's agent　生产代理商
channel design　渠道设计	merchant wholesaler　商业批发商
channel partnership　渠道伙伴关系	purchasing volume　采购量
channel relationship　渠道关系	resale restriction　转售限制
channel structure　渠道结构	selective distribution　选择分销
contractual system　契约型体系	selling agent　销售代理商
corporate system　公司型体系	target market coverage　目标市场覆盖
disintermediation　去中介化	trying arrangement　搭售安排
exclusive dealing　独家经营	vertical marketing system　垂直营销体系
exclusive distribution　独家分销	
forward integration　前向一体化	vertical integration　纵向一体化
franchising　特许经营	

Unit 19
Collaborative Strategy

We all admire the "strong individual salesperson", uncovering qualified prospects, closing deals ... making it look easy.[1] We all aspire to be that kind of sales person. The truth is, however, that this is a rare breed and most of us can't be that person. We don't like cold calling; we stumble through closes; we think we know why we shouldn't follow-up, and we hope the last prospect will come back on their own because of our offering.[2] These are real and very common feelings. The type of actions just noted accounts for the majority of sales activities in our business. A lot of people make a living following this activity pattern. It can be better and the tools we need are all around us: our managers, co-workers, competitors, agents, and even our customers and prospects ... all these resources will help you if you just ask.

Asking for help is one of the best ways to get engagement from someone. The scientific studies and real experiences show that if you ask someone to give a little help, there is very strong likelihood that they will help and you will strengthen the bond between parties.[3] Humans are social beings, and we are inclined to naturally help one another. Experience tells us that asking is better than hiding, and that collaboration is better than quiet "self-talk".

The web has changed many things about business, but one thing's for sure—it's dramatically enhanced our ability to collaborate with every important constituency group. In the past, it was generally considered very natural for small business owners to collaborate with partners and the occasional vendor in order to complete a project. A marketing consultant, for instance, might collaborate with a graphic designer, copywriter and print shop to complete a direct mail campaign. In the new world of marketing the notion of collaboration is expanded dramatically.

Most leaders agree that effective collaboration is more important than ever in today's turbulent business environment. In a "do more with less" reality, it takes ongoing teamwork to produce innovative, cost-effective and targeted products and services. Many organizations are planning or are already in the middle of adopting collaboration technology to their global organization.

Collaboration between businesses can happen between corporations, or between nonprofit organizations and corporations. To survive in a competitive business world, a company needs as much help as it can get.

The collaborative process combines different perspectives. When individuals from various professional and technical backgrounds come together to work on a project, the result is that all angles are considered. This is a particularly attractive outcome, especially in situations where the project is expected to command a huge budget, because it eliminates the possibility of errors arising from failures and considers the effect of contributing elements.[4]

Workplace collaboration encourages creativity. The adage "two heads are better" is true. When you have different people collaborating on a project, then you get a greater sense of creative input. You are able to tap into the creative combination of several employees in one group. The collection of different ideas, approaches to the project and brainstorm can spur innovative results that can in turn raise the visibility and quality of the products or services offered by your company. Bringing together several different voices from an organization helps to raise the profile of ideas. It may never have come to the forefront without the collaborative effort. Teams that are well-structured consist of staff members from various levels of the company. Creative solutions are often the result of simply looking at challenges from a different angle.

Collaboration takes advantage of synergies.[5] The formation of collaborative teams often involves the separation of duties. Within the structure of the team, certain members may be asked to focus on particular elements and put forth a recommendation based on their expertise. This kind of separation of responsibilities helps to bring the benefit of synergy to the project because areas of overlap are more easily identified and the incidences of re-doing work can be eliminated.

Workplace collaboration brings balance to decision making. The influence of several different stakeholders that may comprise the overall team helps to ensure that the decisions made are ones that consider the effect of all the interested parties. This means that workplace collaboration can root out the occurrence of biased or partisan decisions because each stakeholder has a presence around the table.

Collaboration helps you keep up with the fast global pace. With so much global competition and advanced technology, things happen at a faster pace and you have to keep up in order to be successful. Building a team of individuals with diverse strengths allows them to accomplish a variety of complex tasks. A competent team can accomplish much more than any one person alone—helping them adapt to a fast marketplace. In addition, companies can gain access to new skills as the various organizations that have these skills come on board.[6]

It's a good opportunity to expand your own market. Both companies can use the opportunity to reach target markets that may have previously been difficult to sell to. For example, if your product appeals to an age group of between 35 and 55, but you want to reach a younger audience to develop a longer cycle of repeat sales, then having a company with a younger target market introduce your product can help gain credibility with a younger audience.

One of the advantages of collaborative effort between companies is the complementary ways in which personnel can enhance the relationship. For example, if your company has strong software development skills, and you collaborate with a company that makes high-end computer hardware, you both benefit from creating products with strong software and hardware components. Nonprofit organizations can also benefit from the collaboration by an increase in volunteers from the partner company.

Workplace collaboration can be an instrumental part of the decision-making process within an organization, but this tool needs to be properly implemented to maximize its benefits and downplay potential negatives. In other words, collaboration is generally a good idea, for all the reasons mentioned above. However, there are some circumstances where you at least need to be careful and to put safeguards in place to overcome a few potential problems.[7]

Collaborations can mean that your campaign moves more slowly, because you need to get consensus or check with the other players regarding every decision, so make sure you have a good understanding of the levels of autonomy that you have.

You'll be more restricted in what you can do. Certain tactics your group might follow, or positions that your group might ordinarily take, may not be agreed on by other members of your collaboration.

In-fighting between parties may emerge, and could be more damaging to a booming business. These squabbles often become public, people in the organization often finish up acting according to their own micropolitical agendas rather than on the basis of what's good for the campaign.

Collaboration, the ability to work together especially in business is raising key concerns for organizations taking on new approaches to improve performance and outcome. It is a sophisticated skill that asks people who work together to look beyond personal interests towards outcomes benefiting the whole. It is a great way to address complex challenges, since it has the potential to tap communal creativity and unleash true innovation and earn genuine buy-in.[8] Despite an increasing desire for collaboration in the workplace and the prolific use of this buzzword, effective collaboration is rarely occurring in most work environments.

Here are some strategies for better collaboration that help us have more productive collaborative relationships.

● **Put team success ahead of personal gain**

As an individual, you always want to do your personal best, but learn that team success will always achieve greater results. Olympic athletes are the best example of team success, where individuals are striving not only for their own performances, but for the whole group.

● **Tap into a broad range of resources**

You've probably heard this expression, the whole is greater than the sum of the parts, which was established by Gestalt psychologists. Everyone brings something to the table, whether it is intellectual, creative, or financial, among other things. Instead of always telling, try asking questions. When you start a conversation with a question, you immediately bring someone else in and add something bigger than what one individual can do.

● **Keep commitments**

For personal and professional development, follow through with your promises.[9] People will know and remember they can count on you.

● **Connect authentically with each other**

Be genuine in your approach to collaborate with people. Working collaboratively can strengthen your connections. As you learn to collaborate better, you will be helping others along the way, too.

● **Thrust yourself into collaboration**

When you approach a collaborative opportunity, explain what you are doing with as much clarity as possible and express why you feel this way. Open up the possibilities—people will believe in you, and both sides will see the benefits.

Vocabulary

inaction *n.* 不活动，不活跃	credibility *n.* 可靠性，可信性
copywriter *n.* 广告文字撰写人	complementary *adj.* 互补的，补充的
turbulent *adj.* 骚乱的，混乱的	downplay *n.* 贬低，轻视
ongoing *adj.* 不间断的，前进的	negative *n.* 否定的观点
innovative *adj.* 创新的，革新的	safeguard *n.* 保护，保卫，防护措施
cost-effective *adj.* 划算的，合算的	consensus *n.* 一致同意
eliminate *vt.* 根除，消除	regarding *prep.* 关于
contributing *adj.* 起作用的	autonomy *n.* 自主，自治
adage *n.* 谚语，格言	in-fighting *n.* 混战，暗斗
spur *vt.* 鞭策，激励	damaging *adj.* 破坏性的
well-structured *adj.* 结构良好的	squabble *n.* 争吵，口角
synergy *n.* 协同，配合	micropolitical *adj.* 微观政治的
overlap *n.* 重叠部分，交叉部分	unleash *vt.* 释放
incidence *n.* 发生，发生率	buy-in *n.* 买进
interested *adj.* 有利害关系的	prolific *adj.* 多产的，众多的
occurrence *n.* 出现，发生	buzzword *n.*（报刊等的）时髦术语，流行行话
biased *adj.* 有偏见的	
partisan *adj.* 偏袒的	Gestalt *n.*（心理学上的）格式塔

Phrases and Expressions

close deal　达成协议，完成交易
cold calling　推销电话
be inclined to do sth.　倾向于做某事
for sure　毫无疑问
graphic designer　平面设计师
tap into　进入，利用，开发
come to the forefront　成为焦点，成为中心
takes advantage of　利用
put forth　提出
root out　根除
keep up with　赶上

gain access to　可以进入，可以使用
come on board　加入
repeat sales　重复销售
put ... in place　将……置于合适的位置；实施，实现
agree on　就……达成一致意见
finish up　结束
strive for　奋斗，争取，谋求
follow through　坚持，进行到底
count on　依赖，依靠

1. We all admire the "strong individual salesperson", uncovering qualified prospects, closing deals ... making it look easy.　我们都对"能干的推销员"羡慕不已，发现有资历的顾客，完成一次又一次的交易……这一切都看似很简单。
在本句中，后面的"uncovering qualified prospects""closing deals"和"making it look easy"都是分词短语来修饰前面的 salesperson。

2. We don't like cold calling; we stumble through closes; we think we know why we shouldn't follow-up, and we hope the last prospect will come back on their own because of our offering.　我们不喜欢冷不丁地给潜在顾客打电话；在整个交易过程中错误百出；我们认为自己知道为什么不应该像这样继续下去了，我们提供了优质的产品和服务，希望最后一个潜在顾客会因此而再次光顾。
在本句中，短语 cold calling 的意思是"冷不丁地给潜在顾客打电话，电话推销"，在电话销售中，销售技巧的重要性自然不言而喻。

3. The scientific studies and real experiences show that if you ask someone to give a little help, there is very strong likelihood that they will help and you will strengthen the bond between parties.　很多科学研究和真实的实践经验表明，如果你请别人帮个小忙，他们很可能会愿意帮助你，这样你就能加强团队之间的联系。

在本句中，第一个 that 引导的是宾语从句，作谓语动词 show 的宾语。在宾语从句中，if 引导的是条件状语从句，第二个 that 引导的是同位语从句，用来解释说明 likelihood。在这里，likelihood 的意思是"可能性"，例如：

There is every likelihood that his promotion plan will work. 他的促销计划完全可能发挥作用。

That, as we all know, is not only a possibility but a likelihood. 众所周知，那不仅可能发生，而且是很可能发生。

4. This is a particularly attractive outcome, especially in situations where the project is expected to command a huge budget, because it eliminates the possibility of errors arising from failures and considers the effect of contributing elements. 这种结果是特别引人注意的，在项目需要巨额预算的情况下尤为如此，这样做不会因为各种失败而出现失误，考虑到了方方面面的相关因素。

在本句中，where 引导的定语从句用来修饰限定先行词 situations，because 引导的是原因状语从句，在该从句中，and 连接了两个并列的谓语动词 eliminate 与 consider。后面的分词短语 arising from failures 用来修饰 errors，arise from 的意思是"产生于，起因于"，例如：

Accidents arise from carelessness. 疏忽大意往往会引发事故。

5. Collaboration takes advantage of synergies. 合作采用了协同的形式。

在本句中，短语 take advantage of 的意思是"利用"，例如：

He took advantage of the good weather to conduct market research. 他趁着天气好去进行市场调查。

在市场营销领域，协同效应（synergy effect）就是"1+1>2"的效应，可分为外部协同和内部协同两种情况。外部协同指的是一个集群中的企业由于相互协作共享业务行为和特定资源，比一个单独运作的企业具有更高的盈利能力；内部协同指的是企业在生产、营销、管理的不同环节、不同阶段、不同方面共同利用某一资源而产生的整体效应。

6. In addition, companies can gain access to new skills as the various organizations that have these skills come on board. 此外，公司还可以采用许多新的技术，因为各种掌握这些技术的机构都出现在合作团体之中。

在本句中，that 引导的是定语从句，用来修饰限定先行词 organizations。access 的意思是"进入，获得，利用"，例如：

Mortimer Hotel offers easy access to central London. 从莫蒂默旅馆去往伦敦市中心交通很方便。

They have only recently been able to gain access to the market. 直到最近他们才得以进入该地区。

7. However, there are some circumstances where you at least need to be careful and to put safeguards in place to overcome a few potential problems. 然而，在某些情况下，你至少需要小心谨慎，采取防护措施，克服一些潜在的问题。

在本句中，where 引导的定语从句修饰限定前面的 circumstances，在该从句中，and 连接两个并列的结构 to be careful 和 to put safeguards in place，短语 put safeguards in place 意思是"采取防护措施"，例如：

We're going to put in place new safeguard to make sure that customers will frequent our store. 我们要采取新的防护措施，确保顾客还会不断地光顾我们的店。

8. It is a great way to address complex challenges, since it has the potential to tap communal creativity and unleash true innovation and earn genuine buy-in. 这样做有助于应对各种错综复杂的挑战，因为合作可以充分利用集体的创造力，释放真正的创新精神，从而真正实现买进。

在本句中，it 是形式主语，真正的主语是后面的不定式 to address complex challenges。从属连词 since 引导的是原因状语从句，在该从句中，tap communal creativity、unleash true innovation 和 earn genuine buy-in 是并列的结构。address 的意思是"处理，应对，设法了解或解决"，例如：

Mr King sought to address those thorny problems when he spoke at the meeting. 金先生在会上讲话时试图解决那些棘手的问题。

9. For personal and professional development, follow through with your promises. 为了个人和职业的发展，务必要信守诺言。

在本句中，主句是祈使句。短语 follow through 的意思是"坚持到底"，例如：

David is determined to follow through with his plan. 大卫决定把自己的计划进行到底。

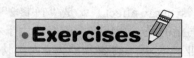

I Answer the following questions according to the text.

1. What can we learn from the first paragraph?
2. What is the main idea of the second paragraph?
3. What changes have happened to the notion of collaboration?
4. Why is collaboration so important?
5. How does collaboration take advantage of synergies?
6. How can you understand that collaboration helps to enhance relationships in a complementary way?
7. What are the disadvantages of collaboration?
8. Why is collaboration likely to delay your campaign?
9. What strategies for better collaboration are mentioned in the text?
10. What is the writer's attitude towards team success and personal gains?

Unit 19　Collaborative Strategy

II Decide whether the following statements are true or false.

1. As long as we work even harder than before, we can become the "strong individual salesperson".
2. As social beings, we tend to help each other.
3. The web had played an important role in improving our ability to collaborate with each other.
4. Business owners used to depend upon collaboration to finish a project.
5. Collaboration exists in both nonprofit organizations and corporations.
6. With individuals from various professional and technical backgrounds, the possibility of making errors will be eliminated.
7. With collaboration, members may be asked to finish different tasks based on their own expertise.
8. Collaboration ensures that effects of different parties who are interested in the matter are all considered.
9. For all the benefits of collaboration, people should be aware of some potential problems.
10. Collaboration is time-consuming in that people become lazier than before.

III Fill in each blank with the proper form of the word in the bracket.

1. There didn't seem much _____ (likely) of its happening.
2. He was one of the most creative and _____ (innovation) engineers of his generation.
3. The food queues have become a daily _____ (occur) across the country.
4. Managers are naturally _____ (bias) towards projects showing a quick return.
5. He hardly seemed to notice my _____ (present).
6. He warned that the action was _____ (damage) the economy.
7. There have been minor _____ (squabble) about phone bills.
8. Recommendations from two previous clients helped to establish her _____ (credible).
9. Two discussions from different points of view may _____ (complementary) each other.
10. The administration may put more emphasis on _____ (spur) economic growth.

IV Fill in each blank with a proper preposition.

1. For us, it's something that we may aspire _____ but can never attain.
2. If we tap _____ the children's market before our competitors, we will make a lot of money.
3. Subscribers to the magazine can take advantage _____ this special offer.
4. This kind of mistakes should be rooted _____.
5. Finally they agreed _____ the terms of transportation.

6. We must finish _____ this business in a day or two.
7. We encourage all members to strive _____ the highest standards.
8. Don't count _____ other people to help you out of trouble.
9. The software enables you to gain access _____ the Internet in seconds.
10. After careful consideration, he put _____ a five-point plan.

V Fill in the blanks with the words and phrases given below. Change the form where necessary.

| breed | cost-effective | consensus | come to the forefront | put in place |
| downplay | instrumental | for sure | be inclined to | keep up with |

1. In his first years as chairman he was _____ in raising the company's wider profile.
2. The issue of innovation has _____ with the fierce competition in the global market.
3. The manager is trying to _____ the complaints from the customers.
4. The new _____ of products puts the emphasis on enjoyment, not endurance.
5. A successful company must _____ the pace of technological change.
6. The newly appointed manager _____ communicate with others before making an important decision.
7. Any business must be run in a _____ way.
8. You can't say _____ that he will lose.
9. More policies and measures are _____ in this regard.
10. The _____ amongst the world's scientists is that the world is likely to warm up over the next few decades.

VI Cloze.

It's no surprise 1_____ marketing is in the early stages of a massive shift. 2_____ with the rise of social technologies, we can no longer embrace the strategies of the past. The evolution of marketing necessitates a new playbook, and marketers need to embrace new tactics fast. Marketers must begin to embrace collaboration now. The below five steps will 3_____ marketers with a clear plan to begin consumer collaboration and have clear results for their efforts.

Audit your audiences. Look at all of your brand's existing communities and databases, including CRM, Facebook and Twitter. Every brand has consumers 4_____ want to participate at different levels. Some love to tell you 5_____ they think of your brand, and others want to 6_____ from the rooftops. Brands need to understand all of these consumer segments and ensure they have plans to 7_____ the value of each.

Unit 19 Collaborative Strategy

Engage your core. Marketers must empower their loyal consumers to amplify their messages for them. In the article "How Valuable is Word of Mouth?" the authors write, "A company's most valuable customers are 8_____ who are both excellent buyers and marketers." These brand advocates have a 9_____ lifetime value than loyal customers who don't advocate but purchase more.

Align your content. Earned media is a popular buzzword these days, but most advertising content is still not 10_____ for the social world. Many marketers now attempt 11_____ the next viral hit, which often causes them to lose focus 12_____ what actually makes content shareable. Content is largely shared in small groups—not via an elite group of influencers. Developing content more frequently and targeting that content more accurately is becoming the new formula for achieving scale in communications.

Do it faster, smarter, better. It simply does not make 13_____ to develop a yearlong marketing plan anymore. Attempting to forecast spend and messages on a yearly or even quarterly 14_____ simply doesn't fit with how content is now consumed or how quickly culture evolves. Marketers today must operate more like tech companies 15_____ like advertisers. According to Steven Cook, former chief marketing officer of Samsung, "The new model is more akin 16_____ a startup mentality. The CMO will need to learn what it's like to move fast and do things on the cheap. The future is, after all, about doing more with less."

Commit to collaboration. Marketers must 17_____ to marketing with consumers in the long run. Collaboration cannot be thought 18_____ as a campaign. With each success, brands can develop a deeper relationship with consumers and build a long-term asset that will derive increasing value.

Marketing won't change overnight, but look back five or even three years, and it's clear how quickly our industry evolves. Technology grows quickly, and we can bet that the changes that happen over the next three to five years 19_____ a far greater impact than those we've just experienced. Why stand alone, when you can collaborate? Get 20_____ today.

1. A. why	B. how	C. what	D. that
2. A. But	B. And	C. However	D. Therefore
3. A. offer	B. give	C. provide	D. send
4. A. what	B. that	C. /	D. which
5. A. how	B. what	C. that	D. why
6. A. cry	B. stand	C. jump	D. shout
7. A. maximize	B. improve	C. enhance	D. raise
8. A. ones	B. the ones	C. those	D. these
9. A. bigger	B. higher	C. larger	D. fewer
10. A. developed	B. developing	C. being developed	D. underdeveloped

11. A. to creating   B. to create   C. creating   D. being created
12. A. to   B. into   C. for   D. on
13. A. progress   B. profits   C. sense   D. difference
14. A. basis   B. basics   C. ground   D. floor
15. A. other than   B. rather   C. rather than   D. than
16. A. to   B. after   C. with   D. in
17. A. resort   B. take   C. commit   D. aim
18. A. at   B. for   C. with   D. of
19. A. have   B. would have   C. will have   D. will be having
20. A. started   B. starting   C. began   D. beginning

VII Translation.

1. Once your organization has established business reasons for an enterprise collaboration strategy and is ready to deploy a system, it is essential to get employees invested in learning about the technology and how best to use it.
2. These tools offer the ability to reach huge audiences that you otherwise would have difficulty and high costs to touch.
3. Even if employees see the benefits of a collaboration system, it is all too easy to slip back into old habits, so continue to offer incentives for using the system and make improvements to collaboration processes.
4. Technology will not make an organization collaborative if it does not already support the notion of teams from different business units working in concert on common projects.
5. Analysts say that by carefully preparing for a deployment in this way, you'll be better positioned to confirm that all levels of the enterprise understand the importance, and business outcomes of the collaboration system; doing so, in turn, can help ensure that the organization derives optimum benefit from its investment.

Extended Reading

In a complex business environment where organizations are made up of more and more specialists, a great value is placed on leaders who can bring diverse groups together in a spirit of cooperation to get things done. As collaboration experts, these leaders must guard against "tribalism"—an attitude that arises when subgroups focus on their own activities and fail to look at the organization as a whole.

Tribalism starts when employees and leaders view their organization as divisible. They see their immediate coworkers and their part of the organization as special, alienating people from other "tribes" within the same organization whom they paradoxically rely on to get things done.

Whether it is departmental, hierarchical, generational, geographical, categorical or gender-specific, tribes are formed in organizations every day. The old-timers resent Gens X and Y for being fickle and disloyal, while the young people impatiently throw their arms up in frustration because they can't dislodge the organization from its dinosaur ways. The creatives resent the suits, and the suits can't believe they have to put up with people who think "business casual" means cargo shorts and flip-flops.

Tribalism chews up physical and emotional energy that distracts people from their jobs, wastes resources, disconnects people and stops the flow of information, severely weakening your organization's ability to compete.

Use the following strategies to banish tribalism and lay the groundwork for cross-departmental collaboration.

- **Understand why tribes exist**

A "tribe" is any part of the organization that has turned inward, functions as a unique, separate identity and is loyal to its own department, division or section rather than to the organization as a whole. Why do tribes exist and why are they so powerful? Here are a few thoughts: tribes provide identity; tribes create emotional ties in a world where people have a deep need for belonging; tribal pride usually causes members to think their ideas and practices are superior. People are typically motivated by self-interest first, then allegiance to the tribe and finally loyalty to the common good of the larger organization or community.

- **Do your homework—become a "tribal" expert**

To break down the walls of tribalism you have to understand the tribe. Don't automatically assume you know them just because they are part of the same organization. What do they do? Why do they exist? Who do they rely on to get work done? Who relies on them? What pressures, roadblocks and barriers do they face in carrying out their mission? What do you know about the culture of the tribe? What language do they speak? Who are the key players in the tribe? The more you empathize with them and understand the tribe, the more prone they will be to cooperate and collaborate with you.

- **Create a clear, compelling and urgent cause**

It has been pointed out that firefighters, police forces and special units teams rarely get caught up in tribalistic behavior because the mission at hand is laser clear and the consequences of mission accomplishment are compelling and urgent—often a matter of life and death. Just because you take a team member out of a tribe doesn't necessarily mean you will take tribalism out of the team member. You've got to give that person a gripping reason to be a part of what you are doing. Make your cause exciting, build a solid business case for what you're trying to do and inspire them to care as much as you do.

- **Never burn a bridge**

The person, department or functional area you criticize today may be the ally you need tomorrow. Even if you are grinding gears with another part of the organization, never diminish, disparage or dehumanize people from another tribe. Remember the real opponent is out there, not in here.

- **Create small wins**

Small wins have a way of breaking down barriers. Small wins create momentum. It feels good to win and if winning requires the participation of two tribes that have been "warring" with each other, both tribes now have a reason to work collaboratively.

- **Promote meetings between department heads**

Something positive happens when people meet together. Thinking and brainstorming together, problem solving together, celebrating together, and assuming collective responsibility for the organization's success is a powerful catalyst for building trust and making collaboration a way of life. Of course, busy people who compete for scarce resources or think they really have no reason to build rapport will resist this effort, but don't back down, it could be the single biggest thing you can do to foster creativity, collaboration and cross-functional accountability.

- **Recognize, reward and celebrate collaborative behavior**

The legends of athletic dynasties consist of incredible collaborative efforts. Players sit in locker rooms and clubhouses reminiscing about the key play "when it all came together". Whether told through video, newsletter, podcast, annual report or webinar, stories of great collaboration break down the walls of tribalism and honor collective accomplishments. Attaching performance metrics and bonuses to collaborative efforts sends a very strong message to everyone about what values are driving the business.

- **Make innovation a preeminent focus**

Creativity and innovation by necessity requires different people with diverse perspectives to "cross-pollinate" the organization with fresh ideas. When the bar for innovation is set extremely high and creative breakthroughs are an expected part of the culture, people have no choice but to start silo-busting.

- **Walk a mile**

Create opportunities for people from different parts of the organization to work together. Establish a rotation system where employees can work in another area to develop empathy and gain a big picture perspective. Invite people from other departments into your team meetings for an outsider/insider point of view.

- **Honor requests—keep your promises**

Most requests and promises are held sacred within the tribe, but considered optional between tribes. There are some questions every person and every business unit asks of another . Can I count on you? Will you be there when I need you? Do you care about this as much as we do?

Unit 19 Collaborative Strategy

Words and Expressions

tribalism   *n.* 集团意识，部落意识，宗族意识
subgroup   *n.* 小团体，小集团
divisible   *adj.* 可分开的
paradoxically   *adv.* 自相矛盾地
departmental   *adj.* 部门的
hierarchical   *adj.* 按照等级划分的，等级制度的
generational   *adj.* 两代之间的
gender-specific   *adj.* 针对不同性别的
old-timer   *n.* 前辈，老手
resent   *vt.* 憎恶，讨厌
fickle   *adj.* 易变的，无常的
disloyal   *adj.* 不忠诚的
dislodge   *vt.* 移动，把……逐出
creative   *n.*（广告）创意人员，创作者
suit   *n.* 追随者
flip-flop   *n.* 人字拖鞋
disconnect   *vt.* 切断，断开
weaken   *vt.* 削弱
banish   *vt.* 消除
belonging   *n.* 归属，归属感
tribalistic   *adj.* 部落的
compelling   *adj.* 非常强烈的，不可抵抗的
gripping   *adj.* 吸引注意力的
ally   *n.* 同盟，支持者
disparage   *vt.* 轻视，贬低，批评
dehumanize   *vt.* 使失去人性
momentum   *n.* 势头，动力
war   *vt.* 作战，同……处于交战状态
catalyst   *n.* 催化剂
scarce   *adj.* 缺乏的，罕见的
foster   *vt.* 培养
accountability   *n.* 责任，义务
reminisce   *vt.* 追忆，回忆
podcast   *n.* 播客
webinar   *n.* 在线研讨会
metric   *n.* 度量标准
preeminent   *adj.* 卓越的，杰出的
cross-pollinate   *vt.* 异花授粉
bar   *n.* 障碍，阻碍
silo-busting   *n.* 消除壁垒
outsider   *n.* 局外人
insider   *n.* 知情人
sacred   *adj.* 神圣的
optional   *adj.* 可选择的，随意的，任意的
guard against   避免，预防
view ... as   把……看作
business casual   商务便装，商务休闲装
chew up   消耗
distract ... from   把……的注意力转移开
burn the bridge   破釜沉舟
lay the groundwork for   为……做准备
cross-departmental collaboration   跨部门合作
function as   充当，担任
empathize with   产生共鸣
be prone to do sth.   倾向于做某事，易于做某事
laser clear   清晰，清楚
back down   放弃
locker room   衣帽间，更衣室
rotation system   轮换制度

Comprehension

I Answer the following questions according to the passage.

1. What is the topic of the first paragraph?
2. What is tribalism according to the passage?
3. When does tribalism start according to the passage?
4. Since tribes can be departmental, hierarchical, generational, geographical, categorical or gender-specific, then which type of tribe does the example of old-timers and young people belong to?
5. What are the disadvantages of tribalism?
6. Why do tribes exist according to the writer?
7. Why is creating a clear, compelling and urgent cause a must?
8. How to understand the strategy of "never burn a bridge"?
9. Why should meetings between departments be promoted?
10. What is the purpose of a rotation system?

II Write "T" for true, and "F" for false.

1. Leaders are responsible for fighting against tribalism.
2. It's contradictory that some employees and leaders view their part of the organization as different from other parts while relying on the latter to get things done.
3. Since tribalism can take different forms, it will do great harm to the organization's ability to compete.
4. A tribe is likely to turn outside and loyal to other organizations instead of its own organization.
5. The knowledge of the tribe will facilitate your cooperation and collaboration with others.
6. If we take a team member out of his tribe, then we can get rid of tribalism in his mind.
7. In order to collaborate with others, we cannot do damage to the bridge.
8. All people don't favor meetings between department heads.
9. It's suggested that collaborative efforts should be rewarded and encouraged.
10. To invite people from other departments into your team meetings, sometimes we have to walk a long way.

Unit 19 Collaborative Strategy

Additional Terms

break-out area 突破区域	insider knowledge 内部知识
business efficiency 经济效率	knowledge flow 知识流
collaboration program 合作计划	knowledge capture 知识获取
collaborative culture 合作文化	knowledge sharing 知识共享
collaborative filtering 协同过滤	measurable value 可测定数值
collaborative influence 协同影响力	merger scenario 合并方案
collaborative intelligence 群体智慧,协同智能	non-competition agreement 竞业限制合同
collaborative marketing 协作营销	open collaboration 开放式合作
collaborative platform 协同平台	operating cost 营业成本
collaborative selling 协作销售	organizational force 组织力量
collaborating thinking 合作思考	organizational objective 组织目标
collaborative workspace 协同工作区	process collaboration 流程型协同作业
collective action 集体行动	sales proposal 销售建议
commercial value 商业价值	silo mentality 孤岛思维,竖井心理
core group 核心团体	social networking capacity 社会网络能力
corporate commitment 企业承诺	succession management 后续管理,继任管理
customer data processing 客户数据处理	tacit knowledge 隐性知识
dynamic collaboration 动态联盟	technology collaboration solution 技术协作解决方案
end point 终点	touch point 接触点
enterprise collaboration system 企业协作系统	transactional service 交易服务
explicit knowledge 显性知识	

PART V

Marketing Management & The Future of Marketing

Unit 20

Marketing Management

Marketing management[1] is a business discipline focused on the practical application of marketing techniques and the management of a firm's marketing resources and activities. Globalization has led firms to market beyond the borders of their home countries, making international marketing highly significant. Marketing managers are often responsible for influencing the level, timing, and composition of customer demand. In part, this is because the role of a marketing manager can vary significantly based on a business's size, corporate culture, and industry context. For example, in a large consumer products company, the marketing manager may act as the overall general manager of his or her assigned product. To create an effective, cost-efficient marketing management strategy, firms must possess a detailed, objective understanding of their own business and the market in which they operate.

The key objective of marketing management is to determine how to appropriately allocate the resources of the organization towards marketing related activities. If someone has the job title of a marketing manager, he/she will tend to be the person whose responsibility is to control and direct the expenditure of funding that has been specifically set aside for marketing purposes.

Marketing management tends to go hand in hand with marketing strategy, which is a term that tends to refer to the long-term goals a company has in terms of marketing. For a firm engaged in marketing management, the whole concept of marketing is important for the following reasons. Marketing activities need to collect information that will inform a firm's production plans, so that they can decide, what quantity of good they produce based on a perception of anticipated demand. Marketing helps firms to establish a successful relationship with their customers. If firms produce the right product, make it available at the right price and distribute it properly, they can expand and diversify the exchange relationship. Marketing aims at maximizing customer satisfaction, which in turn should result in an increased demand for products. An increased sales volume will, in turn, help a firm achieve increased profits. Marketing helps in reducing the cost per unit of production. In addition, communication between the firm and society can be improved through advertising campaigns, sales promotions and publicity.

Marketing management employs various tools from economics and competitive strategy to analyze the industry context in which the firm operates. These include Porter's five forces, analysis of strategic groups of competitors, value chain analysis and others.[2] In competitor analysis, marketers build detailed profiles of each competitor in the market, focusing especially on their relative competitive strengths and weaknesses using SWOT analysis.[3] Marketing managers will examine each competitor's cost structure, sources of profits, resources and competencies, competitive positioning and product differentiation, degree of vertical integration, historical responses to industry developments, and other factors.

Marketing management often finds it necessary to invest in research to collect the data required to perform accurate marketing analysis. As such, they often conduct market research to obtain this information. Marketers employ a variety of techniques to conduct market research, but some of the more common include qualitative marketing research, such as focus groups and various types of interviews; quantitative marketing research, such as statistical surveys; experimental techniques, such as test markets; and observational techniques, such as ethnographic observation. Marketing managers may also design and oversee various environmental scanning and competitive intelligence processes to help identify trends and inform the company's marketing analysis.

If the company has obtained an adequate understanding of the customer base and its own competitive position in the industry, marketing managers are able to make their own key strategic decisions and develop a marketing strategy designed to maximize the revenues and profits of the firm. The selected strategy may aim for any of a variety of specific objectives, including optimizing short-term unit margin, revenue growth, market share, long-term profitability, or other goals.

After the firm's strategic objectives have been identified, the target market has been selected, and the desired positioning, product and brand have been determined, marketing managers focus on how to best implement the chosen strategy. Traditionally, this has involved implementation planning across the "4Ps" of marketing: product management, pricing, place, and promotion. Now a new P has been added making it a total of 5Ps. The fifth P is politics, which affects marketing in a significant way.

Taken together, the company's implementation choices across the 5Ps are often described as the marketing mix, meaning the mix of elements the business will employ to go to market and execute the marketing strategy. [4]The overall goal for the marketing mix is to consistently deliver a compelling value proposition that reinforces the firm's chosen positioning, builds customer loyalty and brand equity among target customers, and achieves the firm's marketing and financial objectives.

In many cases, marketing management will develop a marketing plan to specify how the company will execute the chosen strategy and achieve the business objectives. The content of marketing plans varies from firm to firm, but commonly includes: an executive summary; situation analysis to summarize facts and insights gained from market research and marketing analysis; the company's mission statement or long-term strategic vision; a statement of the company's key objectives, often subdivided into marketing objectives and financial objectives; the marketing strategy the business has chosen, specifying the target segments to be pursued and the competitive positioning to be achieved; implementation choices for each element of the marketing mix.

Marketing management employs a variety of metrics to measure progress against objectives. It is the responsibility of marketing managers—in the marketing department or elsewhere—to ensure that the execution of marketing programs achieves the desired objectives and does so in a cost-efficient manner. Marketing management therefore often makes use of various organizational control systems, such as sales forecasts, sales force and reseller incentive programs, sales force management systems, and customer relationship management (CRM[5])tools.

Vocabulary

timing	*n.* 计时，定时	diversify	*v.* 使不同
composition	*n.* 组成	oversee	*v.* 监督，监管

Phrases and Expressions

in part 在某种程度上
industry context 行业背景
set aside 留出，挑出
go hand in hand with 并肩齐步
anticipated demand 预期需求
exchange relationship 交换关系
sales volume 销售总量
competitor analysis 竞争对手分析
cost structure 成本结构
product differentiation 产品特色化，产品差异化
vertical integration 纵向整合
qualitative marketing research 定性市场研究
focus group 焦点小组
quantitative marketing research 定量市场研究
statistical survey 统计调查
experimental technique 实验方法
test market 市场试销
observational technique 观察技术
ethnographic observation 族群观察法
environmental scanning 环境扫描
unit margin 单位收益
revenue growth 收入增长
product management 产品管理
executive summary 执行摘要
situation analysis 形势分析
organizational control system 组织控制系统
sales forecast 销售预测
reseller incentive program 分销商激励计划
sales force management system 销售管理系统
customer relationship management 客户关系管理

Unit 20　Marketing Management

1. Marketing management：营销管理。营销管理是指为了实现企业或组织目标，建立和保持与目标市场之间互利的交换关系，而对设计项目进行分析、规划、实施和控制。营销管理的实质是需求管理，即对需求的水平、时机和性质进行调解。在营销管理实践中，企业通常需要预先设定一个市场需求水平，然而，实际的市场需求水平可能与预期的市场需求水平并不一致。这就需要企业营销管理者针对不同的需求情况，采取不同的营销管理对策，进而有效地满足市场需求，确保企业目标的实现。
2. These include Porter's five forces, analysis of strategic groups of competitors, value chain analysis and others.　这包括波特五力分析、竞争对手战略集团分析、价值链分析等。
在本句中，波特五力分析（Porter's five forces）是迈克尔·波特在1979年提出的架构，其用途是定义一个市场的吸引力程度。波特认为影响市场吸引力的5种力量由密切影响公司服务客户及获利的方面组成，任何力量的改变都可能吸引公司退出或进入市场。4种力量为来自消费者的议价能力、来自供应商的议价能力、来自潜在进入者的威胁和来自替代品的威胁，共同组合而创造出影响公司的第5种力量，即来自现有竞争者的威胁。
战略集团（亦称战略群组）就是一个行业中沿着相同的战略方向，采用相同或相似战略的企业群。只有处于同一战略群组的企业才是真正的竞争对手。因为他们通常采用相同或相似的技术，生产相同或相似的产品，提供相同或相似的服务，采用相互竞争性的定价方法，其间的竞争要比与战略群组外的企业的竞争更直接、更激烈。
价值链分析法是由美国哈佛商学院教授迈克尔·波特提出来的，它是一种寻求确定企业竞争优势的工具，即运用系统性方法考察企业的各项活动和相互关系，从而找寻具有竞争优势的资源。
3. In competitor analysis, marketers build detailed profiles of each competitor in the market, focusing especially on their relative competitive strengths and weaknesses using SWOT analysis.　在竞争对手分析中，营销商搜索市场中每位竞争者的详细资料，尤其是利用态势分析法，侧重分析他们的相对竞争优势和劣势。
SWOT分析法又被称为态势分析法，它是由旧金山大学的管理学教授于20世纪80年代初提出来的，SWOT 四个英文字母分别代表：优势（strength）、劣势（weakness）、机会（opportunity）、威胁（threat）。所谓SWOT分析，即基于内外部竞争环境和竞争条件下的态势分析，将与研究对象密切相关的各种主要内部优势、劣势和外部的机会和威胁等，通过调查列举出来，并依照矩阵形式排列，然后用系统分析的思想，把各种因素相互匹配起来加以分析，从中得出一系列相应的结论，而结论通常带有一定的决策性。
4. Taken together, the company's implementation choices across the 5Ps are often described as the

marketing mix, meaning the mix of elements the business will employ to go to market and execute the marketing strategy. 这些综合在一起，公司实施 5P 的选择经常被描述为市场营销组合，指的是公司进入市场、实施营销战略所利用的各种因素的总和。

市场营销组合指的是企业在选定的目标市场上，综合考虑环境、能力、竞争状况等因素，加以最佳组合和运用，以完成企业的任务。市场营销组合是企业市场营销战略的一个重要组成部分，是指由企业可控的基本营销措施组成的一个整体性活动。市场营销的主要目的是满足消费者的需求，而消费者的需求很多，要满足消费者需求所应采取的措施也很多。因此，企业在开展市场营销活动时，必须把握住那些基本性措施，并合理组合，充分发挥整体优势和效果。

5. CRM：客户关系管理。最早开展客户关系管理的国家是美国，这个概念最初由 Gartner Group 提出。在 1980 年便有所谓的"接触管理"，即专门收集客户的所有信息，到 1990 年则演变成包括电话服务中心在内的客户关怀。

I Answer the following questions according to the text.

1. What is market management according to the passage?
2. What is the key objective of marketing management?
3. How can we understand the first sentence in paragraph 3?
4. Why is the whole concept of marketing important for companies engaged in marketing management?
5. What tools does marketing management employ?
6. What factors will marketing managers examine?
7. What techniques do marketing managers use to conduct market research?
8. What are the 5Ps of marketing?
9. What can be called the marketing mix?
10. What is usually included in marketing plans?

II Decide whether the following statements are true or false.

1. Globalization is an integral part of a firm's marketing strategy.
2. A business's size, corporate culture, and industry context have a bearing on a marketing manager's role.

Unit 20 Marketing Management

3. The responsibility of a marketing manager is to create an effective, cost-efficient marketing management strategy.
4. Porter's five forces makes use of SWOT analysis.
5. Marketing management invests in research to collect the relative data out of necessity.
6. An adequate understanding of the customer base and its own competitive position helps marketing managers to make strategic decisions.
7. Traditionally, the implementation of the chosen strategy calls for 5Ps.
8. The overall goal for the marketing mix is to develop a marketing strategy designed to maximize the revenues.
9. The marketing plans are not necessarily the same in different firms.
10. Marketing management employs a variety of metrics to measure progress rather than objectives.

III Fill in each blank with the proper form of the word in the bracket.

1. We are going to _____ (execution) our campaign plan to the letter.
2. He has not _____ (specify) what action he would like them to take.
3. The new systems have been _____ (optimize) for running Microsoft Windows.
4. The company's troubles started only when it _____ (diverse) into new products.
5. The price increase has had no _____ (perception) effect on sales.
6. Television has transformed the size and social _____ (compose) of the audience at great sporting occasions.
7. This sense of privilege tends to be _____ (reinforce) by the outside world.
8. Husband and wife were similarly successful in their _____ (choose) careers.
9. Basically, the article can be _____ (summary) in three sentences.
10. The technique is _____ (experiment), but the list of its practitioners is growing.

IV Fill in each blank with a proper preposition.

1. The employment outlook for the next year is based _____ part on contracts signed this year.
2. What he has done for us can not be measured _____ terms of money.
3. The hotel manager set _____ two pleasant rooms for us.
4. Industrial progress should go hand in hand _____ the development of agriculture.
5. You can use sales organizations to subdivide markets _____ regions.
6. This report refers _____ what has happened to the poor families in this area.
7. I'm a professional and I have to conduct myself _____ a professional manner.
8. It would be imprudent to invest all your money _____ one company.

9. The newly invented machines vary in color _____ almost black to yellow.
10. Please inform us _____ your decision and we will act accordingly.

V Fill in the blanks with the words and phrases given below. Change the form where necessary.

oversee	go hand in hand with	in part	as such	in terms of
publicity	set aside		produce	in turn	discipline

1. All this _____ has had a snowball effect on the sales of their latest album.
2. Winter _____ will cost more for the next few weeks.
3. You've got to make sure that people work together across _____.
4. Theory is based on practice and _____ serves practice.
5. These areas are _____ for public recreational use.
6. As the owner of the factory I'm like the head of a family, and _____ I can't allow any black sheep among my employees.
7. He thought of everything _____ money.
8. The failure of the promotion was due _____ to the infeasibility of his plan.
9. I set up a separate department for George to _____ quality.
10. Production must _____ technological improvement.

VI Cloze.

Marketing management is an important part of the business field that concentrates on 1_____ marketing techniques to the management activities of an organization. Marketing managers are highly trained professionals responsible for 2_____ the marketing activities. A big part of a company's success or failure is directly tied to the 3_____ of its marketing efforts. In the last few months, I 4_____ the privilege to meet and work with some truly exceptional marketing managers and have pulled 5_____ a list of the qualities that seem 6_____ in all of them; some that you're 7_____ with, some you learn at university, and some you develop every day.

Great marketing managers are vision creators. This ability to communicate the 8_____ clearly will give not only their employees a clear understanding of what the product does, but will help get the best out of their advertising agency. "Our company will be selling a new product. This product will be more expensive, but it's a more 9_____ product and it's easier to use—saving time and money. This is our 10_____ in the marketplace."

Good marketing managers need to have a very strong understanding of what is happening in the marketplace and what influences people's buying decisions. They 11_____ the prospective markets, oversee product development, help their organization 12_____ the amount of profit

Unit 20 Marketing Management

and market share, and make sure they are meeting customers' 13_____. They are also responsible for constantly monitoring 14_____ to identify the need 15_____ new products and services. Understanding both market and customer base is critical to 16_____ the essential, clear vision and getting to your core customer.

Successful marketing managers listen to people inside and 17_____ of the company. They listen to their customers, co-workers, and salespeople. By having their ears 18_____, marketing managers better understand the marketplace. 19_____, they must be flexible, goal-oriented, and have the ability to work under pressure. They often complete continuing education and participate in seminars and conferences 20_____ a regular basis.

1. A. putting   B. applying   C. changing   D. devoting
2. A. overseeing   B. managing   C. controlling   D. participating
3. A. efficiency   B. effect   C. impact   D. effectiveness
4. A. had   B. have   C. have had   D. having
5. A. up   B. together   C. for   D. on
6. A. strange   B. familiar   C. popular   D. apparent
7. A. born   B. filled   C. burdened   D. provided
8. A. qualities   B. techniques   C. vision   D. needs
9. A. durable   B. fashionable   C. practical   D. profitable
10. A. policy   B. strategy   C. edge   D. success
11. A. identify   B. recognize   C. realize   D. supervise
12. A. enlarge   B. increase   C. expand   D. maximize
13. A. standards   B. needs   C. wants   D. requirements
14. A. production   B. trends   C. sales   D. distribution
15. A. for   B. with   C. on   D. of
16. A. create   B. be creating   C. having created   D. creating
17. A. external   B. internal   C. outside   D. out
18. A. closed   B. open   C. closing   D. opening
19. A. Besides   B. However   C. Therefore   D. Hence
20. A. with   B. in   C. at   D. on

VII Translation.

1. In fact, one study showed that dissatisfied customers may bad-mouth the product to 10 or more acquaintances; bad news travels fast, something marketers that use hard selling should bear in mind.
2. Marketing management is an integral part of any business venture. It is therefore very vital for all managers to master all essential skills in this field in order to realize the goal of their

businesses.
3. The sole purpose of studying this discipline is to enable the market managers to know the ideal customers, the appropriate time to market a product, the ideal price, and the most appropriate product to market.
4. In order to create an effective marketing management strategy, a firm needs to have a strong understanding of their own business and the market in which they operate.
5. Winning in the marketplace requires managers to have an in-depth understanding of all areas of marketing—from formulation to execution.

 Extended Reading

Marketing Management Philosophies

Firms and businesses, approach and conduct business in different ways in order to achieve their organizational goals. There are different philosophies or concepts that guide sellers to conduct their marketing activities. For example, sellers can only focus on production and try to reduce their cost of production, or focus on the quality of product. Similarly, they can pay more attention to promotion. In this way different concepts have evolved to help the organizations in managing their marketing activities. The most practiced marketing philosophies are: production, product, selling, marketing and societal marketing, which guide firms and business in their marketing effort. The first three concepts, namely, production, product and selling, focus all on the product. The last two concepts, marketing and societal marketing, focus on the customer. However, the commonality in all five philosophies is that they all have the same goal which is organizational profit.

The first concept, the production concept, refers to the philosophy that consumers will favor products that are available and highly affordable. This philosophy states that any amount of goods produced will sell if it is available and affordable to customers. When firms adopt this concept, generally they produce goods on a mass production level, to be able to produce large quantities, therefore make it more available; investing in technology is essential, to reduce the costs of production and make it more affordable. In such a case the management is required to focus mostly on improving the production and distribution. It is one of the earliest marketing concepts where goods were just produced on the belief that they would be sold because consumers need them. Practiced by earlier industrials, it soon became a standardized practice. But with the continuous industrialization and increasing number of players into the market, too many people were selling the same product. The mass production of goods which is the heart and soul of production concept can no longer work. Therefore, it is a concept where goods are produced without taking into consideration the choices or tastes of target customers. It focuses on the internal capabilities of the firm rather than on the desires and needs of the market place. A production orientation falls short because it doesn't consider whether goods and services that the firm produces meet the needs of the market place.

Product concept states that sellers should focus on improving the quality of their products as well as the performance, and adding more innovative features and so on. So basically, this concept holds that a good product creates its own market, and does not require heavy marketing expenditure. However, its main drawback is that it may lead to marketing myopia in which the organization overlooks the importance of other substitutes available in the industry. The concept is applicable in some situations such as electronics and mobile handsets.

The selling concept is an idea in marketing which proposes that costumers will not automatically buy something if they are left to themselves, unless they are swayed to do so through selling effort. In other words, the demand for a product is equal to the supply for that product. It dictates that companies and organizations should be aggressive and persuasive in promoting and selling their products to the typically inert customers. It focuses on the large scale selling and promotion activities in order to attract more customers. Industries that sell products which are not normally considered for purchase by buyers must practice the selling concept. There is high risk in such marketing. If the buyers do not like the product, then it can really spoil the reputation of the organization. So the fundamental problem with this concept is the lack of understanding of the needs and wants of the market place.

The marketing concept states that the organizational goals are based on the wants and needs of the target markets. This concept highlights that the supply is greater than the demand. According to marketing concept, organizations should focus on analysis of the needs and wants of target markets and providing the desired satisfaction more effectively than competitors. Marketing concept is often confused with selling concept. Selling concept starts with the production of goods, focuses on promotion and sales, and ends with getting profits. In contrast, the marketing concept starts with a well-defined market, focuses on customer needs and wants and ends with creating long-term customer relationship by effectively satisfying the needs and wants of customers. Thus through marketing concept, organizations could be benefited in the long run.

Societal concept focuses on improving the well-being of customers and society as a whole. Therefore, those organizations which are practicing this concept try to analyze the needs, wants and demands of target markets and deliver superior value to customers which results in overall well-being of customers and society. Societal concept is really new as compared to other marketing management philosophies. One reason a market-oriented organization may choose not to deliver the benefits sought by consumer is that these benefits may not be good for individuals or society. So some of the companies practice societal marketing philosophy which preserves individual's and society's long-term best interests.

Different companies use their own marketing management philosophies. The choice as to which concept or philosophy to adopt depends on the circumstances of the company. The equity analyst should understand these philosophies to identity which companies are good to invest for long-term.

Words and Expressions

commonality n. 共同特征	product concept 产品观念
affordable adj. 买得起的，负担得起的	marketing concept 营销观念
applicable adj. 适当的，可适用的	selling concept 推销观念
sway v. 影响，左右	societal concept 社会观念
dictate v. 规定；认为	internal capability 内在能力
inert adj. 迟钝的，不活泼的	production orientation 生产导向
highlight v. 强调，突出	fall short 缺乏，不足
well-being n. 幸福，福利	marketing expenditure 营销支出
drawback n. 缺点，不足	marketing myopia 营销近视症
production concept 生产观念	equity analyst 股票分析师

Comprehension

I Answer the following questions according to the passage.

1. What role do the marketing management philosophies play?
2. What are the differences and similarities of the five philosophies?
3. How can companies make products available and affordable?
4. Why can't the production concept work any longer?
5. What are the characteristics of product concept?
6. How to understand "marketing myopia"?
7. What does the selling concept focus on? What are the demerits of this concept?
8. What do companies with the marketing concept focus on?
9. What are the differences between selling concept and marketing concept?
10. How to distinguish societal concept from other concepts?

II Write "T" for true, and "F" for false.

1. There are five philosophies or concepts that guide sellers to conduct their marketing activities.
2. The first three concepts focus on the product, while the other two concepts focus on marketing.

3. Different as five philosophies, they still have something in common.
4. As the earliest marketing philosophy, the production concept has been a standardized practice.
5. The selling concept holds that a good product creates its own market, and does not require heavy marketing expenditure.
6. The selling concept is popular among those industries that sell products buyers are unwilling to buy.
7. Without consideration of the needs and wants of the market place, organizations run the risk of spoiling their reputation.
8. For firms practicing marketing concept, demand is equal to supply.
9. In the long run, organizations can benefit from selling concept rather than marketing concept.
10. Societal concept aims at improving the well-being of both individuals and society.

Additional Terms

anticipative marketing　预期营销
brand competition　品牌竞争
broad environment　大环境
communication channel　沟通渠道
competitor orientation　竞争者导向
creative marketing　创意营销
customer attraction　顾客吸引力
customer cost　顾客成本
customer database　客户数据库
customer identification　客户识别
customer orientation　顾客导向
customer share　顾客份额，客户占有率
customer solution　顾客问题解决
demographic environment　人口统计环境
dialogue channel　对话渠道
ecological imperative concept　生态准则观念
economic environment　经济环境
entrepreneurial marketing　创业营销
exchange relationship　交换关系
expenditure tracking system　开支跟踪系统
external market orientation　外部市场导向
financial accountability　财政责任
form competition　形式竞争
formulated marketing　惯例化营销，制式化营销
generic competition　愿望竞争
holistic marketing concept　全方位营销观念
human concept　人类观念
implied need　隐性需求
industry competition　行业竞争
integrated market orientation　整合市场导向
intelligent consumption concept　理智消费观念
interfunctional coordination　职能协调，功能间协调
internal market orientation　内部市场导向
internal marketing orientation　内部营销导向
market offering　市场供应品

marketing network　营销网络
marketing task　营销任务
model-based decision making　基于模型的决策
organizational culture　企业文化
performance marketing concept　绩效营销观念
political-legal environment　政治法律环境
product orientation　产品导向
product substitutability　产品替代风险，产品替代度
real need　真实需求
relationship marketing orientation　关系营销导向
responsive marketing　响应营销
sales orientation　销售观念
secret need　秘密需求
social-cultural environment　社会文化环境
social marketing orientation　社会营销导向
supply chain　供应链
target audience　目标受众
target marketing　目标营销
trade channel　贸易渠道，营销渠道
technological environment　技术环境
task environment　任务环境
value delivery system　价值传送系统

Unit 21

The Future of Marketing

The marketing landscape is changing fast. The marketers who understand what's coming next have a distinct advantage over their competitors. They are constantly faced with changes, which is neither a new situation, nor one to be feared because changes provide opportunities for the emergence of new marketing activities and market positions.[1] Being aware of the importance of changes and adapting creatively to new conditions are the daily bread of marketing professionals. In other words, the world of marketing is in a constant state of flux, always on the lookout for the newest trends and opportunities. Technology is certainly providing marketers a lot to think about these days. Old models are gradually making way for new ones and businesses are quick to act on it. The great thing about the technologies is that they provide more personalized data on usage and purchases. This allows marketers to get a clearer picture of what customers want. This depth of insight can lead to a better relationship between businesses and consumers, leading to higher profits.

The future of marketing is going to look quite different from the marketing of today. Marketing will become more tactical. In the last century, marketing was often seen as a strategic investment, so important to corporate success that there was not much point in measuring it. With the exception of direct marketing, it was difficult to measure many marketing activities anyway, so few companies tried. Today, however, companies gather far more data than in the past and have become far more sophisticated about measuring just about everything. There are now very few marketing activities that aren't "sliced and diced" to see whether they're actually making money. This is not to say that companies don't need a marketing strategy. However, now that activities under the marketing rubric are measured, the marketing group itself must become ever more tactical in order to make the metrics improve. In other words, there will be a lot less of "the ads must be working because the revenue went up" and a lot more of "27% of our website leads converted into paying customers."

Commoditization will drive marketing investment. There's a growing awareness that product categories go through four distinct stages, each requiring a different level of marketing investment.[2]

- **Entry phase**

Sales plays the primary role, explaining the concept to buyers, getting them excited about it, following up to get reference accounts, and so forth. By comparison, marketing plays a minor role, at best.

- **Consulting phase**

Once the product category is established, the salespeople continue to cultivate new accounts while marketing helps sales to identify new leads. Marketing acts as a service organization to sales, with sales still "leading the charge".[3]

- **Service phase**

When several vendors provide essentially the same product, customers decide which product to buy based on the ability of vendors to precisely respond to their specifications, their delivery requirements, payment convenience and so forth. During this phase, marketing and sales are of roughly equal importance.[4]

- **Commodity phase**

Once a product becomes a commodity, sales moves into the background (or goes away completely) while marketing moves to the forefront, locating potential customers and setting up of fulfillment channels that do not require the overhead of a dedicated sales team.

As companies better understand this inexorable process of commoditization, they can allocate marketing budgets based upon the phase of the product category, rather than a preconceived notion of appropriate marketing investment. In other words, there will be a lot less of "this product is our future, so let's spend marketing dollars on it" and a lot more of "it's time to shift responsibility for this product from sales to marketing".

Marketing will be more reactive and less proactive. Traditionally, marketing has been seen as a "proactive" activity where marketing activities "create" a brand. That's beginning to turn upside down now that customers play a far more visible and powerful role in brands.

Marketers will be increasingly dependent on information technology to create their campaigns. Close integration is necessary for successful implementation. With the right tools for data gathering and analysis, marketers may soon be able to know customers so well that they can predict what people want before they want it.

By 2020, most interruptive marketing will be gone. Instead, marketing will be personalized and customized. Data will be essential, and as users, we'll be paying with our data—bartering a bit of our personal information in return for the use of platforms and services. Customers will be forming relationships with brands that are built on trust, and if a company breaks that trust, it will be very quickly viral and very quickly over. By 2020, unauthorized targeting of consumers will essentially be useless.

The idea of having a separate marketing department is going to vanish. In the future, the "reason to buy" will be socially motivated. If a product is great and everybody loves it, it will sell. And you're going to stop buying things from companies that don't fit your values, just because you can't see giving them the money.

Companies are going to try to predict how people feel about their brand, and then adjust in real time by changing features, and starting new conversations with customers in real time. In the future all of the companies will have one big job: to make sure that the customer feels cherished and safeguarded. As Amazon calls it, "customer delight" will be the number one mission. If you screw that up, everyone will leave.

The future of branding is to use the latest technology, such as mobile devices and smart TVs, to create unique and compelling images so that members of the target audiences only want to buy your products. The technology is available to enable companies to find an open space in the minds of customers and fill it with the right image that satisfies their needs.⁵ There are a lot of innovative technologies that will be used to create the products of the future. For instance, 3D printers are being used to create products from a software program or blueprint. Innovations will also help marketers to make better decisions on products including the styles, shapes, and colors.

Even though customers have the ability to shop the lowest price for a particular brand, technology will also enable marketers to dynamically reveal hidden costs and add them to the list price to minimize the showrooming effect. For example, a retailer such as Best Buy will not have to lose a customer to an Internet retailer because of price. ⁶It could add the hidden costs related to wasted time, gas, traffic stress, waiting for the products, and shipping charges to advertised prices. The same technologies that facilitate calculating hidden costs in pricing can be used to help customers and companies select the most effective distribution channel. Much of the future innovation in marketing will be in the area of promotion. Companies are already shifting to Internet, mobile, and social media promotion channels. Using GPS and other location technology, promotion will find customers that are physically near the store (if given permission by customers) and send them a text or a voice message telling them about items they typically buy that are on sale.

Companies can collect all the data they want, but data alone will never be enough. You still need to reach consumers on an emotional level. The bottom line for marketers will be that if a product or service isn't humanized, it won't sell—because buying something isn't an intellectual process of saying "this could be useful"; it's saying "I really want this".

Vocabulary

flux *n.* 变动，波动	preconceived *adj.*（观点等）事先形成的
rubric *n.* 说明，规定	viral *adj.* 病毒性的
commoditization *n.* 商品化	unauthorized *adj.* 未经授权的
inexorable *adj.* 不可阻挡的，不容变更的	humanized *adj.* 人性化的

Phrases and Expressions

on the lookout for	寻找，密切注意	product category	产品类别
make way for	让路	marketing investment	营销投资
get a picture of	了解	entry phase	进入阶段
corporate success	企业成功	at best	充其量
with the exception of ...	除……之外	consulting phase	咨询阶段
service phase	服务阶段	screw up	弄糟，搞乱，毁坏
commodity phase	商品化阶段	showrooming effect	先逛店后网购的现象
lead the charge	打头阵		
in return for	作为回报	voice message	语音信息
customer delight	感动顾客		

1. They are constantly faced with changes, which is neither a new situation, nor one to be feared because changes provide opportunities for the emergence of new marketing activities and market positions. 营销商不断面对各种变化，这既不是什么新鲜事，也不需要害怕，因为变化可以带来机遇，催生新的营销活动和市场定位。
在本句中，which 引导非限制性定语从句，指代的是前面整个主句，因此看作单数。在该从句中还使用了 because 引导的原因状语从句。

2. There's a growing awareness that product categories go through four distinct stages, each requiring a different level of marketing investment. 人们越来越意识到产品类别要经历 4 个不同的阶段，每个阶段都需要不同水平的营销投资。
在本句中，主句使用了常见的 there be 句型，其中 that 引导的是同位语从句，解释说明 awareness。此外，句子中的 each requiring a different level of marketing investment 使用了独立主格结构，动词 require 与其逻辑上的主语 each（each one of the four stages）之间是主动关系，故使用了 -ing 形式。

3. Marketing acts as a service organization to sales, with sales still "leading the charge". 营销部门是销售部门的服务机构，而销售部门依然是领头羊。
在本句中，短语 act as 的意思是"充当，担任"。此外，本句使用了 with 的复合结构，因为动词 lead 与其逻辑上的主语 sales 之间是主动关系，故使用了 -ing 形式。

Unit 21　The Future of Marketing

4. During this phase, marketing and sales are of roughly equal importance.　在这一阶段，营销与销售几乎处于同等重要的地位。

在本句中，短语 be of equal importance 的意思是"同样重要"，这是英语学习中常见的一种表达，即 be of+名词（通常是抽象名词），例如：

The meeting is of great importance.　这次会议很重要。

Mary and Lily are of the same age.　玛丽和莉莉年龄相当。

5. The technology is available to enable companies to find an open space in the minds of customers and fill it with the right image that satisfies their needs.　公司可以充分运用技术，在消费者的心目中找到一席之地，满足他们的需求，给他们留下深刻的印象。

在本句中，and 连接了两个并列的宾语，即 find an open space 和 fill it with the right image，后面跟的是 that 引导的定语从句，that 在从句中充当主语。此外，短语 enable sb. to do sth. 的意思是"使某人能够做某事"。后面的 it 指代上文提到的 open space。

6. For example, a retailer such as Best Buy will not have to lose a customer to an Internet retailer because of price.　例如，像零售商百思买就不会因为价格的原因致使其顾客转向网上零售商。

百思买（Best Buy）是全球最大的家用电器和电子产品的零售商，该公司通过物美价廉、易于使用的高科技娱乐产品提高生活品质。本着这一宗旨，从 2002 年下半年起，百思买不仅在美国境内，而且在加拿大开设了分店。

I　Answer the following questions according to the text.

1. What is the writer's attitude towards changes marketers meet with?
2. How can you understand "Being aware of the importance of changes and adapting creatively to new conditions are the daily bread of marketing professionals."?
3. What role does technology play according to the first paragraph?
4. What does the writer mainly talk about in the third paragraph?
5. What are the four stages that product categories go through?
6. What is the difference between being reactive and being proactive?
7. How will the technology influence the future of branding?
8. What is the writer's purpose to mention the example of Best Buy?
9. What new devices are mentioned to facilitate the growth of future marketing?
10. How can you understand the bottom line of marketers?

II. Decide whether the following statements are true or false.

1. The marketing landscape is changing so fast that marketers find it difficult to adapt to changes.
2. The advantages of changes in marketing outweigh the disadvantages.
3. The technology enables marketers have a better understanding of customers and establish better relationship, thus leading to higher profits.
4. In the past it was difficult to measure such marketing activities as direct marketing.
5. Marketing strategy will become less important since activities are carefully measured to see whether they're actually making money.
6. In the four phases that product categories go through, sales is important than marketing.
7. Marketing used to be seen as a "proactive" activity where marketing activities "create" a brand.
8. By 2020, marketing will be personalized and customized rather than interruptive.
9. 3D printers will become increasingly popular in the area of promotion.
10. In addition to collecting data, marketers are expected to reach customers on an emotional level.

III. Fill in each blank with the proper form of the word in the bracket.

1. The company is staffed by capable and _____ (dedicate) employees.
2. They decided to _____ (location) the head company in New York.
3. You had to respect him because he was _____ (authorize) to deal with this matter.
4. The company should be able to _____ (fulfillment) our requirements.
5. The _____ (showroom) shop at conventional shops, but they buy items online for a cheaper price.
6. Our trips are all-inclusive—there are no _____ (hide) costs.
7. The company's leaders had underestimated the _____ (deep) of the crisis.
8. Jo Robinson began by_____ (humanized) the waiting room magazines and tea-making for customers.
9. It's illegal to reproduce the worksheets without _____ (permit) from the publisher.
10. He argued that the economic recovery had been _____ (facilitate) by his tough stance.

IV. Fill in the blanks with the words and phrases given below. Change the form where necessary.

make way for	at best	flux	the bottom line	there is no point in ...
in return for	forefront	screw up	on the lookout for	with the exception of

Unit 21   The Future of Marketing

1. The new factory could put the town back at the _____ steelmaking.
2. _____ talking with her since she was too stubborn to listen to me.
3. Generally speaking, customers are _____ cheap and fine products.
4. Get out! Haven't you _____ things _____ enough already?
5. Our society is in a state of _____, so people have to learn to adapt to changes.
6. I wish I could do something _____ the kindness I have received from him.
7. The old building is being knocked down to _____ a new road.
8. For want of money, we can only finish half of the task _____.
9. It was a day off for everyone, _____ Laura who had draft a contract.
10. _____ is that we have to make a decision today, or it'll be too late.

V   Cloze.

Like any business, the media industry evolves in 1_____. In the past decades, there 2_____ few job openings at media companies, but now, as more media companies are looking for ways to 3_____ out and reach larger population bases, there is an increase 4_____ the availability of highly coveted marketing positions. Today, we are at the top of the business cycle and marketing jobs are plentiful across a variety of industries. Even the media industry, which 5_____ has not provided much career potential for marketing executives, 6_____ its doors. In fact, the media industry is currently exceeding 7_____ industries, such as consumer packaged goods, in career opportunities for marketers. HarperCollins and MySpace, for example, are both media businesses and are owned by the same 8_____, but they go to market in very different ways. 9_____, they have different revenue models that require very different forms of marketing. Marketing opportunities 10_____ in a variety of niche specialties. 11_____, an e-commerce company might be interested in 12_____ marketing professionals to support customer acquisition or product development, 13_____ a magazine might need marketing support in 14_____. Marketers should also be aware of the competition they will face when 15_____ a position at a media company. Typically, marketers must have a plethora of solid experience and a vast understanding of the media industry and the specific changes impacting the industry they are looking to work in. Marketers should already be familiar with 16_____ to communicate their messages across a variety of mediums and how to connect with a large customer base. Marketers will also need to enhance their skills in Internet marketing, as many media companies now want marketers to have at 17_____ 10-15 years of Internet marketing experience. Because the Internet industry is relatively young, and has not always valued marketing as 18_____ as other functions, there are few marketers with much Internet experience. However, for those who can 19_____ their Internet marketing skills, or have the experience, the demand has completely outstripped the supply. There are currently two 20_____ of Internet marketing that offer the greatest growth potential: search engine marketing and advertising sales marketing.

1. A. order   B. sequence   C. advance   D. cycles
2. A. has been   B. have been   C. were   D. had been
3. A. branch   B. turn   C. make   D. put
4. A. on   B. with   C. in   D. for
5. A. seldom   B. traditionally   C. mostly   D. certainly
6. A. is opening   B. are opening   C. is closing   D. are closing
7. A. less developed B. more developed C. more mature   D. less mature
8. A. parent   B. owner   C. boss   D. person
9. A. However   B. In addition   C. Therefore   D. Hence
10. A. lie   B. exist   C. abound   D. persist
11. A. For example B. In other words   C. Therefore   D. Nonetheless
12. A. enrolling   B. training   C. interviewing   D. hiring
13. A. and   B. while   C. but   D. as
14. A. production   B. circulation   C. Edition   D. compiling
15. A. pursuing   B. pursued   C. to pursue   D. to pursuing
16. A. what   B. how   C. when   D. which
17. A. best   B. most   C. least   D. length
18. A. few   B. less   C. much   D. many
19. A. increase   B. enhance   C. boost   D. promote
20. A. areas   B. scopes   C. fields   D. ranges

VI Translation.

1. The decisions and products of Apple, Amazon and other innovators will affect how we live in the years to come.
2. While privacy issues surrounding location services will need to be resolved, consumers are still demanding that marketers understand all of their daily contexts and find ways to make their lives easier.
3. In this increasingly interconnected world, consumers are not necessarily thinking in terms of silos.
4. Smart marketers can succeed by engaging with the trends that are resonating with the emerging consumers of today.
5. In the face of the unknown, it is courage that carries us forward and creativity that opens new doors.

Unit 21　The Future of Marketing

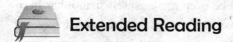
Extended Reading

Market Research Fails to Predict the Future

Don't believe market research—it can't predict the future. Market research only tells us about today. It tells us nothing about tomorrow.

There's a growing feeling that something is not working with market research, where billions are spent every year but results are mixed at best. Some of the problems relate to the basic challenge of using research to predict what consumers will want (especially with respect to products that are radically different). Turning to market research as a tool to predict the future has no more scientific validity than using astrology. It isn't a good idea to entrust your product development to a market researcher any more than it would be wise to consult your horoscope before crossing a busy road. Many companies will not survive in the new millennium because they are relying on surveys conducted before to plan future products and services. They will land up with the wrong products, designed for consumers who no longer exist.

Most people see the future as more of the same: faster computers, better cars, more TV channels. They can't see the big picture—how life itself will change. A classic example is aircraft design. In the mid 1990s airlines such as British Airways asked business fliers what they wanted and they said good food and wine, comfortable seats, more video choices and personal screens. Hardly anyone mentioned data sockets on satellite phones, and even fewer asked for power supplies in arm rests so they could use PCs without clusters of spare batteries. Now these things are regarded as number one essentials for any world class airline—but it's too late. They won't be widely available on British Airways flights until the next millennium. In contrast, those with longer range of vision have won a competitive advantage. Over 1,700 aircraft world-wide already have in-seat power, not one owned by British Airways.

So what went wrong? Airline chiefs trusted market research and lost sight of the future. Fundamental changes were taking place in three areas. Email replaced fax and people began to expect near-instant answers. Last minute interactive presentations on PowerPoint replaced dusty overheads. Heavier flying schedules meant that many executives were forced to give up in-flight leisure time to catch up on work. Laptops appeared everywhere in departure lounges and during flights.

There is nothing more annoying than being forced to stop urgent work less than three hours into a seven hour flight. What's the point of a data socket when you have no power? Instant access to email is absolutely essential in a world where responding in an hour can make all the difference between signing or losing a multimillion pound deal. It also means you can get vital reports out of the plane seconds after completion at 33,000 feet.

The trouble is that behaviour is changing far faster than lead time for new products and services, and the gap is getting worse. That means market research will be even more useless than it has been over the last decade. So why doesn't predictive research work? First, more decisions today are affected by what we call O sources of information—"other" information sources, such as user reviews, friend and expert opinions, price comparison tools, and emerging technologies or sources—whereas market research measures P sources—"prior" preferences, beliefs and experiences. Consumers have limited insight into their real preferences. This is especially true with respect to products that are radically different. What market researchers often underestimate, though, is the degree to which consumers have difficulty imagining or anticipating a new and very different reality. What makes the task of a market research firm even trickier is that just as consumers' expectations may be wrong, there are many cases where expectations about what consumers will buy are wrong.

Indeed, trying to predict where things are going has become more challenging. While traditional consumer research can still tell a marketer if their next toothpaste will do better with purple or black stripes, it is not of great help for more radical, unfamiliar changes. There is no effective way to use market research to predict consumer reaction to major changes. When assessing new concepts, consumers tend to be locked into what they are used to, which makes them less receptive to very different concepts and more receptive to small improvements over the current state.

The current environment does not mean the end of market research, just a shift in focus with some silver linings. We expect that future market research will focus more on tracking and responding to consumers' decisions as they occur, and less on long-term preference forecasting. Instead of measuring consumers' preferences, expectations, satisfaction and loyalty, marketers should systematically track the readily available public information on review sites, user forums and other social media.

Words and Expressions

radically *adv.* 根本地	in-seat *adj.* 座椅内的
validity *n.* 效力，有效性	in-flight *adj.* 飞行中的，飞行过程中的
astrology *n.* 占星术	multimillion *n.* 数百万
entrust *v.* 委托	predictive *adj.* 推测的，预言性的
horoscope *n.* 星象	stripe *n.* 条纹
flier *n.* 飞行员	systematically *adv.* 系统地
socket *n.* 窝，孔，插座	satellite phone 卫星电话
cluster *n.* 组，群	range of vision 视野
spare *adj.* 多余的，备用的	lead time 交付周期
essential *n.* 必需品，基本要素，必不可少的东西	user review 用户评论
	silver lining 一线希望

Unit 21　The Future of Marketing

Comprehension

I　Answer the following questions according to the passage.

1. What is the main idea of the second paragraph?
2. Why does the writer say that many companies fail to survive in the new millennium?
3. What is wrong with most people's attitude toward future?
4. What is the purpose of the writer to mention the example of British Airways?
5. Why are data sockets and power supplies so important?
6. In what areas are fundamental changes taking place?
7. Why does market research fail to work properly?
8. How does O sources of information influence businesses?
9. What should marketers do to cope with such unfavorable circumstances?
10. What advice does the writer give with respect to the future market research?

II　Write "T" for true, and "F" for false.

1. According to the writer, market research is useless to predict anything.
2. Marketers' investment in market research goes to nothing in the end.
3. Turning to market research as a tool to predict the future is more scientific than using astrology.
4. The British fliers didn't ask for data sockets and power supplies because they were too expensive.
5. Information sources, such as user reviews, friend and expert opinions, price comparison tools will influence consumer's purchasing decision.
6. According to the writer, consumers' expectations are not necessarily right.
7. O sources of information is likely to change so that it is bound to become out of date by the time actual purchase decisions are made.
8. It's difficult for marketers to predict consumer reaction to major changes.
9. Future market research is expected to focus more on tracking and responding to consumers' decisions as they occur rather than on long-term preference forecasting.

Additional Terms

adaptive strategy　适应策略	corporate structure　公司结构
competitive environment　竞争环境	customer engagement　顾客契合
corporate location　公司位置	environmental change　环境变化

financial environment 金融环境	regulatory environment 监管环境
interactive marketing 互动营销	societal environment 社会环境
near field communication 近距离通信	strategic planning 战略计划
online community 网络社区	technological environment 技术环境

参 考 文 献

[1] 阿姆斯特朗，科特勒. 营销学导论 [M]. 何志毅，改编. 北京：中国人民大学出版社，2006.
[2] GILBERT A. Marketing: creating value for customers [M]. Illinois: Burr Ridge, 1995.
[3] MARTIN C, MALCOLM M. Marketing: an introduction [M]. London: Macmillan Press, 1995.
[4] 法拉尔，林斯利. 剑桥市场营销英语 [M]. 北京：人民邮电出版社，2010.
[5] 李洪涛. 市场营销英语实用教程 [M]. 天津：天津科技翻译出版公司，2013.
[6] 滕美荣，许楠. 市场营销英语 [M]. 北京：首都经济贸易大学出版社，2010.
[7] 张初愚. 市场营销基础教程 [M]. 成都：西南交通大学出版社，2012.
[8] 张惠华，郑琦. 市场营销英语基础教程 [M]. 天津：南开大学出版社，2010.
[9] 张琳琳，DONALD G. 市场营销英语 [M]. 天津：南开大学出版社，2008.
[10] 赵娟. 市场营销英语 [M]. 北京：中国劳动社会保障出版社，2008.
[11] 郑琦，李桂华. 市场营销专业英语 [M]. 天津：南开大学出版社，2009.
[12] 朱曦，高伟. 市场营销专业英语 [M]. 武汉：武汉大学出版社，2011.